A. J. Ayer
Memorial Essays

ROYAL INSTITUTE OF PHILOSOPHY SUPPLEMENT: 30

EDITED BY

A. Phillips Griffiths

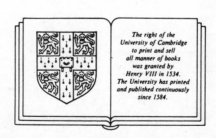

The right of the University of Cambridge to print and sell all manner of books was granted by Henry VIII in 1534. The University has printed and published continuously since 1584.

CAMBRIDGE UNIVERSITY PRESS

NEW YORK

Published by the Press Syndicate of the University of Cambridge
The Pitt Building, Trumpington Street, Cambridge, CB2 1RP
40 West 20th Street, New York, NY 10011-4211, USA
10 Stamford Road, Oakleigh, Victoria 3166, Australia

*A catalogue record for this book is available
from the British Library*

ISBN 0 521 42246 9 (paperback)

Library of Congress Cataloguing in Publication Data

A. J. Ayer memorial essays/edited by A. Phillips Griffiths
p. cm.
Also published as second 1991 supplement to the journal
Philosophy and as v. 30 in the series
Royal Institute of Philosophy lecture series.
Includes bibliographical references and index.
ISBN 0 521 42246 9
1. Ayer, A. J. (Alfred Jules), 1910– . 2. Philosophy
I. Ayer, A. J. (Alfred Jules), 1910– . II. Griffiths A.
Phillips.
B1618.A94A63 1991   91-32637
192-dc20   CIP

Origination by Michael Heath Ltd, Reigate, Surrey
Printed in Great Britain by the University Press, Cambridge

Contents

Contents

Preface

Sir Alfred Jules Ayer was for many years a member of the Council of the Royal Institute, and gave generously of his help and advice. It was therefore particularly fitting—while appropriate, in any case, for one of the most distinguished British philosophers of this century—that the Institute should devote its annual lecture series of 1990–1991 to his memory; and it is on these lectures that the essays in this volume are based.

The first lecture, 'A Defence of Empiricism' by Ayer himself, was written to be given to the closing plenary session of the quinquennial World Congress of Philosophy held in Brighton in 1988. He was not well enough to travel from the south of France to be present at the Congress, but very readily gave his permission for the lecture to be read for him. We judged that he would have been equally pleased for it to be read again as the first in the series of his own memorial lectures. It is printed here for the first time with the kind permission of his executors, Lady Ayer and Professor Ted Honderich.

We have also included in this volume the transcript of a broadcast interview with Ayer by Ted Honderich, now printed for the first time. We are most grateful to Professor Honderich for making this available to us.

A Defence of Empiricism

A. J. AYER

I am very much honoured to have been asked to make the closing speech at this Conference.[1] Since this is the first time for over fifty years that a philosophical congress of this scope has been held in England, I hope that you will think it suitable for me to devote my lecture to the revival of the empiricist tradition in British philosophy during this century. I shall begin by examining the contribution of the Cambridge philosopher G. E. Moore. Though he first owed his fame to his book *Principia Ethica* (Moore, 1903) regarded as a work of genius by the Cambridge Apostles and their associates in Bloomsbury, who did not venture to question Moore's mistaken view of 'good' as an unanalysable non-natural quality, his reputation now chiefly rests on his subsequent defence of common sense.

The core of Moore's defence of common sense was that he knew the truth of a huge number of propositions of kinds that we all accept without question in the course of our everyday concerns, such as that I am standing in a room with walls and a ceiling and a floor, that I have two arms and two legs, that I am perceiving the furniture and the other people in the room, that I have a variety of memories and beliefs, and that the other people in the room are having or have had experiences which are counterparts of my own. It is true that Moore diminishes the force of his position by adding that no one knows the correct analysis of these propositions of which we all know the truth, and still more by admitting as possible analyses interpretations of the propositions in question that one would suppose him to have ruled out of court, but I shall ignore this complication in the present context.

As he himself made clear, the point of Moore's proceeding was not so much to come to the rescue of common sense, which he cannot suppose to have been widely endangered, as to demolish a certain type of metaphysics, namely the neo-Hegelianism which had come to the fore in Britain in the latter half of the nineteenth century, its foremost representatives being F. H. Bradley in Oxford and J. Ellis McTaggart at Cambridge. Moore was the more anxious to put paid to this doctrine as both he and Russell had temporarily succumbed to it as philosophical apprentices at Cambridge under McTaggart's influence. The neo-

[1] This lecture was written in April 1988 for the closing plenary session of the World Congress of Philosophy held in Brighton in August of 1988.

1

Hegelians did not take the same view of Reality. For example, Bradley believed that it consisted in what he called an Absolute, a whole of Experiences, somehow embracing in a coherent fashion all the appearances which he had previously stigmatized as self-contradictory. McTaggart believed that it was a community of immortal souls. Where they agreed was in denying the reality of matter, space and time. Bradley tried to hedge by saying that they were real as appearances, but since his charge against them, as I have just remarked, was that the very conceptions of them were self-contradictory, he must be held to have maintained that they were not real.

Now obviously if space and time and matter were unreal, Moore's common-sense propositions could not be true. If space is unreal, I cannot be standing in this room.[2] If time is unreal, I could not have arrived here yesterday. If matter is unreal, since we are all embodied persons, none of us exists.

There Moore was content to leave it. He thought it strange that philosophers should assert propositions which were straightforwardly inconsistent with what they knew to be true, but he did not speculate as to how this came about. He dismissed the metaphysical pronouncements which he had refuted by drawing out their practical implications as being simply false as indicative statements of empirical fact.

His disciples reacted in various ways. Those of us who had been influenced by Wittgenstein's *Tractatus* (Wittgenstein, 1922) and, in my own case, by the productions of the Vienna Circle, rejected metaphysical utterances as being not even false but nonsensical. Returning in fact to Hume, we divided sentences, said to be literally meaningful, into two classes: those that expressed *a priori* propositions—what Hume had called relations of ideas—the validity of which was purely formal, depending wholly on the meaning of the signs which the sentences contained, and those that expressed propositions which were empirically verifiable, that is to say, confirmable or disconfirmable through sense experience, dealing with what Hume had called matters of fact. Utterances which did not fall into either of these classes might have some poetic appeal but they were literally nonsensical. This was taken to apply not only to the work of the neo-Hegelians but to that of Hegel himself and indeed to a very large part of what had traditionally passed for philosophy.

This limitation of literally significant sentences into two classes was deduced from an axiom which became famous as the Principle of

---

[2] Ayer was at this time not well enough to attend the World Congress, and this lecture was read for him by another. This enabled one of the less incompetent journalists reporting the Congress to make a joke. Freddie was good-naturedly, if not vastly, amused.

Verification: a principle somewhat cryptically couched by Moritz Schlick, the leader of the Vienna Circle, as 'The meaning of a proposition consists in its method of verification'. As the American philosopher Morris Lazerowitz was quick to point out, the principle was a *petitio principii* in the sense that it did no more than summarize the criteria of significance that it was designed to underpin. No attempt was made to prove it independently and indeed it is not easy to see how it could be proved.

Lazerowitz also complained that our use of the word nonsensical to characterize metaphysical utterances was itself a misuse of language, but here I am not in agreement or at least not in full agreement with him. It is true, as we shall see in a moment, that his criticism may apply to his own re-interpretation of the utterances of Moore's metaphysicians, but Moore obtained his results by treating these utterances as empirical and, though I agree with Lazerowitz that this was an error, it is not clear to me what sense they retain as he reconstructs them. What I want to say now is that the main contentions of such a work as Bradley's *Appearance and Reality* (Bradley, 1897) are literally nonsensical and that the same is true of much of Hegel's own work, not to speak of the outpourings of such modern charlatans as Heidegger and Derrida. It makes me very sad to learn that their rubbish is acquiring popularity in this country, appealing to those who mistake obscurity for profundity, and find the serious work of such first-rate American philosophers as Quine, Goodman, Putnam and Davidson too difficult.

Before embarking on my main theme, I should like to say a final word about Morris Lazerowitz who took a line of his own. In his view, the metaphysicians whom Moore attacked and indeed metaphysicians of every type, such as Plato, when he maintained that what he called Forms and we now call Universals alone were real, or Spinoza who claimed to reduce the nature of reality in geometrical fashion from the definition of a few key terms like Substance, Cause and Attribute, did not really mean what they seemed to be saying. They were neither making empirical assertions, in the literal way that Moore had foisted on them, nor were they making *a priori* claims, which would need to be vindicated by an accurate account of our actual use of language. If their assertions were interpreted in either of these ways, the most simple investigation would show them to be false. With a few exceptions, these metaphysicians are not charlatans. In most cases they have been highly intelligent men. Why then should they advance theories which are so easily disproved? Lazerowitz's answer was that they were not advancing any such theories. What they were doing, whether they were aware of it or not, was making linguistic recommendations, and their motive for making these recommendations lay in their unconscious desires.

I admire the boldness of this theory and I wish that I could accept it, if only because it would supply a solution to what still remains very largely an open question. Nevertheless I do not accept it. I do not mind admitting that not only metaphysicians but philosophers of all sorts have unconscious motives, which may intrude into their work, though I should need to be convinced, by much stronger evidence than I have yet seen produced, that they wholly accounted for it. What I find very implausible is the view that the metaphysicians's statements, or what masquerade as such, are linguistic recommendations in disguise. Indeed, I am not sure that it is even coherent.

Let me support this charge by examining one of Lazerowitz's own examples, the contention of Parmenides and his school, including the celebrated Zeno, that nothing changes. Lazerowitz interprets this as a proposal to denude the language of any expression which implies that things suffer any alteration whether in quality or in position; hence Zeno's denial of the reality of motion. Now I can see that one might have an unconscious resistance to any form of change, just as one may have an unconscious desire for perpetual novelty, as expressed in the Heraclitan conception of everything as being in a constant state of flux. But if you fulfil the first of these desires by removing all words implying any process of change from the language, then so far from ensuring the triumph of stability, you abolish the contest. If there is no longer even the possibility of saying that something changes, the assertion that nothing changes loses its meaning.

Lazerowitz was disposed to extend his account of the practice of metaphysics to that of philosophy in general, accusing philosophical analysts, especially myself, of obvious misuses of languages if their words were taken literally. Though I shall be defending myself against these accusations, I admit without further ado that Moore did pose a serious problem for his followers concerning the function of philosophy. The problem arose initially because it was obvious that Moore's claim to know the truth of the propositions which he assigned to common sense was not made in the void. He did not say how he knew that they were true, but if the question had been put to him he could have answered it. In the case of the propositions relating to his current situation, such propositions as that he was seated in a room containing such and such items of furniture and a number of other human beings, his answer would have been that he was relying on the present evidence of his senses, reinforced no doubt by his memory of having often had similar experiences. What is more, his assumption that this evidence gave him the right to claim knowledge of the truth of the propositions in question implied that he took it to be sufficient evidence. There might be some queries about the interpretation of the propositions which it established, upon which enlightenment could be sought, but none about their truth. In particular, it was not to be impugned by any philosophical argument.

What Moore did not point out, though it should have occurred to him, was that this conclusion could be generalized. There is no reason why the truths of common sense should be the only ones to be immune from philosophical attack. Every branch of knowledge employs its own criteria of evidence. They may indeed differ in the degree of credibility which they bestow upon the propositions which satisfy them. The researches which meet the standards which are required of a modern historian get more secure results than the paleontologist is commonly in a position to claim. Even so, each discipline is master of its own territory. If mistakes are made, they are corrected internally. There is no special source of information, available only to philosophers, which would enable them either on the one hand to over-ride pure mathematics or, on the other, to say that the conclusions reached, each in their own way, by classical scholars, modern linguists, lawyers, historians, physicists, chemists, botanists, and biologists are empirically false.

We shall see later on that the position may not be quite so simple. Doubts about analysis, which Moore allowed to be legitimate, may foster doubts about truths. Nevertheless, the position which it seemed to us that we were facing in the nineteen thirties was what I have just outlined. If the entire domain of knowledge was self-sufficiently occupied by the formal, natural and social sciences, what role was there for philosophy? There were those who took the same road as Lazerowitz, or perhaps I should say a similar road, to the point of saying that philosophy was an activity, not a doctrine, but still they regarded it as a cognitive activity. What kind of cognition could it possibly yield?

The authoritative answer had been given by F. P. Ramsey in one of the 'Last Papers' reprinted in his posthumous *Foundations of Mathematics*:

> Philosophy must be of some use and we must take it seriously; it must clear our thoughts and so our actions. Or else it is a disposition we have to check, and an inquiry to see that this is so; i.e. the chief proposition of philosophy is that philosophy is nonsense. And again, we must then take seriously that it is nonsense and not pretend, as Wittgenstein does, that it is important nonsense!
>
> In philosophy we take the propositions we make in science and everyday life, and try to exhibit them in a logical system with primitive terms and definitions, etc. Essentially, philosophy is a system of definitions or, only too often, a system of descriptions of how definitions might be given. (Ramsey, 1931, p. 263)

Ramsey goes on to raise the question what definitions we feel it up to philosophy to provide, and answers that philosophy 'does not propose to define particular terms of art or science, but to settle e.g. problems which arise in the definition of any such terms or in the relation of any terms in the physical world to the terms of experience' (ibid. 264). He admits that we seldom get actual definitions but have to be content with explanations of the use of the symbols and sees a difficulty in the fact that the explanation may refer to entities for which we have no names. This applies particularly to descriptions of definitions of sensory characteristics, in reference to which our language is very fragmentary. 'For instance, "Jane's voice" is a description of a characteristic of sensations for which we have no name. We could perhaps name it, but can we identify and name the different inflections of which it consists?' (ibid. 265).

Finally, Ramsey considers the question whether we can avoid committing a *petitio principii*. The difficulty is that there are terms and sentences about which we cannot get clear without getting clear about meaning and that we cannot understand meaning without understanding, for example, 'what we say about time and the external world' (ibid. 268). He finds this circularity unavoidable and so do I. For example, the Principle of Verification commits one to a certain view of the world, and conversely a certain view of the world is secured by the Principle of Verification.

Ramsey's reference to Wittgenstein is of course to the well-known passage at the end of the *Tractatus* in which Wittgenstein states of his own characterizations of the relation between language and reality, which is the main theme of the book, that they are nonsensical, but goes on to remark that the reader will recognize them as nonsensical only when he has used them as steps to climb beyond them. He then throws away the ladder and sees the world rightly. This is patently disingenuous and it is interesting that Ramsey in his critical notice of the *Tractatus*, which was also reprinted in *The Foundations of Mathematics*, made a valiant attempt to reinterpret many of Wittgenstein's sayings in such a way that they did not violate his conditions of significance. Russell did the same in his Introduction, although in an altogether different fashion. Wittgenstein insisted that both Russell and Ramsey had misunderstood him, but that was common form.

Ramsey died in 1930, an irreparable loss to British philosophy, and I do not know how he would have reacted to the steps by which Wittgenstein gradually moved from the position of the *Tractatus* to that of *The Philosophical Investigations* (Wittgenstein, 1953) and its sequels. So far as I know, Wittgenstein did not say of the vast quantity of material which constitutes this development that it was nonsensical and I think that he would have rejected any general characterization of it. I shall be dealing with one important feature of it later on.

Before I abandon Ramsey I have to remark that his programme was never carried through. The most successful contribution to it had already been made by Bertrand Russell, with his Theory of Descriptions, which Ramsey himself hailed as a paradigm of philosophy. Russell's achievement was to show how nominative expressions could be systematically transformed into predicates, thereby disposing of the problem how the sentences which contained them could be meaningful even when there was nothing that the expressions denoted. The theory has been criticized on the ground that it obliges us to count propositions as false which we should be more naturally inclined to view as lacking in truth-values, the point turning on the question whether in the case of a sentence like 'The present King of France is bald' the existence of one and only one present King of France is covertly asserted, as Russell would have it; or merely presupposed; and it is open to the objection that more often than not, when we make use of definitive descriptions, the target of the description is not wholly identified by our utterance, but is picked out by the context in which the utterance is made, with the result that Russell's reformulations need to be amplified if they are to pass as translations of the sentences which they replace. Nevertheless, I believe that Russell's theory continues to be important, not only as eliminating a problem which perhaps should not have been taken very seriously in the first place, since it depended on a rather crude identification of meaning with denotation, but as supplying us with a method of getting rid of singular terms.

Perhaps Carnap's *Logische Aufbau der Welt* (The Logical Structure of the World) which had been published in 1928, an extraordinarily valiant attempt to show how the whole body of factual concepts could be created on the basis of the single relation of remembered similarity between the total momentary experience of the author, with no other assistance than the apparatus of Russellian logic, would have met Ramsey's requirements if it had been successful. Unfortunately, it was not successful. As Nelson Goodman showed in his book *The Structures of Appearance*, first published in 1951, Carnap did not even bring about the adequate definition of sensory kinds, and the really difficult task of passing from the experiential to the physical domain was not seriously attempted by him.

A point which Goodman brings out is that the characterization of our sense-impressions is not so straightforward a matter as it had been taken to be, at least by a great many philosophers who have taken a professional interest in the nature of perception. The same point has been made by Michael Dummett (1979) in his contribution to *Perception and Identity*, a volume containing a set of dozen essays, commenting on various features of my philosophical work, and my replies to them (Macdonald, 1979). Dummett went further than Goodman, in that having defined a simple observational quality as one the presence of which could be described simply by observing it, in the sense that a judgment affirming its presence could be over-ridden only by a judgment made on a similar basis but possibly under different circumstances, he denied that there could be such qualities. His argument was that his definition implied that the qualities needed to satisfy what he called *the indiscernibility condition* 'namely that, if one object possesses the quality, and no relevant difference between it and another object can be perceived, then the second object possesses it'. At first sight we may be inclined to take it for granted that this condition is satisfied by a great many predicates like 'red' and 'sweet' but it turns out that the supposition 'that any quality always satisfies it is incoherent' (op. cit. 9).

The reason why it is incoherent depends on the empirical fact that sensory qualities constitute a continuum, with the result that the relation of indiscernibility between qualities of the same kind is not transitive. Thus, for example, in the case of colour, one discovers a series of patches A, B and C such that A is indiscernible in colour from B and B from C but A is discernible from C. Consequently if we assume that things are of the same colour if they are indiscernible in colour from one another, and also that colours are continuous throughout the spectrum, we reach the conclusion that there is only one colour, since the colour of B being indiscernible from that of A will be of the same colour as that of A, and so will the colour of C since it is indistinguishable from that of B, and so *seriatim*. This conclusion is no worse than empirically false, but since we can also start at the other end of the spectrum or indeed at any point in it with a patch of a different colour from that of A, and go backwards to A, we do get a contradiction.

Goodman has shown that the contradiction can be avoided if we require for X and Y to be of the same colour not only that they be indiscernible in colour but that there be no other patch Z from which either X or Y is discernible in colour and the other not. This proposal meets the difficulty of the continuum, but it does have the disadvantage that we are debarred from asserting with complete confidence that any two patches are of the same colour until we have examined every patch of colour that there is.

Dummett himself sees no need to follow Goodman, since he sees no point in developing what Goodman calls a language of appearance, and makes our ascriptions of colour and other observational qualities depend not only on the way things look or feel or sound or smell or taste to different observers in different circumstances but also on the applications of scientific theories. This is another point to which I shall return later on.

The view that there are no simple observable qualities runs counter to a long tradition in philosophy, going back at least to Descartes. The theory of sense-data has gone out of fashion increasingly since the war, but in one form or another it was taken for granted by Descartes, Locke, Berkeley, Hume, Kant, John Stuart Mill, Husserl, G. E. Moore, Bertrand Russell, Moritz Schlick, C. D. Broad and Henry Price, and considered seriously by Rudolf Carnap and Ludwig Wittgenstein though they both finally turned against it. Its cardinal feature is the assumption that our everyday judgments of perception, such perceptual judgments as Moore assigned to common sense, are founded on the reception of sensory items which are luminous either in the strong sense that one's assessment of their character allows no possibility of error or in the slightly weaker sense that one's assessment is authoritative: one may be uncertain about its character, while it is still present, or even revise one's original judgment, but one's decision cannot be over-ridden by anybody else. This has been taken to be true of the entities, variously denominated as ideas of sense, sensible qualities, impressions, representations, sense-data, sensa, sense-contents and sense-qualia, and what is common to them all is that they or their instances in the cases where sensible qualities, or qualia, are taken as primitive, is that in the process of perception they are objects of what Russell called direct acquaintance.

Is every theory of this sort demolished by Dummett's argument against the possibility of there being simple observational qualities? I do not think so, because I do not agree that the theory commits one to the indiscernibility condition. I admit that if two mutually indiscernible patches of colour are presented in the same sense-field, with no third instance in relation to which they could be differentiated, it would be inconsistent to describe them differently. I do not, however, believe that the inconsistency extends to the case where the colours are instantiated in different sense-fields and one is merely going on the supposition that if they were brought together one would not be able to discriminate between them.

But does not Dummett's argument prove that any characterization of sensory qualities, purely on the strength of their appearance, is inconsistent? Not unless one accepts his condition of indiscernibility or rather his interpretation of it. My view is that it forces us to conclude not that the use of simple observational predicates leads to contradiction but that at numerous points it is bound to be arbitrary. Consider, for example, a colour atlas which runs through the colours in a continuous fashion, so that between any two specimens which are distinguishable in colour there is one that is indistinguishable from each of its neighbours. Let us suppose that blue runs into green in this fashion. At a certain point we are going to encounter an item which on the basis of its similarity to its neighbour we shall be equally justified in calling blue or green. We then take an arbitrary decision. In Quine's terminology there is no fact of the matter that we shall be contravening.

There is a similarity between this case and the sorites paradox. It seems obvious that if n is some large number, and a crowd of n persons is present on some occasions, the number of those present does not cease to be a crowd if one is added or one removed. Yet if one adopts the general principle that if n persons form a crowd so do $n-1$, we shall gradually reduce the crowd to nobody at all. Our only resort is to fix arbitrarily on some number m, and say that anything less than that number of persons does not constitute a crowd, though the choice of $m+1$ or $m-1$ would have been equally acceptable. The same applies to other vague terms like 'warm' or 'bald'. It does not follow that we have no use for them.

If reference to colours and other sensory items can be made in a purely observational way, without the assistance of terms which imply the existence of physical objects, then I think that a very simple argument justifies their choice as a basis for a theory of perception. We need only consider the range of assumptions which our ordinary judgments of perception carry. I am not now embarking on an excursion into scepticism. I have no doubt that I can see a door at the further end of the room. I am merely remarking that for there really to be a door there, or indeed any other physical object in the room that I could mention, it is not enough that it be visible to me. It has to be accessible to my sense of touch and it has to be accessible to other observers. It has to occupy a position in three-dimensional space and to endure throughout a period of time. Moreover, if it is correctly identified as a door it has, at least potentialy, to fulfil a certain function: it needs to be solid; there is a limit to the sort of material of which it can be made. And similar considerations would apply to any other physical object that I had chosen for an example.

But now can it possibly be the case that all this can fall within the content of a single act of perception? Can it follow from the appearance of a door in my present visual field that I am seeing something that is also tangible or perceptible by other observers? Can it follow even that what I am now seeing persists beyond the brief duration of my present visual experience, let alone that it possesses all the other properties with which my perceptual judgment endows it? Surely not. But then it follows that my judgment of perception embodies a set of inferences, which do not cease to be inferences because I am not conscious of making them. Their existence is established by the fact that I reach a conclusion which, as I am accustomed to put it, 'goes beyond' the sensory experience on which it is based.

Now the contention of the philosophers who have adopted, in one version or another, what I have been calling the theory of sense-data is that these inferences can be made explicit. This contention has two implications; first, that it is possible to give a description of the premises, which is, as it were, strictly tailored to the experiences which they record. Secondly, that the inferences to which they give rise can be analysed in a more illuminatory way than merely by saying that they are perceptions of the physical objects and other public items such as voices, mirror images, and shadows that figure in our everyday discourse. The currently fashionable view is that neither of these aims can be achieved. I, on the other hand, regard them both as possible.

In upholding the first of my two contentions I am not allying myself with Nelson Goodman who has succeeded in laying the groundwork for a language of appearance, using only the primitive concepts of colours, sensory places and sensory times. For Goodman, so far from maintaining that his language is basic in the formulation of our perceptual claims, attaches no meaning to the question whether sensory or physical descriptions come first in the order of knowledge; nor does he suggest that his vocabulary is tailored to our actual experiences, even if it is extended to include data of the other senses. Since my purpose is to achieve fidelity to experience, and since our descriptions of our sensations are normally buried in the references to physical objects to which they give rise, I do not scruple to raid our physical terminology for my sensory descriptions. My device is to speak of our seeing such things as door-patterns, hearing patterns of bird song, and so forth. Sir Peter Strawson, in his contribution to *Perception and Identity* (Macdonald, 1979), objects to this manoeuvre on the ground that I eventually represent the physical world of common sense as the embodiment of a theory with respect to a basis of sense-qualia and that 'in order for some belief or sets of beliefs to be correctly described as a theory in respect of certain data, it must be possible to describe the data on the basis of which the theory is held in terms which do not presuppose the acceptance of the theory on the part of those for whom the data *are* data' (op. cit.). My answer to this is simply that even if Strawson were justified in laying down this requirement, which could be disputed, my procedure does not violate it. For my descriptions of sensory patterns do not entail that the physical objects from which the descriptions are purloined actually exist.

Carnap in the *Aufbau* does claim to pay respect to priority in the order of knowledge. He argues that, had he been concerned only with what was technically possible, he could equally well have founded his construction on a physical basis, but by adopting the initial standpoint of what he called 'methodological solipsism' he did better justice to our actual experience. The use of the word 'methodological' in this context was intended to ward off the charge that his approach committed him to actual solipsism, or at least required him to offer some proof that he escaped it. In this it was ineffectual, so much so that within a few years Carnap himself was publishing papers, in which he argued that it was only by taking a 'physical language' as primitive that one could arrive at the conception of a common world.

I believe that Carnap's change of front was justified to this extent that the bugbear of solipsism cannot be evaded if one begins with sense-data which are defined from the outset as private entities. I have long been surprised at the indifference to this problem which was displayed by the classical empiricists. Neither Locke nor Berkeley nor Hume nor John Stuart Mill nor even Bertrand Russell appears to have thought that there was any great difficulty, on their principles, in establishing one's right to ascribe experiences to persons other than oneself. Berkeley, for example, credited himself with having a notion of other spirits. These spirits were somehow attached to other bodies, but since these bodies were composed of Berkeley's own ideas, it is not at all clear that any provision was made for the accompanying spirits also to perceive ideas.

The problem of one's justification for ascribing experiences to other persons is going to arise at some point in any case, but the way to circumvent it at the outset is to treat the elements on which one bases one's theory of knowledge as neutral with respect to persons. It would, indeed, be incorrect to do otherwise, since persons enter the picture only at a later stage. The need to affirm the neutrality of one's starting point is the main reason why I now prefer to start with sensory qualities or qualia. Being universals they are not confined to the experience of any one person. It is true that they are particularized by their manifestation in given sense-fields and that these sense-fields are not shared, so that they can eventually be transmuted into private mental or even physical states. But this happens when they have given rise to a theory which governs our conception of reality and interprets into itself the elements out of which it grew. The cardinal point is that priority in the theory of knowledge is compatible with quite a modest position in an acceptable account of the way the world is constituted.

If we can agree that the particularization of qualia is to be our starting point, we can pass to the second question how we characterize the inferences that lead us from the set of premises to the judgments of perception which Moore assigned to common sense. And here the main problem, to which Moore himself never found an answer that satisfied him, is how our descriptions of everyday physical objects should be analysed.

I take there to be three serious possibilities. One is to identify physical objects with actual and possible sense-data. The second is to treat them as external causes of sense-data, corresponding to them in one way or other, but not themselves directly perceived. The third is to extract from what Hume called the constancy and coherence of our sense-impressions a standardized model of what we judge to be the various appearances of one and the same physical object and posit it as continuing to exist when no representative of it appears in any sense-field, for the most part occupying the same position, and lasting so long as perceptions of it are thought to be at least theoretically obtainable.

The first of these possibilities has traditionally gone by the name of phenomenalism. This is the theory that statements about physical objects can be shown to be equivalent to sets of statements about actual and possible sense-data. It was casually mentioned by Berkeley, as if it were something on which we could fall back if God relaxed his vigilance. It can be foisted on Hume if his grounds for our suffering from the illusion that our sense-impressions have a continual and distinct analysis are treated as the outline of a reductive analysis. The theory was adopted by John Stuart Mill with his characterization of physical objects as permanent possibilities of sensation and for a period by Bertrand Russell. It became fashionable in the 1930s and I myself advocated it in my first two books. The most conscientious attempt to work it out in detail was made by Henry Price in his books *Perception* (1950) and *Hume's Theory of the External World* (1940), though he himself did not wholly subscribe to it.

Phenomenalism still has one or two advocates, but I am convinced that its programme cannot be carried out for reasons which I first set out in a paper published in the Proceedings of the Aristotelian Society for 1947–8 and reprinted in my *Philosophical Essays*. They are, briefly, that the protases of the hypothetical statements into which statements about physical objects need to be translated, when the objects are not actually being perceived, cannot be unambiguously expressed in purely sensory terms, and that the constant need to guard against illusion leads to an infinite regress.

The second possibility is what, following Eddington, I call the two-world theory. I take it to have been held, if not consistently, by Locke and it was maintained by Bertrand Russell in the periods before he adopted, and after he gave up phenomenalism, and by others including yet another Cambridge philosopher, C. D. Broad. The objections to it were first set out by Berkeley in his criticism of Locke's distinction between ideas of primacy and ideas of secondary qualities and in my opinion they are still cogent. The fatal defect in this type of theory is not that it takes the inferences from sense-data to physical objects to be causal, even though I do in fact believe that these are not what they initially are, but that the causality in question is taken to be of such a character as to put an impenetrable veil between the phenomena with which we are directly confronted and the physical objects which are partly responsible for them. On this view, physical objects are inferred entities which cannot be directly perceived. Even more damagingly, so are the spatial relations between them. For if you put all phenomena on our side of the curtain, they do not leave the positions which they occupy behind. We have to postulate a set of particles, or whatever, dwelling in a space of their own, the system bearing some structural correspondence to the deliverance of our senses which may possibly be equated with events in our brains. Russell indeed did not shrink from drawing this conclusion, enjoying no doubt the freedom which it gave him to put forward the paradox that when a physiologist believes himself to be examining the brain of his patient he is actually looking at his own. But even if we accept all that the scientists tell us about the etiology of perception, and there is no good reason why we should not, the implications of a two-world theory are so unacceptable that Russell must have been mistaken in supposing that we are thereby committed to it.

This leaves my third possibility in possession of the field, but even though it yields the best account of perception that I have been able to devise, I cannot pretend that it immediately conjures all the old problems away. One of them which goes back to Locke and Berkeley is that of reconciling our belief in the existence of what I have been calling the phenomenal world with the world which is depicted in the theories of physics. It is the apparent discrepancy between them that principally motivates a belief in the two-world theory which we have just rejected.

In his contribution to *Perception and Identity* (Macdonald, 1979), and again in his Woodbridge lectures, delivered at Columbia in 1983 and published under the title of *Scepticism and Naturalism: Some Varieties* (Strawson, 1985), Sir Peter Strawson makes light of this problem. Speaking of the ostensible discrepancy between what he calls common sense and scientific realism he says that 'the impression, of irreconcilable antagonism between the two views disappears as soon as we are prepared to recognize . . . a certain ultimate relativity in our conception of the real: in this case, of the real properties of physical objects. Relative to the human perceptual standpoint, commonplace physical objects really are what Ayer calls visuo-tactile continuants, bearers of phenomenal visual and tactile properties. Relative to the standpoint of physical science (which is also a human standpoint) they really have no properties but those recognized, or to be recognized, in physical theory, and are really constituted in ways which can only be described in what, from the phenomenal point of view, are abstract terms. Once the relativity of these "really's" to different standpoints of "the real" is acknowledged, the appearance of contradiction between these positions disappears; the same thing can both be, and not be, phenomenally propertied' (op. cit. 44–45).

While I am favourably impressed by Strawson's speaking of the relativity of our 'really's', I am not entirely convinced that the perceptual and physical standpoints can be quite so easily reconciled. The model on which he is drawing is that of the relativity of our judgments within phenomenal standpoints. To use an example of Strawson's own, blood is ordinarily seen as red, but seen through a microscope it is mostly colourless. This does not cause us to trouble ourselves over the question what colour blood really is. Clearly if we are going to treat this as a question deserving of an answer, we are free to choose either standpoint. If we have a scientific bias, we shall say that it looks red to the naked eye, but that it is really colourless, but this shows no more than that we have a scientific bias. And here in speaking of a scientific bias I am not forsaking the perceptual standpoint. It is anyhow linked to science in that it incorporates the use of scientific instruments.

The question now arises whether the shift from the perceptual to the wholly scientific standpoint can properly be treated, in the way that Strawson does, as simply analogous to the shift from one stance within the perceptual standpoint to another. I am not sure that it can. The reasons for my doubt are, first, that the two versions compete for the same areas of space and, secondly, that there appear to be grounds for holding that perceptible objects are literally composed of scientific particles, even though the most minute of these particles are credited with properties that render them imperceptible. At the moment I am undecided whether to adhere to this view or to take a position, closer to that of Strawson, whereby the scientific standpoint 'takes over' the perceptual, retaining the spatio-temporal framework which would act as a link between them. Here again, there would be no fact of the matter, except in so far as the propositions which belonged to either standpoint would be required to satisfy their respective criteria of truth. We should then be free to choose which set of criteria to employ in deciding how things really were.

As I remarked earlier, one great advantage of setting one's theory of knowledge on a neutral foundation is that it diminishes the danger of one's dropping into the pitfall of solipsism. Having transformed sense-qualia into external objects, one can identify what Peirce calls the central body with one's own body and distinguish other human bodies by their similarities to the central body, especially their command of signs. We are still left with the problem of one's justification for treating these other bodies as other persons, inasmuch as this requires one to think of these persons as having experiences which are similar to one's own. I have not yet found a solution to the problem which entirely satisfies me, though I believe that it is to be found in some combination of the admittedly shopworn argument from analogy with the theory that the ascription of conscious states to others supplies the best explanation for their overt behaviour.

If this problem is widely thought to have been solved it is for two reasons, neither of which I consider to be valid. One of them is the acceptance of the hypothesis that mental states are identical with states of the central nervous system. I have yet to discover an argument in favour of this hypothesis which seems to me cogent, but that is not the objection on which I am now relying. My point is rather that while the hypothesis does render the contents of a person's mind observable by others in so far as it is possible with the right resources to inspect another person's brain, it goes no way towards explaining how the physical states that are thereby detected are apprehended by the owner of the brain as states of consciousness.

Probably more people have been convinced by the argument which Wittgenstein develops in his *Philosophical Investigations*. It purports to prove that one could not intelligibly ascribe sensations to oneself unless one had been taught to ascribe them to others. Wittgenstein employs the sensation of pain as his principal example mainly, I think, because it allows him to draw on such goodwill as behaviourism commands, without committing himself to it. For the sensation of pain has a characteristic set of physical stimuli and physical expressions. This is, however, not true of states of consciousness in general. It is not true of our musings, our memories, our hopes and our dreams. With regard to these, the Wittgensteinian slogan 'an inner process stands in need of outward criteria' has very little plausibility. But this is not the principal point that I wish to make against Wittgenstein, withholding my objection to the so-called private language argument which I have repeatedly set out elsewhere. The point I now wish to make is that Wittgenstein writes as if there were no problem at all about one's crediting other persons with perceiving physical objects in the same way as one does oneself but only a problem about their having similar sensations. The truth is, however, that the distinction which we make between public and private objects is based on empirical contingences and if there is a problem about our attribution of sensations to others it extends to the assumption that they share our perception of physical objects and their properties. In short, my present charge against Wittgenstein and his more or less critical disciples is that they pocket what Russell once called 'the advantages of theft over honest toil'.

Ayer: the Man,
the Philosopher, the Teacher

RICHARD WOLLHEIM

I have told elsewhere the story of my first meeting with Freddie Ayer, but I shall re-tell it. It made a great impact on me, though, I believe, none on him. Certainly at no point in our friendship did he ever bring it up.

It was mid or late 1946. I was an undergraduate at Balliol, having returned from three years in the army, and I was reading for Part II of the History Schools. Most of my friends, most of my intellectual friends, were reading philosophy, and there was a necessity, which I already sensed, for my returning to Oxford once again to follow in their footsteps. This happened later in the autumn of 1947. Post-war Oxford was a very different place from the Firbankian hothouse of wartime Oxford, at least as I knew it. We were all said to be 'more mature', but within the confines of austerity, we were determined to enjoy ourselves. Oxford was not, in the famous words that Max Beerbohm put into the mouth of Mrs Humphrey Ward, 'wholly serious'.

I was living in Holywell Manor, the Balliol annexe, at the time. If I had been out late, or sometimes for no particular reason, I would climb into Holywell Manor. 'Climb into it', I say, but the truth of the matter is that this involved no more than walking across the pretty churchyard of St Cross, raising one leg sharply, and stepping over the wall. The walk took me past the gravestone of Walter Pater, one of my heroes. On this particular evening, having climbed in, I walked straight back to the Porter's Lodge to see if there were any messages for me. The porter was on the telephone. It was for me oddly enough; would I take it in the little box?

I had known Phyllis Young during the war through more florid friends of mine in the Slade. She was small, of immense delicacy of feature, with a tiny slightly husky voice, and she generally dressed in the manner of Sarah Bernhardt. To a boy of 18, she was the fullest expression of glamour and inaccessibility. She lived in a tiny, very old frame house in Holywell, which inside was all white, something very rare in those days: white walls, white rugs, white sofas, in spring enormous bowls of white lilac with the leaves pulled off, and on the walls her paintings which were very gifted in a kind of pastel version of the Euston Road School. The house was always heated to the point of suffocation. When I returned from the war, I somehow found courage to renew our acquaintance, and after a while I took to dropping in in the evening. She liked entertaining, though there was never anything in the house except china tea and chocolate digestive biscuits. The guests mustn't be 'boring'—a great word with her. Isaiah Berlin I saw there: far more frequently, David and Rachel Cecil, who loved her: Tom Brown Stephens, the ancient historian: Gilbert Ryle: and usually, some incredibly decadent, almost totally silent undergraduate, who would play with his rings.

The voice on the telephone begged me to come round. There was a man there. He might, he *might*, be a bore. I left the lodge, walked out into the garden, stepped over the wall of the churchyard, and in two minutes was knocking at the door. The man there, who was perhaps not altogether pleased to see me, was, I quickly realized, no ordinary person. He was in his late thirties, not tall, with dark wavy hair, parted near the centre of his head, which from time to time he combed back— combed back rather than brushed back—with his fingers. He was very delicate-looking, slightly swarthy, with very hooded brown eyes, and the general Modigliani cast of his face was enhanced by the two upper front teeth being slightly longer than the others. When years later modern dentistry substituted an even row of teeth, the face was always for me, for the first second or so, unfamiliar. But it was the movement, the constant movement, of head, hands, fingers, hair—the playing with the watch-chain, one bit rubbed against another, the feet going backwards, forwards, shuffling, tapping, turning on his heel and *sotto voce* a stream of 'Yes, yes, yes'—it was this incessant movement, this constant stream of excitement, that so impressed me. It convinced me that I was in the presence of someone quite remarkable, and it was also it that led to a curious misunderstanding. The ballet was in Oxford that week, and I was almost convinced that my hostess had introduced the man as 'Freddie Ashton', the dancer, the choreographer, who had made something out of English Ballet. Certainly I had, for a start, never seen anyone else in 4 Holywell quite so unoppressed by the heat. The stamina of all that training, I thought. I have no idea what the three of us found to say, but, about half an hour later, as the man was making to go, I followed him into the night air and down the two steep steps on to the pavement, when suddenly with a daring balletic movement he leapt round me, jumped back into the house, and slammed the door behind him. I was confirmed in my misunderstanding. Within minutes I climbed back over Holywell Manor wall for the third time that night.

I learnt my error from, I believe, my close friend Marcus Dick, later my tutor. Many years later, when I met Freddie Ashton I told him the story and he was, I think, amused. He then suddenly said to me, 'Do you know that your father gave me my first job.' If the identity of

Ayer: the Man, the Philosopher, the Teacher

Freddie Ashton and Freddie Ayer, which the world rejected, had been sustained, the first part of this lecture would have had, as you will soon see, a neatness, a symmetry, which, things being as they are, it lacks.

Over the next two years I saw Freddie socially a few times. I went, amusingly enough, to the ballet with my great Oxford friend, Mark Bonham Carter and his sister Cressida, and Freddie came too. When I was living in London in 1947 I used to see Freddie at the Gargoyle Club, a drinking club founded in the 1920s by David Tennant, decorated by Matisse, and frequented by the more bohemian writers, painters, journalists, and girls of good family, and also by respectable couples who came to watch the entertainment. It is by now an anthropological fact that there was introduced, around the early 1920s or perhaps earlier, into a certain section of English society a form of epigrammatic rudeness taken to a high art. According to some, it was the brainchild of that great barrister, the most famous of all *raté* politicians, F. E. Smith, later Lord Birkenhead. After the last war it hung on till about, I would say, 1960, and its practitioners were people like Randolph Churchill, Brian Howard, Evelyn Waugh, Guy Burgess, the painter Dennis Wirth-Miller, and at times Cyril Connolly. It was not confined to men. The Gargoyle Club was one of its sanctuaries.

Freddie liked the Gargoyle very much, though he hated the rudeness. He liked it basically for being London, and he liked it for a reason that he shared only with the couples who had come to watch the fun, and a humorous, then well-known, writer called Stephen Potter, who was one of the most assiduous supporters of the Gargoyle: Freddie loved the dancing. Freddie, for many years at any rate, loved dancing with a fervour equalled in my experience only by Hugh Gaitskell.

I do not remember any particular conversations with Freddie during all this period, except one: it was momentous. My friend Benedict Nicolson had around this time organized an 'ordinary'. 'Ordinary', I take it, is an eighteenth-century term, which was revived by various hostesses of this century and in this context it meant a group of people who met in the private room of a restaurant, ate very badly, paid for their meal, and after dinner listened to a speaker, often a guest, and other guests would be invited to match the speaker. I do not remember who most of the members of Ben's ordinary were, and I do not remember if Freddie was one. He might have been, but he was certainly present at by far and away the oddest of our meetings. Pastor Niemöller, German war hero of the First War, a great voice of resistance during the Second War, spoke, and to match the speaker Ben had invited his friends and acquaintances whom he took to be interested in religion. Canon Hussey, a clergyman from Northampton who loved modern British art and had commissioned works from Graham Sutherland, Henry Moore, and Benjamin Britten: Frank Pakenham, as he then was: Evelyn Waugh: Charles Morgan, the doyen of upper middle brow literature: and Ben's mother, Vita Sackville-West. Pastor Niemöller spoke in very poor English. Looking up from his brandy in a drunken rage, Evelyn Waugh said that the Pastor had for reasons of his own chosen to omit the most important difference within religion: that between the true faith and other faiths. Believers in the true faith descend—or so, he said, *we* believe—from those who at Pentecost received from God the gift of tongues. As people left the dinner table, Freddie came up to me and said, 'When you finish Schools, and you do all right, I intend to give you a job'. Freddie, I must explain, was now at University College, London, I was back at Oxford reading shortened P.P.E. in four terms, and 'doing well' meant, or so I supposed, getting a First.

Of course, I was totally amazed by Freddie's remark, though it never occurred to me to wonder who, if anyone, Freddie had consulted. I think I thought of him as such an autonomous character that I would not have been surprised if he had asked no-one's advice. I took Schools in December 1948, my philosophy examiners were Grice and Ryle, and, seeing Ryle in the High about twenty minutes after the viva, I was told the result. I had been given a formal viva, of which I remember only one question. Possibly it was the only question. 'Mill,' Ryle said to me, 'claimed that all knowledge is arrived at by deduction or by induction. What's a counter-example?' I hesitated. 'What's two times two?' he asked me. 'Four', I said. 'How did you arrive at that?', he asked me. I hesitated again. 'Multiplication', he said, 'So there's your answer'.

I rang Freddie to tell him the result. He was in China. I went away by myself, to Paris, to Zurich, to Florence, all in the grip of a white winter. I returned, and Freddie was still in China. Term was to begin in less than a week. Then I got my summons. I was due to be interviewed by Freddie and John Neale, the great Tudor historian, who ran a postgraduate research factory on the old German academic model. Neale had a cherubic appearance, and his manner to *me* was always one of great sweetness. I was offered a job, I think on the spot, which was to be joint between the Philosophy and the History departments. So here I now was, with only four terms of philosophy behind me, moreover those spent during a period at Oxford when any form of scholarship, whether in the history of philosophy, or in logic, or in science, was looked upon as superfluous, standing up to lecture to undergraduates in their eighth term of philosophy who had had the chance to acquire from Freddie some pretty tough forms of self-defence. I never took in the enormity of my situation, though I was a bit scared, but I found my new department fascinating. At first I thought I would miss the dreamworld of Oxford, and perhaps I did, but it is easy to feel, after quite a short time, that one has lived in Oxford too long.

At University College big things were going to happen. You could feel that. The staff when I arrived consisted of three people: Freddie, Stuart Hampshire, who, to Freddie's great credit, was employed by him at a moment when no-one else would employ him for reasons that Freddie might have taken seriously if anyone was going to, and Dr Keeling. Dr Keeling lived in Paris and came over weekly (or so it was said), wearing his beret, to deliver his lectures. He did not permit discussions in his classes (or, again, so it was said). He wrote on Descartes and Spinoza, and he thought deeply about the Greeks. He was a disciple of McTaggart whom he thought right on nearly all topics except one which left him with a bitter taste: Keeling was a pacifist, and McTaggart was rabidly militaristic. Freddie liked Keeling: he particularly liked talking to him in French. The feeling was not reciprocated, and when, some time around 1955, Keeling decided to retire and an expensive dinner was given for him, which we thought he would like, and which Freddie paid for, Keeling, without waiting for Freddie's panegyric, announced to us all that he had been chased out of philosophy by some new wave, of which 'you' he said pointing at Freddie, 'are a major agent—no', he went on, 'I flatter you, you could never be more than a minor agent.' Freddie laughed. He was amused. 'What a rogue' he used to say afterwards—'rogue' being quite a term of endearment which he applied to most of his older philosophical colleagues in the other London colleges. Sometimes he called someone 'a very bad man', and that meant for him what it seems to say. At this period of his life, Arthur Koestler apart, there were very few people whom Freddie really disliked.

Stuart Hampshire, the other member of the staff, had been a friend of mine for several years. To my deep regret he left to go back to Oxford in the early 1950s, and after me Freddie appointed only his own students: James Thompson, Johnny Watling, Basson as he then was, Peter Long, and Peter Downing. He did this as a point of policy just as others refuse to do it as a point of policy, and exactly why he did it is an interesting question, and it takes us, I believe, to the core of his conception of the department and of his role as its Head. He certainly did not do it in order to hear his views parroted back to him. With these appointments he stood no chance of that, and vain though Freddie was—and he was very very vain, and those who have attempted to deny this do history no service—this was not a form his vanity took.

To appreciate Freddie's conception of the Grote Chair and what the twelve years or so during which he held it meant to him, we have to take stock of the formidable reputation he enjoyed in the late 1940s. It was important to others, it got him his Chair. But also it was important to him. It was the mirror into which he looked when he wondered what to do.

Freddie's reputation, the world's opinion of him, rested in effect on two struts.

In the first place there was his fame as a philosophical writer of great brilliance. He was the author of *Language, Truth and Logic. Language, Truth and Logic* is a very remarkable tract. It combines views of great iconoclasm and vertiginous scope with a very pure style, cadenced, subtle, neat. In the way he dressed, some of the same timeless fastidiousness came out. Freddie prided himself on his style, and once he told me how he wrote. He never put pen to paper until he had the sentence he wished to write down fully formed in his head. Then he wrote it down and moved on to the next sentence, which he similarly perfected in his head. And so on, until he had 500 words down on the page. Then his day's work was over. He never never crossed anything out, he told me.

With one part of himself Freddie thought that the literary side of his reputation *was* his reputation. He was not, after all, a mere teacher: a beak, an usher, a dominie, a hack. In London and Paris he moved amongst writers, some of his closest friends were poets, and, if he was to be circumscribed at all, it was to be, as with his great predecessor David Hume, as a citizen of the republic of letters.

But just here was the rub. The name of Hume tells all. It was a boast of Freddie's, and no mean boast, that he had written, *Language, Truth and Logic* at the same age as Hume had written his great revolutionary *Treatise of Human Nature:* twenty-four. Both were works of amazing precocity. But precocity is not a bird to be snared and kept captive. A book remains precocious, its writer does not. A book does not age, its writer does. As the years passed, *Language, Truth and Logic* receded into the past and the question was, Could Freddie write another book that he would find equally satisfying? I believe that the answer he gave to this question was, Not yet, not in the foreseeable future, No. Of course Freddie went on seeing himself as a writer, and he went on writing. In his later years he aimed, he told me, at writing a book a year. Partly it was to show the young. 'What books', he said to me once, 'does Gareth Evans write? Where are John MacDowell's books?' Certainly before this last period he did indeed write a number of books of great philosophical interest, of which the best is *The Problem of Knowledge.* He borrowed from his great hero Russell the idea of writing books, part historical, part theoretical, and his books on pragmatism and on Russell and Moore will almost certainly come back into favour. But of necessity none of his other works, late, middle, earlyish, could give Freddie the satisfaction of his very first work, and that necessity lay in his overall idea of philosophy.

The overall idea of philosophy for Freddie was to articulate a vision of the world, and to do so through the unaided use of reason—'analysis' being of course the favoured term for reason in its modern manifestation. Philosophy then was partly a matter of content, partly a matter of method.

Language, Truth and Logic certainly articulated a vision of the world. It is a vision of startling clarity in which the pursuit of knowledge, in particular the pursuit of prediction, through the accumulation of well-articulated propositions, is the central aim, and metaphysics and emotion are the two great dangers. Freddie, of course, never refers to the visionary nature of philosophy as such, and the various formulations he attempts of what he took the nature of philosophy to be are probably the least successful and the least consistent part of *Language, Truth and Logic*.

However by the time the second edition of the book appeared—and, though it had a great immediate success it was only in the second edition, in post war Britain, that the book was widely diffused, becoming perhaps the last Bible of British Nonconformity—that vision was no longer so bright or so clear. It may be some time since some of you have looked at the second edition of *Language, Truth and Logic*. Let me encourage you to do so. It is a very extraordinary work. For in the new Introduction specially written for this edition Freddie sets out, end to end, all the criticisms of the original text offered by friends, by colleagues, by himself, which cumulatively stop the book's argument in its tracks. Freddie, I have said, was a vain man. He was also a highly competitive man—anyone who ever played chess or tennis with him knows that. But read this introduction, and you can see exactly where for this man, torn as he was between a childish egotism and a guileless honesty, the point came at which vanity and competitiveness count for nothing.

Of course there is more than one way to look at the Introduction to the second edition of *Language, Truth and Logic*. It was a work of great honesty, but it was also a work of great audacity and ambition. The Introduction is suffused with the conviction that the vision can be restored, and, when it is restored, when it is re-established in a form that takes account of everything that criticism has to offer, then the finality of the vision will be asserted. Vision and finality went for Freddie hand-in-hand. In the Introduction to *Philosophical Essays*, which came out in 1954, we find him writing, 'While I have not reprinted anything that I now believe to be false, I should certainly not claim that all the questions treated had been satisfactorily disposed of.' 'Satisfactorily disposed of'—what an idea! But I quote this passage here, only to make the point that in the late 40s, early 50s, Freddie believed two things: that the definitive vision was still the one proper aim of philosophical writing, and that he, as things stood, was not in a position to catch its detail. The nature of necessary truth in a natural language seemed very remote from Freddie's grasp: and he increasingly realized, much to his distaste, that a vision of the world that could not account for value, in however negative a way, was not viable. Freddie must also have realized that, if philosophy was to sustain its commitment to liberal values in personal life and in politics—something which was very important for him—it needed something more than the emotive theory or the principle of utility: for all the truth in both these views.

It was at this juncture, when the immediate reworking of *Language, Truth and Logic* seemed out of the question, that Freddie's mind moved back to the second strut—that is my metaphor—on which his fame rested. In the 1930s, at the very same time as Freddie was establishing himself as a virtuoso writer of philosophical prose, he was also securing notoriety for himself—not as a teacher—but as a converter, as a proselytizer. When still an undergraduate he was supposed to have converted his tutor, Gilbert Ryle, a lapsed phenomenologist, deeply dispirited, as he himself used to tell the story, from his visit to Husserl and the idolatrous Frau Husserl. Freddie's next move, no less momentous at least in its indirect consequences, was to convert the most remarkable, the most independently minded undergraduate, of more or less his own age. It was a conversion that did not last long, and John Austin, having abruptly fallen under Freddie's sway, was soon to become what he remained until his death: Freddie's most dedicated critic.

Friends have described to me the meetings of a small group of colleagues who in the mid and late 30s met, and discussed the philosophical agenda that positivism had set them. In addition to Freddie and Austin, there was Isaiah Berlin, in whose rooms the meetings were held, Stuart Hampshire, McNabb, and sometimes Woozley and MacKinnon. At the centre of these discussions was the heightened conflict between Freddie, the devoted defender of general principles, and Austin, who always saw the difficulties, the exceptions, and did not regard these things as Freddie inevitably did, as temporary obstacles to the forward march of philosophy, which would eventually wear them down or work its way round them. Austin saw no reason to believe, or to *want* to believe, this. Wisdom for him lay enshrined in the nuances, in the idioms of ordinary thought and speech, where the past had deposited them. The politically radical Austin was the Burke, not of institutions, but of language. The task was to capture those nuances, not to deny them and not to systematize them: or at any rate not just yet, not for a very long time.

I have said what I have just said with the benefit of hindsight. In the 1950s Austin's mode of philosophy became acceptable. It set a norm. His distinctive shake of the head, and his 'That won't do, that won't do at all' became greeted as marking a breakthrough. The mode fitted in well with the Oxford tutorial system, and Austin's own presence further gave it the air of infallibility. But in the 1930s the mode had not really caught on, and the more natural perception was that it was Freddie who produced the ideas, of which Austin was just the critic. Judicious by-standers like Price and Kneale welcomed Freddie's onslaught on Oxford philosophy.

My suggestion is then that, after the war, though—or perhaps because—Freddie's literary aims were as ambitiously conceived as they had ever been, *but* he saw no immediate way of achieving them, the thought of what he had done so effectively at Oxford in the 1930s returned to him. It came to seem to him the most worthwhile thing he could do. In a way it was teaching, but also it was not teaching: it was not teaching because it was not a matter of simply filling people's heads, it was a matter of *opening their eyes*. What remained was to find somewhere to do this, and the opportunity with which University College London provided Freddie when in 1947 it appointed him Grote Professor was even happier than he initially recognized.

The great thing was that it gave him a department, something Oxford did not have at its disposal. A department meant several things. It meant that all the students were studying just one subject—philosophy—and it meant that they were around all day: they formed a unit. Furthermore, and primarily for these two reasons, they need not be just students. They need not be, and Freddie seized his chance and saw that they were not: they were allies, associates, companions, co-workers, colleagues, and Freddie was their *maestro*. They were, in Freddie's famous phrase, 'my boys', and what I want to consider is how Freddie converted the chance students of the department of philosophy at University College London, a department with not a very distinguished past, indeed with barely a past at all, into his boys.

In the first place they *weren't* chance students. They were a remarkable group of people, older for the war, mostly (as I recall) magnetized out of the psychology department by the powerfully attractive figure of Freddie. When I arrived in the department in 1949 the ablest of them was James Thomson. Thomson was one of the three or four cleverest people I have ever known. A rear-gunner in Bomber Command during the War, Thomson had read the *Critique of Pure Reason* as he sat with his knees hunched up by his chin, high above the German heartland. When I arrived he already had that extraordinary battered look which people who knew him only in later years might have thought had been brought on by the chaotic life he led. I have never known anyone with so few teeth. James was always in the grip of an obsession: psychoanalysis (I first heard of Melanie Klein from James Thomson), logic, chess, the dogs, horse-racing, the Stock Exchange, drink—and the two great constancies, philosophy and chain-smoking. Then there was Peter Newnham, a large sprawling character who looked like Beethoven and had a powerful inconsequential mind. He drank prodigiously and his appetite for philosophy was unquenchable. Somewhat more borderline between the philosophy and the psychology departments were Martin Shearn, a man with a very quick mind who speedily saw the ridiculous side of his opponents' views, Jonckheere for many years in the psychology department, and my friend Johnny Watling, my colleague for three decades.

The material then was rich, but what Freddie offered his students was to educate them. He gave all the tutorials to the finalists and he supervised all the postgraduates. (In 1949, when I arrived, there were, it must be said, not more than four of each.) He undertook their education in two things: in philosophy and in intellectual self-confidence. And this latter he achieved by making his department a hub of philosophy. In contrast to the more casual arrangements that prevailed at Oxford and at Cambridge, Freddie ensured that all the leading philosophers of the day were invited to come and talk at London—it became the sort of invitation people didn't want not to get—and then, when they were there, in the ensuing discussion, there was, or so it seemed, scarcely an argument that could be mounted against what they had said that was not mounted. For an hour, an hour and a half, the scene was like an old-fashioned cavalry battle, assault after assault crashing through the smoke-filled room. Freddie would say proudly, at a party, or in Oxford. 'Yes. Strawson came down the other day, or Herbert read us a paper, or Gilbert gave us something, and my boys gave him a pretty rough time.' And his smile went from ear to ear. That's what I mean by being a *maestro*.

The centre of the department's activity was the Monday five o'clock seminar. Everyone turned up except the first-year students. No-one had to. I once mentioned to Freddie a seminar I knew of in some department at which attendance was compulsory. 'Good God' he said in horror. A book was selected for the term. Week by week someone would either volunteer or be nominated to write something on the reading for the week. Freddie would sit behind his desk, tipping his chair back, with his silver cigarette case in front of him, helping himself to it at regular intervals, pausing between cigarettes only to comb his hair with his fingers or to adjust the knot of his tie or to straighten the silk folds as they fell over his shirt. The paper would end. Freddie's chair would fall forward. He frowned. he took another pull on his cigarette or twiddled his watch-chain. Then he began. His reply was clear, precise, in faultless sentences, touching on every point made or not quite made. Sometimes he would stop himself in mid-flight. 'No, that's not quite right—because you could get out of it by saying . . .' and then he would invent a counter-argument. It was, and it was meant to be seen as, a tour de force. After that the discussion was general, but, if there was a silence, someone would be asked his view. Basson was asked regularly what he thought, because otherwise he never spoke. I was once asked when I was daydreaming. The tone was very different from the running battles with the out-of-town philosophers, it was always generous and always didactic, but the rules of engagement were the same. No position was to be considered better than the arguments presented in its favour. No argument was to be considered better than the weakest link in the form in which it was presented. The most implausible counter-example was a deadly, festering threat.

Freddie, I have said, made the philosophy department a hub of philosophy. This meant that philosophers from abroad staying in London would attend Freddie's seminar. Those whom I remember coming back over the years were Max Black and the Lazerowitzs— Morris Lazerowitz and Alice Ambrose, who were in London on two or three separate occasions. Morris was a great fan of Freddie's, and he brought to our discussions his own psychoanalytically oriented form of philosophy which combined in a unique way profundity and super- ficiality. I remember only this fragment: that philosophers who were realists about universals were, in the last analysis, proposing that the word 'universal' should be written with a capital U. Visitors from London who turned up regularly included E. H. Hutten, a physicist from Royal Holloway, a pupil of Reichenbach, very interested in psychoanalysis, a deeply embittered man who felt (rightly) that his gifts were unrecognized by all, and the eccentric polymath Woodger from the Middlesex Hospital, who had axiomatized biology. David Armstrong frequented the seminar, but perhaps towards the end of the 50s, and amongst students from other departments who attended was the young Jonathan Miller, then a postgraduate medical student. After the seminar it was the habit to go to a pub and the discussion continued. Freddie always drank half a pint of mild and bitter, and then, looking at his watch, would leave abruptly, call a taxi as he was going out through the door, and be off to another world. Freddie was a philosopher in London. It was only by some sort of accident, to which he felt it unnecessary to accommodate, that he was a philosopher *at* London.

Freddie loved his department. It made him very happy. I suspect that for the first time he could put behind him the very real wounds inflicted on his pride at Eton, at Christ Church, in the Welsh Guards. He realized that it was only a place like University College that could allow him to do what he wanted, just as it allowed his other clever remarkable friends to do what they wanted: John Young, Lionel Penrose, Bill Coldstream. But he was not a College man, a 'U.C. man'. I think that he would have thought the idea rather ridiculous, an importation of something from where it was appropriate like Oxford or Cambridge to somewhere where it was grotesque. I doubt if he ever had lunch in College. And he treated the College administration with a feigned ignorance of their existence. Once, on one of the various occasions on which the department was obliged to move, the Bursar, a heavy despondent man, offered to show us some accommodation which he thought we would like. It was on the servants' floor of a handsome house now demolished. Freddie reluctantly agreed to look at it. On the third or fourth floor he was muttering to himself 'I don't think this'll do, don't think this will do at all.' As we got there and Freddie was shown his office, he said 'And where's the sofa to go?', and he was down the stairs before the Bursar had taken in the question he was expected to answer. The sofa, it must be explained, played an extremely important role in the lay-out of the seminar, it was much more comfortable than the chairs and since those who sat on it did so on a first-come, first-served basis, it helped to establish the strictly anti-hierarchical character of the occasion. Some years later, after he had left London, he returned to take part in the election of two professors of philosophy. At one moment things were not going as he wanted them to. He got obstreperous. 'All right', he said to one of the electors. 'Have your way. London philosophy was a slum when I came here, and turn it back into a slum if that's what you want'. Then he added, turning to the very solid Principal of the University 'I don't see why a clerk like you has any say in the matter'. Personally I very much liked this side of Freddie, and it was never just frivolous. What lay behind this outburst with Freddie was the most disgraceful incident in the recent history of London University, which still rankled with him: the rejection of Joseph Needham as Professor of the History and Philosophy of Science at University College because of his political stance in the Korean War. The Principal, according to Freddie, had led the attack.

To members of his staff Freddie was always easy and open. We were all equals and we could do what we wanted—provided only that we respected the one rule that there was to be no teaching before 11 in the morning, and we enabled every student to get at least as good a degree as he deserved.

I have been suggesting that there was a continuity between Ayer the proselytizer of the 1930s and Ayer the Grote Professor of the 1950s in that in the later incarnation the earlier concern with method, with the use of reason, with the criticism of argument, flowered and flourished within the felicitous context of a department. That is right. But, of course, there was a discontinuity, and that difference was just the difference between living under and not living under the aegis of *Language, Truth and Logic*. Freddie's most substantial work of the 1950s was *The Problem of Knowledge*. In the preface to this work, having enumerated some of the problems with which it will deal, Freddie writes, 'I do not suppose that I have said the last word upon any of these problems, but I hope that I have done something to clear the way for their solution.' Note that the notion of the last word is still in there—but contrast this sentence with the famous declaration from the First Edition of *Language, Truth and Logic:* 'I maintain that there is nothing in the nature of philosophy to warrant the existence of conflicting philosophical schools. And I attempt to substantiate this by providing a definitive solution of the problems which have been the chief sources of controversy between philosophers in the past'—and you can measure the retreat involved. The last word was now about as imminent as the last trump.

I am deeply grateful for what I learnt from Freddie's seminars. I reckon that I acquired from them whatever dialectical abilities I possess. But if you discount the high spirits, it could appear a bleak school. It was great to be a philosopher, but was philosophy, shorn of its ultimate attainment, a great thing? Whenever the Monday discussion reached a certain point, we would be told, 'And here we hand things over to the scientist, or to the historian, or to the psychologist.' This point often coincided with the moment at which the discussion got interesting, and at times the sacrifice appeared hard to make when anyhow the reward, what we could count on, seemed to be ever diminishing. There were nights when, waking up, I cursed philosophy.

What topics did we discuss in the 1950s? They were varied, and they were not necessarily those discussed elsewhere: still sense-data, other minds, induction, incorrigibility and the nature of so-called 'purely verbal error', behaviourism, individuals and the identity of indiscernibles, the nature of philosophy. More interesting than any such enumeration is the various pendulism-like swings, endemic to empiricism that our discussions at once manifested and examined. One swing was methodological: it went from the view that philosophy studies the nature of things, or what they are, to the view that philosophy studies how, given what things are, we come to have knowledge of them, *and then back*. The other swing was substantive: it went from the view that the external world is a matter of, or can be reduced to, my experiences to the view that my experiences are a matter of, or can be reduced to, how my body reacts, *and then back again*. The two swings are not, of course, independent of one another, they have not been so in the history of philosophy, and they were not so in our discussions. And finally there was on Freddie's part a revived interest in metaphysics, not the speculative metaphysics he claimed to have eliminated in *Language,*

Richard Wollheim

Truth and Logic, but the reductive metaphysics of scepticism. Is it right to expand the world to the point at which we can reasonably claim to know it, or is it the better course to deflate the claims of knowledge so that the world can meet them? In struggling with these issues in the 50s, Freddie came significantly under the influence of John Wisdom. He found the idea of 'the pointless lament' an effective tool in dealing with the claims of scepticism. Freddie acknowledges his debt to Wisdom in the preface to *Philosophical Essays*, but this influence, which is strongest in *The Problem of Knowledge* has, as far as I can see, gone largely unremarked. On one subject we were seldom asked to give our views: necessary truth in natural language. Freddie had very largely given up on this topic, contenting himself with vague remarks like 'something to do with language'.

Reviewing the topics we used to discuss brings me to what I believe was Freddie's most important philosophical shortcoming: his failure to feel the particularity of particular philosophical problems. Every problem raised brought us back, after one or two moves, to the general nature of philosophy. But since the particular problems had themselves so little substance, there was always the temptation to be stipulative in the answer we gave to the general problem. In the last resort, philosophical method remained untested. At any rate it was too little tested.

Freddie decided to go back to Oxford in 1960, largely, as far as I could see, in order to resume his duel with Austin. By now the stakes had for Freddie become serious. Whole generations of philosophers had become Austinians. Blindfolded they could point to the errors in *The Foundations of Empirical Knowledge*. Just when Freddie had made his decision and his successor had been appointed, Austin died. A vocation was gone.

Some time in the autumn of 1960 I drove Freddie down to Oxford. He was in high spirits all the way there. As we approached the Headington roundabout, he spotted the carved wooden sign which says 'City of Oxford'. Freddie turned towards me. 'My heart sinks', he said. 'It always has at the sight of Oxford.' Another phase in his life was opening.

Ayer's Place in the History of Philosophy

ANTHONY QUINTON

When A. J. Ayer arrived in Oxford in the autumn of 1929 he had no thought of becoming a professional philosopher. He intended to go to the Bar, but, in the manner of an Etonian, by way of Literae Humaniores rather than the study of law. He had read a couple of philosophical books. The first of them was Russell's *Sceptical Essays* (Russell, 1928), which he bought on its first appearance in 1928. The other was *Principia Ethica* (Moore, 1903), to which he had been led by a reverent aside in Clive Bell's *Art* (1914). These choices were significant. Ayer always thought of himself as Russell's successor. He modelled his thought on that of Russell, both in its content and in its unguarded expression and also, to some extent, his manner of life, both political and amorous. What he got from Moore is less obvious, although his respect for Moore is evident, as is shown by the preface to *Language, Truth and Logic* and by his devoting a book to a close examination of his ideas, along with those of Russell. An important likeness is that both Moore and Ayer were provoked to philosophize by the assertions of other philosophers, not by problems arising outside philosophy in mathematics or the sciences, in history or everyday life.

Ayer avoided the full rigour of an Oxford training in the classics, devoting one term only to the acquisition of a minimal requirement in them. So, at the beginning of 1930, he started on the formal study of philosophy. The philosophical scene in Oxford at that moment was, for the most part, drab and wintry. Adherents of Cook Wilson, who had died in 1915, exercised a fairly oppressive intellectual authority: H. A. Prichard from the chair of moral philosophy, H. W. B. Joseph as an overwhelmingly energetic college tutor. (For what it is worth, at least as an index of their subsequent reputations, neither is honoured with an article in Edwards's *Encyclopaedia of Philosophy* (1967) and Joseph does not even secure a mention.) British Hegelianism, in opposition to which the school of Cook Wilson originally defined itself, was represented by H. H. Joachim. He, like most Oxford philosophers of that time, had given himself over to the historical study of the subject. There was also the wayward and defiantly isolated R. G. Collingwood. The only notable books published by Oxford philosophers in the 1920s were Collingwood's *Speculum Mentis*, of which nobody took any notice, in 1924 and, in 1926, *Statement and Inference*, the posthumous compilation derived from the lectures of Cook Wilson and used by his followers as a kind of textbook.

By the 1920s orthodox idealism was more or less extinct outside Scotland. The Cook Wilsonians had turned their antiquated artillery on to what they saw as the even worse errors of the Cambridge philosophers, who had done so much more than they had to undermine it. Prichard had vehemently criticized Russell's theory of knowledge in an article in *Mind* in 1915 and he and Joseph were persistently hostile to Russell's logic. Moore, as an ethical consequentialist, was one of those who, in Prichard's view, had committed a fundamental mistake in moral philosophy. The only book Prichard published in his lifetime, *Kant's Theory of Knowledge* had come out in 1909: Joseph's main work, his *Introduction to Logic* as long ago as 1916.

There were, however, signs of renewed life. H. H. Price, Prichard's favourite pupil, in a disconcerting betrayal, had been converted to the theory of sense-data advanced by Russell and Moore. Ayer, as an undergraduate, attended the lectures that were to be published by Price in 1932 as *Perception*. The more influential of Ayer's philosophy tutors was Gilbert Ryle. After an early interest in the phenomenological movement, revealed in a respectful, if finally suspicious, review of Heidegger's *Sein und Zeit* (1929), Ryle was, by the beginning of the 1930s, showing marked Russellian tendencies. 'Are there propositions?' of 1930 presents a reductionist account of propositions that was to be echoed in the second chapter of Ayer's *Foundations of Empirical Knowledge* ten years later and in his London inaugural of 1946: *Thinking and Meaning* (TM). Ryle then laid out a comprehensive programme of analysis on Russellian lines in 1932 in his 'Systematically Misleading Expressions'.

Cambridge was unquestionably livelier as a philosophical centre, in spite of its comparatively minute population of philosophers. From 1922 it had Wittgenstein's *Tractatus* to discuss and, until 1927, Ramsey to discuss it with. Also in 1922, Moore's *Philosophical Studies* had brought together a number of influential essays. C. D. Broad published his *Scientific Thought* a year later and in 1925 *The Mind and its Place in Nature*. At a geographical distance, but not at a very large spiritual one, Russell brought out his *Analysis of Mind* in 1921 and *Analysis of Matter* in 1926.

Not much was going on in other British philosophy departments. The most imposing product came from Manchester: Alexander's *Space, Time and Deity* in 1920. Exported fruitfully to Australia by John Anderson, it was respectfully ignored in its country of origin. Kemp Smith's *Prolegomena to an Idealist Theory of Knowledge* (1924) and some elegantly written works by Laird were all that Scotland had to offer. The United States supplied little in the way of exact or minute philosophy in the 1920s. It was an era of massive constructions: Whitehead's *Process and Reality* (1929), Dewey's *Experience and Nature* (1929) and *The Quest for Certainty*, the first volume of Santayana's *Realms of Being* (1928).

The disparaging tone of these judgments of the philosophy of the English-speaking world in the 1920s calls for justification. The decade surely does look weak when it is compared with the effectively preceding period from 1900 to 1914. That roughly Edwardian epoch had contained the early and best works of Russell and Moore. Wittgenstein had come to Cambridge and electrified it. McTaggart's *Hegelian Cosmology* (1901) and *Some Dogmas of Religion* (1906) had provided exemplary displays of argumentative rigour. In Oxford idealism was still quite lively with Joachim's *The Nature of Truth* in 1906 and Bradley's *Essays on Truth and Reality* in 1914. Prichard and Joseph, as has been mentioned, published their most substantial work at that time. In the United States William James was copiously productive up to his death in 1910. The early, less amorphous, Dewey was at work. Santayana's five-volume *Life of Reason* (1905) belongs to this period, as do Royce's *The World and the Individual* (1900) and the collective volume *The New Realism* (Holt, 1912).

The large and altogether more adventurous philosophical activity of the Edwardian age as compared with the 1920s is to be explained—to the extent that it can be or needs to be explained—by the general spiritual devastation of the first World War. That suggestion is confirmed if one looks further afield to continental Europe. It was in the Edwardian era that the main and characteristic works of Croce and Bergson were published, as were the earlier and better works of Husserl, Vaihinger's *Als-Ob* (1911), Cohen's *System der Philosophie* (1915) and Cassirer's *Erkenntnisproblem* (1906). By the 1920s Croce and Bergson had moved to the margins of the subject and the orthodox academic philosophers of importance were Husserl, Cassirer and, perhaps, Nicolai Hartmann. Only near the end of the decade did Heidegger sound a new, arresting note.

From an Anglo-Saxon point of view a more promising publication than *Sein und Zeit* came a year later in 1928 with Carnap's *Logische Aufbau der Welt*. In the United States a sign of a livelier period to come was C. I. Lewis's *Mind and the World-Order* in 1929. These two books coincide approximately with the return of Wittgenstein to philosophy, and Cambridge, and the emergence of Price and Ryle in Oxford. Ayer's philosophical career, then, began after a period of comparative sterility, but at a moment when, in Britain, the United States and Europe, the first indications of renewal are to be discerned.

It might also be said that not only had the recent philosophical past been comparatively sterile, but the immediate philosophical present was, to vary the image, a bit of a vacuum. Russell's best work was behind him and, so far as philosophy is concerned, he was a spent force. Readers of Raymond Chandler will remember Big Willie Magoon, head of the vice squad of the Bay City police. He failed to come across with something for which he had been paid and was seriously worked over by some heavies. As a result he was never much use afterwards. Something of the same kind happened to Russell when Wittgenstein demolished the ideas in his large and ambitious manuscript of 1913 on the theory of knowledge, in the course of a series of painful conversations in May and June of that year. 'I saw', Russell wrote to Ottoline Morrell three years later, 'that I could not hope ever again to do fundamental work in philosophy'. Moore had little new to say, however emphatically and persuasively he said it, as was shown by the publication in 1953 of lectures he had given as far back as 1910 and 1911. Broad confined himself to elaboration and criticism of the ideas of Russell, Moore and, in the 1930s, McTaggart. Wittgenstein had been invisible for more than a decade. Ramsey was dead. The Vienna Circle had only just come into being. The field was wide open.

Ayer's account of his philosophical education in the first volume of his autobiography is rather sketchy. He recalls being introduced to the *Tractatus* by Ryle. He read Russell's *Our Knowledge of the External World* (1914) and *The Analysis of Mind* (1921). The origins can be discerned in these three books of his later central doctrines about necessity, perception and the mind. He also read Ramsey and Broad, James's *Pragmatism* (1907), Poincaré and Nicod. He does not say what problems preoccupied him. Nor does he say anything much about the development of his thinking up to the point in 1936 of its first, strikingly finished and comprehensive expression.

There is little echo in his writings of any influence of the thought of Prichard and Joseph, apart from two negative reactions. The first of these is his repeated insistence that, as he puts it in *The Problem of Knowledge*, 'from the fact that someone is convinced that something is true, however firm his conviction may be, it never follows logically that it is true' (*PK*, 15). That is hardly consistent with his conclusion in the following chapter that statements in the present tense about one's own immediate experience are incorrigible. For that is to say that, if I genuinely believe I am in pain or aware of a red patch, it follows that I am. The original thesis seems to be aimed at the Cook Wilsonian doctrine that knowledge is something unique and indefinable and such that we must know when we have it. Another echo is to be heard in Ayer's treatment of the doctrine of internal relations. In *The Founda-*

tions of Empirical Knowledge it is examined in connection with an argument quoted from Joseph (*FEK,* 200–2).

In November 1932 Ayer went to Vienna and was courteously invited to attend meetings of the Vienna Circle. It was what he learnt there and from the pages of *Erkenntnis*, which had started publication, under the editorship of Carnap and Reichenbach, in 1930, that he was inspired to the extraordinary *tour de force* of *Language, Truth and Logic*. A good way of bringing out the depth of Ayer's involvement is to compare the impact of a similar visit by an American contemporary at much the same time.[1] Ernest Nagel, a few years older than Ayer, spent the academic year 1934–5 in Europe, his principal stops being Cambridge, Vienna and Warsaw. News of the existence of logical positivism had already been brought to American philosophers by an article about it in the *Journal of Philosophy* in 1931 by Albert Blumberg and Herbert Feigl. Nagel's report of his intellectual expedition is, as one might expect, thorough, serious and reliable. He became a recognized associate of the Circle, but more as a fellow-traveller than as a fully committed zealot. He had contributed a boiled-down version of his doctoral thesis on the logic of measurement to *Erkenntnis* three years earlier and also an article on reduction in the sciences around the time of his European trip. Perhaps he was already, in his mid-thirties, too much involved with American naturalism to undergo a major conversion.

Ayer, on the other hand, completely ingested the four main doctrines subscribed to by the Vienna Circle: the identification of meaning with verifiability; the reductionism which that implies if subjective experience is taken to be the basis of knowledge; the theory that necessity is analytic, a matter of linguistic convention; and a radically non-cognitive account of judgments of value. In taking on these views he was not content simply to report them. He had even in his mid-twenties an established intellectual allegiance to the philosophical analysis of Russell, Moore, Wittgenstein and Ramsey. The special achievement of *Language, Truth and Logic* was the remarkable, almost seamless unification of his initial philosophical inheritance with the whole range of the main ideas of the Vienna Circle. Where he differed with the orthodoxy of Carnap, Neurath and Hempel, rejecting what he labelled as its 'formalism', it was with ideas developed by Schlick. Where Carnap and his allies denied that statements can be compared with extra-linguistic fact and so took basic statements to be adopted by convention, Schlick saw them as direct reports of the facts of experience.

[1] Ernest Nagel. 'Impressions and Appraisals of European Philosophy' (first published 1936), in Nagel, 1956.

Anthony Quinton

A survey of the contents of *Language, Truth and Logic* will show how comprehensive Ayer's reliance was on the doctrines of the Vienna Circle. The title of the first chapter is 'the elimination of metaphysics'. That phrase is a translation of the first words of an article by Carnap in *Erkenntnis: Uberwindung der Metaphysik durch logische Analyse der Sprache* (1932). There Carnap identifies the meaning of a sentence, first, following Wittgenstein, with its truth-conditions and then with its method of verification or, in the case of a word, with the criteria of its application. He goes on to say 'in the domain of *metaphysics*, including all philosophy of value and normative theory, logical analysis yields the negative result that the alleged statements in this domain are entirely meaningless'.[2] That and a few other references to value in Carnap were developed, with the aid of some apparatus from Moore, into the notorious sixth chapter of *Language, Truth and Logic*: critique of ethics and theology.

In his *Uberwindung* Carnap admits that the problem of the given, of the empirical basis of knowledge or, as he would prefer to put it, of the nature of protocol statements, is not yet solved. He soon went on to opt for the conventionalist view that they are statements about what is observed that are agreed upon by that shadowy, but quite cosy-sounding group, the 'scientists of our culture-circle'. In 1934 in 'Uber das Fundament der Erkenntnis', Schlick effectively criticized that position.

Although Ayer agreed with Schlick that basic statements are to be verified by the experiences to which they demonstratively refer, he denied that they are absolutely certain and incorrigible. His reason was 'that a sentence cannot merely name a situation, it must say something about it. And in describing a situation one is not merely "registering" a sense-content: one is classifying it in some way or other, and this means going beyond what is immediately given'. He goes on to say that to apply a word such as 'white' to an element of one's experience is to say that it is similar to other contents of experience: 'those which I should call, or actually have called white' (*LTL*, 126, 128–9). He did not support this view for very long. In 'Verification and experience' within a year of *Language, Truth and Logic* he was expressing doubts about it and in the second chapter of *Foundations of Empirical Knowledge* in 1940 and in the introduction to the second edition of *Language, Truth and Logic* in 1946 he explicitly rejected it.

In claiming that all necessity is analytic Ayer depends as much on the *Tractatus* as on the Vienna Circle. But like Carnap, and unlike Wittgenstein, he took the truths of mathematics as well as those of logic to be tautologies. He wisely did not follow Carnap in defining 'tautology' in a

[2] Translated in *LP*, 60–1.

narrowly truth-tabular way. The idea that logic and mathematics are useful because we, as finite intelligences, cannot trace all the implications of our thoughts was, as a footnote shows, derived from Hans Hahn's *Logik, Mathematik and Naturerkennen* of 1933. Ayer's refutation of Mill's account of mathematical truths as empirical generalizations of the widest possible scope was not dependent on Frege, whom, by 1936, he does not appear to have encountered. He unfortunately ascribes to Mill the view that the truths of logic, as well as those of mathematics, are empirical, fixing that mistake firmly in the heads of several generations of students. Mill, in fact, acknowledged what he called 'propositions merely verbal'; held that all essential propositions are identical propositions; and that deduction gives no new knowledge, says no more in its conclusions than is already contained in its premises.

Ayer's fifth chapter on truth and probability follows Ramsey on truth. It advances the theory about the corrigibility of all empirical statements whatever which he soon came to doubt and eventually to drop altogether. In a few concluding pages he had some suggestive things to say about probability. He defines it as the degree of confidence with which it is rational to entertain a hypothesis. He does not specify criteria of rationality, but says they are conventional and vary through time. That is to embrace the kind of conventionalism he rejected in the case of basic statements. Our old friends, the scientists of our culture circle, whose practice determines for Ayer what rationality currently is, are called back from epistemological retirement. The conception of probability as an intrinsic property of a hypothesis and Keynes's view of it as an unanalysable logical relation between hypothesis and the evidence for it are dismissed without argument. The frequency theory is not mentioned.

The significance of his brisk aside about probability is that it sustains the only solution he admits to the problem of induction. It is rational, he says, to be guided by the past in forming expectations about the future because that is what rationality is, by definition. No doubt the current practice of those we should ordinarily describe as scientists is rational in that sense. But as Ayer would surely have insisted we can guarantee their rationality only by defining 'scientist' so that no-one who deviates from being guided by the past counts as one.

His dealings with God and the immortal soul in chapter six derive fairly directly from Carnap's 'Uberwindung'. But the insistence that neither metaphysical sentences nor their negations can be asserted since both are equally devoid of sense is Ayer's own. It has, as he saw, the consequence that neither atheism nor even agnosticism is any better off than theism, a concession that was not much appreciated by its adherents.

The main business of chapter six is the thesis that judgments of value are expressions of feeling and not statements of fact, natural or non-natural. Ayer relies heavily on Moore to dismiss naturalism, although he rephrases Moore's argument. The intuitive non-contradictoriness of 'this is pleasant but not good' is appealed to instead of the intuitive substantiality of the question 'is this pleasant thing good?'. The verification principle is invoked to deal with Moore's positive view about the nature of goodness.

Ayer's own positive account of the matter is a sharper-edged version of Carnap's '*Uberwindung*' (1932) contention that metaphysics (including value judgments) 'serves for the general expression of the attitude of a person towards life'.[3] In his *Philosophy and Logical Syntax* of 1934 Carnap interprets moral affirmations as imperatives, a more plausible view than Ayer's, as subsequent developments in moral philosophy have shown. It seems probable that the main source here was the celebrated distinction of scientific from emotive language in *The Meaning of Meaning* by Ogden and Richards of 1923. They say, in terms Ayer takes over almost word for word, '"(this) is good" serves only as an emotive sign expressing our attitude to *this* and perhaps evoking similar attitudes in other persons, or inciting them to action of one kind or another'.[4] Ayer's account of moral disagreement is taken from W. H. F. Barnes's 'Suggestion about value' of 1933.

In the four chapters so far considered the main borrowings have been from the Vienna Circle. The balance tilts towards Ayer's British, predominantly Cambridge predecessors, in chapters two and three, where a conception of the nature of philosophy is set out and in the two final chapters which are about mind, matter and the self and three 'outstanding philosophical disputes'.

The idea that philosophy should be a business of analysis was affirmed at some length in the last chapter of Russell's *Our Kowledge of the External World* (1914) and it was consistently practised as analysis, with a slightly different inflection, in the writings of Moore. In his neutral monist period from about 1918 onwards, Russell tried to analyse material objects and minds into what he called 'events'. He took material objects to be constructions out of sensations and *sensibilia*, these being gently reified equivalents of Mill's 'permanent possibilities of sensation'. Minds and their states were seen as constructions out of sensations and images, eked out with bodily behaviour where that seemed desirable.

Ayer drew on Price's *Perception* (1950) in his firmly phenomenalist account of our knowledge of material objects in chapter three. But he

[3] R. Carnap in *LP*, 78.
[4] Ogden & Richards, 1923, 125.

restates Price's theory of objects as 'families' of actual and possible sense-data in linguistic form: sentences about objects are translatable into sets of sentences, categorical and hypothetical, about sense-data. No place is found for Price's 'physical occupant', that ghostly vestige of the substratum of Locke.

He follows Russell in holding that sense-data are neither physical nor mental, these being properties of logical constructions. But for the detail of his account of mind he draws, not on Russell, but on Carnap and Hume. In his *Aufbau* Carnap had distinguished the *eigenpsychisch* from the *fremdpsychisch*, the mental states I experience directly from those I ascribe to others on the basis of their bodily behaviour. Ayer was driven to this by his belief that the argument from analogy is unacceptably metaphysical. He was to question that four years later in *Foundations of Empirical Knowledge* and abandon it altogether in 1953. The argument from analogy was rehabilitated by the consideration that, since it is only a contingent fact that I have the experiences I do, there is no logical or necessary obstacle to the possibility that the experiences of others might have been mine. The way out he followed was suggested to him by Ryle's article of 1936 'Unverifiability by me'.

Ayer's Humean view of the self as a series of experiences contained one wholly original element. Hume had been baffled in his attempt to find a relation which could connect a series of experiences into a self. Ayer's suggestion was that the experiences of one self must all 'contain organic sense-contents which are elements of the same body' (*LTL*, 194). That, as he saw, rules out the possibility of the survival by the self of bodily dissolution. It also ensures that no experience can belong to more than one self, which the resemblance and continuity which Hume was inclined to favour failed to do. It makes my identification of my body (under some other description, of course) prior to my identification of myself, which is not too bad. But it also requires that every total momentary experience of mine should contain a veridical organic sensation of my body. That is a very questionable proposal, but I shall not pursue the matter here. It may be noted that later theorists of personal identity—Bernard Williams and Sidney Shoemaker, for example—who have claimed that it entails bodily identity have not done so in Ayer's way.

A final thesis of *Language, Truth and Logic* which was soon dropped was also borrowed. From C. I. Lewis's *Mind and the World-Order* Ayer took the thesis that statements about the past are really hypotheses about future experience, on which we shall have to rely in order to verify them. It implies, I suppose, that our memories are really thoughts about the future. It can be circumvented by the consideration that it is a contingent fact that my experiences occur at the time that they do.

Language, Truth and Logic, then, is almost wholly composed of pre-existing material. It was brilliantly presented, with astounding concision, and its content fitted very well together, despite the geographical remoteness of its two main sources. That is not surprising when one reflects that the philosophers of Cambridge and Vienna continuously interacted. Russell and Wittgenstein were, in a turbulent way, teachers and pupils of each other. The Vienna Circle studied them both and as intently as they studied anyone.

A special virtue of the book, over and above its excellences of style, its force, lucidity and euphony, is its intellectual order. The elements may be borrowed but they are admirably arranged. After *Our Knowledge of the External World* Russell's books became increasingly loose and casual in construction. That can presumably be attributed to the loss of self-confidence caused by Wittgenstein's ruthless criticism. Moore's laborious repetitiveness and his confinement to a minute range of topics, however strategically important, was unsatisfying in a different way. The *Tractatus*, with pretty well all the argument left out, hovers about on either side of the frontier of intelligibility. Ramsey's small, brilliant *Nachlass* was, in its more philosophically interesting parts, largely rough notes. Broad and Price were admirably lucid and thorough and Price's writing had a particular kind of charm. But they were not, as Ayer unquestionably was, exciting.

Presenting the ideas of Vienna Circle in British costume he extricated them from the lavish use of symbolism, the off-putting technical terms and the computer-like detachment of Carnap's writing. More in the manner of Schlick he conceived the philosopher to be, however doctrinally subversive, a citizen of the republic of letters. Also like Schlick, who wrote an article on the Vienna Circle and traditional philosophy, he drew attention to the many anticipations in the philosophy of the past of the ideas he was expounding. Berkeley was invoked for his phenomenalism, so long as its theistic attachments were removed. Ayer was also in sympathy with his slogan: 'Mem, to be eternally recalling men . . . to common sense' (Berkeley 1930, 93). The task of philosophy is not to justify our beliefs but to analyse them. In fact, Ayer probably absorbed that idea from Moore. He saw Hume as right in what he said about meaning, the two kinds of significant proposition, causation and, broadly speaking, the self, even if his thoughts were couched in too psychologistic an idiom. But Ayer's attention to the philosophy of the past faltered when he came to consider examples of metaphysical illusion. Carnap in his 'Uberwindung' had illustrated his thesis with a short passage from Heidegger and a single sentence from Hegel. Ayer made do with a single sentence from Bradley.

It was the fact that Ayer's revolutionary message was expressed in the literary form of a discursive essay and not in the manner of a scientific textbook, together with its elegance and brevity, that give it such an impact. It was addressed to intelligent readers in general, from the then radical publishing house of Gollancz, and in an attractively up-to-date physical form: dumpy in shape with wide margins and a wholly non-Victorian typeface: *Aufbau* by *Bauhaus*. (The move to Macmillan for his next book in 1940—they were to be his publishers for the next thirty-two years—was a turn towards academic respectability and exclusiveness.) Many of the intelligent readers aimed at took it up. No British philosophical book since Russell's *Problem of Philosophy* (1912) a quarter of a century earlier can have been as widely read.

Ayer's later books—*Foundations of Empirical Knowledge, The Problem of Knowledge* and *Central Questions of Philosophy*—and his five essay collections are, by and large, confined to the topics treated in *Language, Truth and Logic*. That is as much a tribute to the superb economy with which they were treated there as a criticism. The book's philosophical agenda covered a wide enough range for anyone's philosophical career. And there are new thoughts presented and new fields explored in the later works. But he did not move far from his starting-point.

The main novelty of *Foundations of Empirical Knowledge*, apart from the limited changes of mind about incorrigibility and the argument from analogy already mentioned, is the contention that theories of perception are not competing substantive doctrines but, rather, proposals of 'alternative languages'. It is not very clear what that amounts to. Does someone who rejects the sense-datum language have to say that some material objects exist only for one person, or intermittently, or have different properties for different people? The arguments used to show that only sense-data are directly perceived could then be mobilized to show that all direct perception is of private material objects and that public material objects, spatiotemporally and causally interconnected in a common world, must somehow be constructed out of them. In that case the alternative offered is of the most trivial, merely typographical kind. What is clear is that nobody seems to have paid much attention to it until J. L. Austin criticized it in *Sense and Sensibilia* (1962). By that time Ayer had explicitly, if quietly, dropped the whole idea. In his essay of 1945 on the terminology of sense-data he accepts the criticism of it by H. H. Price.[5]

Thinking and Meaning, Ayer's London inaugural of 1947, is very properly dedicated to Ryle. For it is a thoroughgoing exercise in dereification, in which the thinking self, the instrument with which it

[5] A. J. Ayer. 'The Terminology of Sense-Data', in *PE*, 103–4.

thinks, the process of its thought, conceived as a sequence of mental acts, and the object of thought, its reference or meaning, are all resolved into the expression of thought in significant sentences. Particularly Rylean is the insistence that what have usually been conceived to be mental acts, such a believing and doubting, are really dispositions to come out with certain sentences or to act in certain ways. There is also a distinct echo of Ryle's 'Systematically Misleading Expressions' in the assertion that for an expression to have a meaning there does not have to exist a thing which is its meaning.

Ayer's remarks about meaning in this lecture indicate a much closer attention on his part to philosophical logic. In his *Philosopical Essays* of 1954 it is the topic of the first three items: on individuals, the identity of indiscernibles and negation. Then four epistemological items rehearse, with minor modifications, the familiar topics of sense-data, basic propositions, phenomenalism and our knowledge of other minds. Finally Quine's ontology is considered, Ayer's ethical theory is presented with greater suavity but without substantial alteration, Bentham's principle of utility is sympathetically explored and the view that freedom and determinism are compatible, affirmed in pellet form in the footnote of *Language, Truth and Logic*, is defended and modified. In its 1946 version, as reprinted in *Philosophical Essays*, freedom is defined as absence of constraint, not as having no cause at all. A group of factors is brought together as constraining causes and thus as cancelling responsibility, but no account is given of what principle links them together and distinguishes them from other, non-exculpating causes of action.

The essay on individuals tentatively puts forward arguments for the eliminability of singular terms and the possibility of a purely predicative language implied by Quine's extension of the theory of descriptions to all referring expressions. The issue is taken up again in an essay on names and descriptions in *The Concept of a Person*, but now what was earlier suggested is categorically affirmed.

Quine's use of his regimented language, in which all reference is carried out by quantifiers, to reinstate ontology in a new, logically respectable form, set Ayer thinking generally about what there is. In his study of William James (*OP*) and again in an essay 'What there must be' in his *Metaphysics and Common Sense* of 1969, Ayer returns to the question. Against Quine and Russell he concludes that reducibility does not imply some kind of inferior existential status, as 'mere constructions' or fictions, in the items to which it applies as contrasted with the unassailably real existence of the elements from which they are constructed. Analysis may eliminate singular terms. It does not fictionalize material things. Here again I think there is a distinct echo of the Vienna Circle, particularly of Carnap's *Scheinprobleme* (1928b) and Schlick's 'Positivismus und Realismus' (1933).

They had maintained that the reducibility of material things to sense-experiences casts no shadow whatever on the reality of the material world. It simply makes clear what the empirical reality of material things consists in. For such things to exist the course of sense-experience must exhibit certain kinds of regularity. If it does there is no further question about the real existence of the material things defined in terms of these regularities. To infer that, as Schlick puts it, 'only the given exists' (*Es gibt nur das Gegebene*) is to fall into unacceptable metaphysics.

In his positive views about ontology Ayer takes an exactly opposite position to Russell. Sense-experiences are not ontologically prior to material things since their occurrence is absorbed into a comprehensive theory of a material world. There they occupy a very modest place, as parts of the histories of sentient organic bodies. Priority for knowledge is one thing: priority of existence another. Ayer takes ordinary material things and the theoretical entities of sciences as competing for the status of being the real components of the material world. He vacillates between the two claimants—intellect urging electrons, sentiment pressing for tables—and concludes that it is a matter for choice and not very important anyway.

The Problem of Knowledge of 1956 has an excellent chapter on memory. It dispels the influence of a radically misguided chapter of Russell's *Analysis of Mind* (1921) on the subject. Memory is having beliefs about the past that do not depend on inference or testimony. It is not images accompanied by feelings of familiarity and pastness, whatever they may be. Some interesting points are raised in the final chapter on myself and others. If a person is simply a contingently related series of experiences, why should an experience not occur on its own, unrelated in a person-constituting way to other experiences? Why, in other words, should there not be unowned experiences? Personal identity is addressed once more, in a guarded, hesitant way. Perhaps Hume's accusation of a circularity in the definition of personal identity in terms of memory can be circumvented. Survival of bodily dissolution seems conceivable. Yet purely psychological criteria of identity seem insufficient.

There are three substantial novelties in the book. First, there is the neat account of what is needed to turn true belief into knowledge as the 'right to be sure'. The question has not been pressed as to why Ayer does not take the ethics of belief to be as non-cognitive as the ethics of conduct, as he did by implication in his account of rationality in *Language, Truth and Logic*.

Secondly, there is the helpful schematization of problems in the theory of knowledge, about perception, other minds, the past, induction and so on as arising from the scepticism generated by a gap between certain kinds of belief—about material things, past events, the minds of others, the laws of nature—and the only evidence that is available for them—sense-data, memories and traces, behaviour and observed regularities. That was not new. It was present in the pre-war writings of John Wisdom and set out clearly in an article about Wisdom by Douglas Gasking (1954). Something along the same lines had also been worked out by Friedrich Waismann. These sources make one wonder if it was not something casually let fall in conversation by Wittgenstein.

Ayer, like the other exponents of the scheme, recognized four standard ways of dealing with the gaps. First, intuition, which claimed direct access to the other side of it. Secondly, the theory of a general principle which could serve as a bridge across it. Thirdly, reductionism, which closed the gap by defining the things concluded to in terms of the evidence for them. Fourthly, the melancholy option of scepticism. Ayer conjured up a fifth contender, grandly called 'the method of descriptive analysis', which seemed to be a matter of admitting the gap and then blithely doing nothing about it.

In fact, once more confronting the question of our knowledge of material objects, he does something rather different, and offers a kind of watered down reductionism. Our beliefs about the material world are not translatable into statements about sense-data. They should be understood as a theory which draws all its support from the evidence of sense-data. There is an air here of trying to settle an overdraft with a cheque drawn on the same account. It shifts the problem to that of the relation of a theory to the evidence for it: is it like the detective's theory that the injury to the deceased was caused by a blunt instrument (later found in the shrubbery) or like Newton's theory that the fall of apples and the orbiting of the sun by the planets are manifestations of the same gravitational force? For better or worse, Ayer stuck to this position until his final treatment of the topic in *Central Questions of Philosophy* in 1973.

By carrying out the ungracious task of tracing most of Ayer's original ideas, and many of those he came to express later, to external sources, I am not suggesting that there is no more to his achievement than the communication of these borrowings. He wrote some lively pieces of philosophical polemic: defending the sense-datum theory against Austin's often captious objections, setting ferociously about Malcolm's view that dreams are stories we are disposed to tell when we wake up and arguing against Wittgenstein's view that a private language is impossible. He expounded Peirce and James, Russell and Moore with thoroughness and distinction. His special kind of clear-headedness proved valuable in his work on probability, a subject often liable to be swamped by fruitless technicalities.

An unstated assumption behind this excavation of Ayer's intellectual borrowings is that a thinker's place in the history of philosophy is determined by the originality of the interesting or influential things that he says. I do, indeed, believe that assumption to be broadly correct. No doubt the more one learns of the history of philosophy the more one realizes that what one had supposed to be the proprietary great thoughts of those commonly reckoned to be great philosophers had often been thought by someone else first. Descartes's *cogito ergo sum*, one learns, is an echo of Augustine's *si fallor sum*. Locke drew heavily on Descartes, Gassendi and Boyle. Nevertheless Descartes put his *cogito* to uses of which Augustine had no conception and, although there are identifiable fragments of other men's ideas in Locke's encyclopaedic *Essay* (1690), the plan and basis of the whole great undertaking were his own. The special greatness of Kant is surely for the most part due to the novelty of his ideas.

Rather than considering the question in general terms it will be better to try to fix Ayer's place in the scheme of things by comparing his achievements with those of his contemporaries who qualify for such a comparison. Broad and Price were lucid and persevering exponents of ideas put into circulation in the first years of the century by Russell and Moore. Broad had the advantage of knowing a good deal about natural science and about the history of philosophy. Price's great merit was his cautious deliberation, his extremely high standard of what the clear understanding of a problem and its proposed solutions consists in. Their main service was to domesticate the inchoate innovations of others. That is something that Ayer accomplished with greater force and comparable distinction.

Two more obviously appropriate comparisons are with Ryle, ten years his senior, and Austin, his near-contemporary. Ryle, too, was an extensive borrower. His philosophical logic derives from Russell and the *Tractatus*, his philosophy of mind from intimations that had come to him of the thinking of the later Wittgenstein. But he put his own stamp very markedly on what he took. That is in part a matter of his breezy, epigrammatic, resolutely non-technical style. That style was in tune with a mode of proceeding that relied heavily on analogy and, in general, avoided the laborious protection of theses from all possible objections. Oddly, in the light of their respective ways of life—collegiate in Ryle's case, metropolitan in Ayer's, it is Ryle who is the less academically respectable and conformist. He steered clear of all the standard etiquette of philosophical writing: the identification of -isms, the footnotes, the polite references to Professor This and Doctor That. In the end I think I should accord him a larger place on the philosophical map than Broad, Price or Ayer, but I admit that it is a close-run thing.

The main reason for it is that, whether by accident or design, his own versions of late-Wittgensteinian doctrine are really very different from the original. The distinction between knowing-how and knowing-that was an insight of great value, however easy it is to take it for granted once it has been pointed out. The boldness with which he dismissed Cartesian dualism, by interpreting all mental life in terms of dispositions to behaviour, has the merit of providing something definite to discuss, rather than endlessly puzzle over.

Austin was the critic who got furthest under Ayer's skin as is clear from the indignant tone of Ayer's response to his criticism of the sense-datum theory. Like Prichard and Moore he was a rigorously minute philosopher whose scrupulous pursuit of exactness gave him an extraordinary personal command over his contemporaries. He went further in that direction than his acknowledged master, Prichard, because of his greater intelligence and general mental agility. But his reputation has not survived him. A later generation finds it difficult to understand. Apart from 'speech acts' his innovations in the philosophical vocabulary are seldom heard.

The two philosophers with whom Ayer is most appropriately to be compared are Quine and Popper. Both, like Ayer, are intellectual by-products of the Vienna Circle; in Quine's case gratefully (*Word and Object* (1960), after all, is dedicated to Carnap), in Popper's with a constant determination to emphasize his differences from it. I think it is fair to say that there is no new idea in Ayer that deserves to receive or has received the kind of attention that has been given to the innovations of Quine and Popper.

Quine's multifarious assaults on the notion of meaning as the chief instrument of philosophical explanation, on the analytic-synthetic distinction, on modal and intentional discourse, on assumptions about translatability, his revival of ontology and his naturalistic account of the theory of knowledge, add up to a major change of direction in philosophy. Not all that many have chosen to follow him very far down the path he has pointed out but his ideas have proved to be inexhaustibly discussable.

Popper's fundamental idea that science progresses by adventurous conjectures, controlled by attempts to overthrow them, is not without forerunners. Something like it is crucial in the philosophy of science of Whewell and it plays a part, if not such a commanding one as for Popper, in the brilliant chaos of the writings of Peirce. But there is no reason to suppose that Popper had the least familiarity with either of them at the time in the early 1930s when he was writing his *Logik der Forschung* (1935). Whewell had been obliterated by Mill in the English-speaking world and was quite unknown anywhere else. As for Peirce, M. R. Cohen's pioneering selection, *Chance, Love and Logic* had come out in 1923 but it did not contain any of Peirce's more Popperian pieces and was anyhow almost certainly unknown to him.

Secondly, and more to the point, Popper's very various developments of his fundamental thought go in directions altogether unexplored by Whewell and only partially by Peirce. Peirce, like Popper, adopts a comprehensively fallibilistic theory of knowledge and rejects determinism. Of Popper's own invention are his attack on the view that there are general laws of historical change, his account of probability as objective propensity, his defence of science as an account of the real nature of things against instrumentalism and essentialism, his application of evolutionary ideas to the theory of knowledge and the connected doctrine of 'World 3', over and above the realms of matter and consciousness.

Quine and Popper arrived at their main new ideas early on: Quine by 1936 in 'Truth by convention' and 1939 in 'Designation and existence', Popper by the date of his first book, 1935. Holding firmly on to them ever since, they have established their fertility by the substantial and interesting body of extensions and applications they have made of them. Ayer, on the other hand, tended to circle round a number of topics, varying his attitude towards them, sometimes opting for one view or another, sometimes concluding that it is a matter for decision, sometimes simply confessing doubt as to what the right answer is. The one thing he never questioned is the primacy of sense-experience, even if, with his later replacement of sense-data by 'qualia', he tried to mitigate the subjectivity of his preferred foundations for knowledge. For all the bold iconoclasm of *Language, Truth and Logic* the abiding impression is one of doctrinal indefiniteness. (It is interesting that he never responded to Quine's rejection of analyticity except in a couple of non-combative pages of *Central Questions of Philosophy*.)

It is that, I think, that must explain the fact that his influence has been so much less than that of the two major contemporaries with whom I have been comparing him. I speak here of influence on philosophers, since Quine is unknown to the part of the general reading public which thinks it would like to know something about philosophy. As every teacher of the subject knows, Ayer has enormously influenced beginning students of philosophy. Since most of them do not go far with the subject, that influence must be, with many, a persisting one. As a paradigm of a philosopher for educated people he is surely exemplary for his unswerving dedication to argument, to explicit reasoning concisely expressed in the clearest language.

It is noticeable that his influence has been comparatively small in the United States. In the post-war years when this country was a net importer of visiting philosophers they crossed the Atlantic to learn about Wittgenstein, Ryle and Austin. That must be partly due to the fact that, from the late 1930s on, the Americans did not need an intermediary to convey the message of the Vienna Circle, since most of its leading exponents were coming to be installed there in university posts. Furthermore Ayer's ideas about necessary truth and phenomenalism had been anticipated in the United States, seven years before *Language, Truth and Logic* in C. I. Lewis's more substantial, if less exciting, *Mind and the World-Order*.

Another possible factor is that philosophers in the United States, as in Cambridge in its greatest days, typically know more mathematics and natural science than philosophers in Oxford. Ayer was always an enthusiast for science, but the enthusiasm was of a generalized, rather ideological kind. I believe it was essentially secondary to his animus against religion. The sensationalism to which he always remained faithful was something he shared with the great generation of late nineteenth-century unbelieving philosophers of science: Mach, W. K. Clifford, Karl Pearson. Present-day philosophers of science—Popper, J. J. C. Smart, the Reichenbach of *Experience and Prediction* (1938), even Carnap after the mid-1930s—take for granted the objectivity of the basis of empirical knowledge. Ayer's distaste for religion seems to be the central vision and object of emotional commitment which it is the office of the brilliantly deployed dialectical manoeuvres to protect, rather as a conviction of the immortality of human souls, related by spiritual love, is the soft centre in need of fascinating ingenuities of argumentative defence in the case of McTaggart.

Ayer thought of himself as the main representative in his own time of the British empirical tradition, running from Hume through John Stuart Mill to Russell. It is a natural and intelligible point of view. His interpretation of the leading ideas of that tradition, in the sharpened form given to them by the Vienna Circle, undoubtedly gave it a new lease of life. But in its most vigorous form at the present time that tradition has moved beyond the doctrinal constraints he accepted from it about necessity, perception and the nature of science.

Although I have come to think his place in the history of philosophy is not as large as I had thought before settling down to write this lecture, I think I understand why I should have thought as I did. In the first post-war decades philosophy in Britain was dominated by Wittgenstein and Austin, one a genius, the other enormously gifted, but both execrable examples in many ways. Confronted by dire imitations of their respective styles of writing and reasoning Ayer stood out as a marvellous champion of the best traditions of rational discourse.

Ayer's Attack on Metaphysics

D. M. MACKINNON

In an article contributed to *Mind* in 1934, the young A. J. Ayer declared war on metaphysics, claiming that his destruction of the metaphysicians' arguments rested on the establishment of the sheerly non-sensical character of their statements. Their errors were syntactical; the combination of symbols in the sentences with which they expressed their propositions violated fundamental principles of significance.

Where statements of fact were concerned, the authority of the principle of verification was absolute. If the often quoted formulation of this principle as the 'meaning of a proposition is the method of its verification' was drastically criticized, its underlying insistence remained that we *must* be able to specify the circumstances which would confirm or discredit the proposition in question. In the case of Moritz Schlick's often quoted example 'There are mountains on the other side of the moon', no one disputed its claim to significance on the ground that at the time of its utterance, it defied verification; it was verifiable in principle, and therefore perfectly intelligible. Whereas the claim that God exists defied any attempt made to specify conditions under which we would suppose it confirmed or refuted. Agnostics and atheists as much as theists were engaged in unintelligible disputes. We could specify conditions under which we would admit the reality of entities totally remote from our immediate experience, or dismiss claims made for their inclusion in the furniture of the describable world, for instance (to take more recent examples) neutrinos or 'black holes'. But with alleged transcendent realities, whether the Judaeo-Christian God or the Platonic 'Idea of the Good', it was altogether otherwise. To entertain their reality as conceivable was to commit oneself to pondering a non-sense; for the combination of the concept of existence with that of a divine substance must destroy any attachment to the conditions under which the notion may alone be employed.

But did Ayer understand the impulses that tempted men of genius into such elaborate essays in non-sense? His answer would have been that he did not deny the possible value of such work as poetry, with more than a hint that he was using the word 'poetry' pejoratively. One was inevitably reminded of Bentham's dismissive dictum: 'Poetry is misrepresentation.' Indeed Ayer once remarked that many philosophers should send their writings to the *London Mercury* rather than to

49

Mind, glossing his remark by suggesting that perhaps *Transition* (an *avant-garde* periodical of the *Thirties*) would be a more suitable recipient of their outpourings than the *Mercury*. It was as if poetry could be regarded as a rubbish-bin to which the vapourings of the intellectually undisciplined might be consigned.

At this point one might quote T. S. Eliot's lines:

> Words strain
> Crack and sometimes break, under the burden
> Under the tension, slip, slide, perish,
> Decay with imprecision, will not stay in place,
> Will not stay still.

But while in *Burnt Norton* Eliot is acclaiming the creativity of linguistic innovation, Ayer might have found in his words, a plea for the sort of rigorous precision in use and understanding of language that the logical positivist programme sought to achieve. In the early years of the *Wiener Kreis*, Professor Moritz Schlick had expressed the hope that one day there would be no more books on philosophy but that all books would be written philosophically. That is to say—the day of the speculative treatise would yield to that of the scientific exposition in which the expositor knew how to give precise cash-value to the terms he was using, and not allow the unfamiliarity of the territory he was mapping to beguile him into supposing that he was opening the doors on to a mysterious ultimate. The essays in popular cosmology of the early *Thirties*—Sir James Jeans' *The Mysterious Universe* (1937), and A. S. Eddington's *The Nature of the Physical World* (1928)—might be judged flamboyant examples of the kind of undisciplined exploitation of cosmological conceptions that Schlick's programme sought to banish. And when later Eddington in his Tarner lectures on the *Philosophy of Physical Science* (1939) sought to establish the authority of a neo-Cartesian rationalism in scientific method, his undertaking might have been regarded as a paradigmatic example of the misunderstanding of the nature and role of necessary or *a priori* truths.

It was indeed this critical programme that Ayer sought to domesticate; and if we are to understand the targets of his anti-metaphysical polemic, it is not enough simply to remark his hostility to the speculative impulse: we must also recall his indebtedness to the Vienna Circle's polemic against the *synthetic a priori*. Schlick in fact wrote his major treatise on the theory of knowledge—*Allegemeine Erkenntnislehre* (1918), before he had read Wittgenstein's *Tractatus Logico-Philosophicus* (1922), and in that work his target had been the Kantian tradition as that tradition had been revived by the so-called Marburg neo-Kantians. And here he argued, not simply (as Kant himself had done) against the possibility of a theoretical demonstration of the reality of God, of human freedom, and of the immortality of the soul; but against the philosopher's claim to have established supposedly universal and necessary truths of fact concerning e.g. the structure of space, the pervasiveness of causal order in the world of our experience etc. The very conception of a universally valid truth of fact was the object of Schlick's polemic, and his welcome to Wittgenstein's work was in no small measure due to the extent to which Schlick believed it had given a definitive solution to the whole problem of necessary truths, in particular by his treatment of logically necessary propositions as tautologies of the two-valued propositional calculus.

In his *Mind* article of 1934 (*IM*) Ayer acknowledged the power of Kant's criticism of transcendent metaphysics. But he claimed a certain superiority for his own critical method in that it proceeded not by way of distinguishing different levels of human intellectual activity (e.g. imagination, understanding, reason) but rather by submitting the deliverances of metaphysicians to the test of verifiability in principle. In fact he was much nearer to Kant than he realized in as much as the notion of verifiability in principle came in practice very near to Kant's 'experience in general'. But it cannot however be denied that Kant had a far greater sympathy with the goals the transcendent metaphysician sought to attain. Indeed it was an important element in his critical programme of 'destroying reason to make room for faith' that he secured for instance, belief in God as 'postulate of pure practical reason' by revealing an intellectual flaw in speculative materialist cosmology no less damaging to its claim than the one which he insisted damaged irreparably supposed theoretical ascent to the reality of a creator *de nihilo*. Kant's deep sympathy with many of the impulses underlying transcendent metaphysical adventure becomes manifest, if one looks at a fair sample of his voluminous output, including the opuscula of his last years. Where however Ayer's fundamental quarrel with Kant lay only becomes clear when close attention is paid to their divergence in the understanding of necessary truth. If they enjoyed a general measure of agreement in their attitudes to transcendent metaphysics, unlike Kant, Ayer had no room for the transcendentally *a priori*: this even though in Kant's understanding of our knowledge of the external world, a strong vein of phenomenalism is discernible, and it is well known how much of his energies Ayer devoted in his early years to testing the phenomenalist programme to destruction, eager if he could by its means rid our commerce with the world around us of any temptation towards admitting that which was unobservable in principle.

And it is to phenomenalism that we now turn. Admittedly Ayer totally rejected Kant's distinction between phenomena and 'things-in-themselves'. But although he found Hume's treatment of causality more congenial than Kant's, he recognized that the latter philosopher's criticism of the cosmological (causal) argument for the existence of God enabled him display with devastating effect, the illegitimacy of speaking of causality in respect of the effect of the unknowable on the familiar. If we could not significantly speak of God's causal activity, nor could we speak of the causal operation of unperceivable material realities in determining the course of our sense-experience. The strength of the phenomenalist's plea to treat physical realities as 'logical constructions' out of actual and possible contents of sense-experience lay in the seemingly opaque unintelligibility of the causality attributed to material reality in any causal theory of perception. We do not know what we are speaking of; the causal activity is something qualitatively totally dissimilar from anything of which we can significantly speak.

It was of course the notion of 'logical construction' introduced into general philosophy by Bertrand Russell from his more technical work on the foundations of mathematics that Ayer employed to give greater rigour and plausibility to Mill's conception of material things as constellations of 'permanent possibilities of sensation'. Indeed in the writings of his own middle period Russell had himself used the same notion in the interest of a modified phenomenalist programme, introducing the notion of 'unsensed sensibilia' to give greater plausibility to his enterprise. The writer Wyndham Lewis had scathingly written off Russell's view of the external world as one of 'a gim-crack world of mere façades', and it might well be thought that Russell's postulation of 'unsensed sensibilia' was aimed at freeing his view from the damage of such sarcastic comment.

The notion of 'logical construction' was fundamental for many years to what has become known as a 'reductionist' method in philosophy: that is a method which sought to reduce the number of independent entities involved in the description of the world by defining through a very subtle method of definition, the relatively unfamiliar in favour of the familiar. 'Reductionism' so conceived was an ontological programme concerned to give an inventory of the irreducible elements of the world; its earliest form was that of logical atomism, a philosophical style given explicit statement by Russell in his famous articles in the *Monist* towards the end of the first world war on *The Philosophy of Logical Atomism* (1918). (The logical atomism of Wittgenstein's *Tractatus* was very different; far more for the most part an essay in philosophical logic.) But with logical positivism 'reductionism' was virtually re-defined as an epistemological programme, aimed at completing the work of Ernest Mach in formulating a descriptive, radically empiricist conception of science, seeking to eliminate as metaphysical non-sense from scientific theories, any assumption of the unobservable. (Mach's criticism of absolute motion remains a classical essay in empiricist philosophy of science.) But the logical positivists, the men of the Vienna Circle, seized not only on Russell's and Frege's work in logic, but on their contributions to the philosophy of language, to give a depth of logical sophistication to a programme aimed at rendering invulnerable the authority of sense-experience. If Mach had practised elimination, the logical positivists substituted a kind of definition, whose paradigm remained Russell's definition of a cardinal number as 'the class of classes corresponding to a given class', but one illustrated perhaps with greater relevant subtlety by Frege in his treatment of the equator and the centre of gravity of the solar system in *The Foundations of Arithmetic* (Frege, 1953).

If I stress the importance of phenomenalism in Ayer's criticism of metaphysics, I do so because in the years he devoted to the topic, he was in fact trying to show that anti-metaphysical polemic yielded a world in which we could feel at home without being distracted by alleged mysteries, whether raised by undisciplined speculation, or by conundra thrown up inevitably by the intellectual triumphs of the exact and natural sciences. A critique of language was here of first importance, and it was a critique which rapidly emancipated itself from the spell of the too rigorously atomist reductionism, while continuing to acknowledge that some forms of description came nearer to actuality than others. And with Ayer (though in later years he came to abandon phenomenalism) it was the world of sense-experience, the world exalted in the tradition of classical British empiricism, that was his home. Sir Isaiah Berlin saw in the style of the *Wiener Kreis*, something akin to the mood of the French Encyclopaedists (in a review of Julius Weinberg's *Examination of Logical Positivism* in the *Criterion* for October 1937); in Ayer's personal hostility to metaphysics there was discernible a passionate re-assertion of the empiricist tradition, extracted from the works of Berkeley, Hume, Mill and Russell. But it was the Mill of the *Examination of Sir William Hamilton's Philosophy* (1865) who inspired him, more than the author of the essays on Bentham and Coleridge, who saw in those two opposed minds, the master-spirits of his age. Again Professor J. L. Austin's criticism of Ayer in *Sense and Sensibilia* (1962) is very well known; but far more perceptive was a searching question I once heard the same J. L. Austin put to Ayer: 'Do you really suppose that we learn more about the world from your phenomenalism than from Einstein's special and general theories of relativity?'

In a review of Sir Geoffrey Warnock's book in the Home University Library on British Philosophy in the first half of the present century (Warnock, 1958), Ayer rightly pointed out that Warnock was wrong to suppose that the logico-analytic tradition stemming from the work of Bertrand Russell and G. E. Moore effectively displaced in Oxford a dominant metaphysical idealism. In the Oxford that Ayer knew as an undergraduate, the dominant school was that stemming from Professor John Cook Wilson, continued by such men as Professor H. A. Prichard, H. W. B. Joseph, and E. F. Carritt. (The differences between Joseph and Prichard are not unimportant.) Their practice was rigorous and minute; but it was also vehemently dogmatic. The two posthumous volumes of Cook Wilson's writings—*Statement and Inference* (1926)—reveal a man who was a passionate realist, at his best a very acute philosophical logician, but a man liable to obsessions, in particular in his later years, the iniquity of non-Euclidean geometry. Indeed in spite of its continued vindication both as a part of pure and in applied mathematics, the whole programme from Lobachewski and Bolyai to Einstein was regarded as something positively evil as well as intellectually destructive. Certainly, although Euclid's parallels postulate had been under criticism since Proclus, the intellectual revolution occasioned by the rejection of Euclid's axioms as absolute was very considerable. But the philosophical resistance to acknowledging its validity focused for Ayer (and indeed for others) the inflexible obstinacy that was judged one of the most damaging aspects of the metaphysical mind. Those engaged in this resistance *knew*, and their supposed knowledge of universal and necessary truth was invulnerable. There is certainly an element of paradox, especially if one recalls the rigour of Ayer's phenomenalist commitment; for it is the hard refusal of intellectual adventure in reconstructing one's understanding of the relation of geometry to the world of ordinary experience that is being rejected as metaphysical. The refusal to launch out into the deep, to accept the need of radical innovation, is being sharply criticized, in a way that seems at the same time to query insistence on the security given by admission of the authority of sense-experience. I say seems; for in his contribution to the volume on Bertrand Russell in the *Library of Living Philosophers* (Schilpp, 1963), Einstein himself had insisted that the creative power of thought (he uses *Schöpfung* in the German text) should be continually checked by appeal to experience. If the empiricist tendency to treat conceptual thought as little more than a *Vorstellungs-ablauf* (a bye-play of presentations) had continually to be resisted by recognition of the innovative power of intellectual construction, such innovation only yielded positive fruit if its suggestions were brought before the bar of actual experience. If the development of non-Euclidean systems of geometry was to prove fertile, the proof of that fertility resided not in any elegance of mathematical construction but in their practical utility in physics.

Ayer found in logical empiricism an understanding of necessary truth that enabled him fuse acknowledgment of its unique authority with a grasp of its rôle that would allow us to regard it as both invulnerable and yet somehow under our control. This theory (or group of theories) is often presented as the conventional theory (or theories) of *a priori* truths, even though the precise sense (or senses) of that conventionality proves elusive and difficult to comprehend. If at first light it seems that Ayer's rejection of metaphysics represents a chapter in the classical empiricist polemic against supposedly self-indulgent intellectual free-wheeling, it is also important to recognize the seriousness of the challenge implicit in the relegation of the necessary to the status of something in the last resort, a matter of convention. For the metaphysical impulse seeks to come to rest in that which cannot be rejected or modified, in that which is suffused with its own self-sufficiency, in that which is ontologically self-authenticating. And here inevitably one turns to the ontological argument for the existence of God. Ayer regarded this argument as finally demolished by the kind of logical analysis provided by Russell's theory of descriptions. It depends for its validity on treating existence as an attribute; and as soon as we recognize that it is only the grammatical form of the sentences by which we affirm or deny existence that conceals from us the fact that in such affirmation or denial we are affirming or denying the application in reality of a description (say: the Loch Ness monster), we are freed from bondage to that mistake. Existence unlike, for instance omniscience, is in no way contained in the concept of God; we can debate his existence or non-existence without being tricked into supposing that by conceiving Him at all, we somehow necessarily posit Him as existing. But further—the realms of actuality and of logical necessity fall apart. The home of the latter is provided by the laws that govern our discourse.

Wittgenstein's dictum in the *Tractatus* (1922) that 'of a non-logical world we could not say how it would look' provided an authoritative summary of its author's view of the logically necessary. Attempts to describe a non-logical world take us beyond the frontiers of intelligibility. Tautology and contradiction constitute the boundaries of significant discourse; in the one case what we entertain is a truth-function true for all truth-combinations of the logical units of its range, in the other one that is correspondingly false for all such combinations. So the one is deducible from any and every proposition; whereas from the other any and every proposition may be deduced. The former is factually vacuous: as e.g. Either it is raining or it is not raining. Of the latter (that is of contradictions) one can say, in less technical language, that if one feeds a self-contradiction into one's premises, one can get anything one likes out of them.

So if one learns anything from such propositions it concerns the rôle of such operators as either-or, if, etc., in our language. What is here presented formally in terms of the sophisticated philosophical logic of the *Tractatus* exhibited necessity issuing from the very notion of significant discourse. Impossibility in the sense of sheer inadmissibility arose out of the fabric of that discourse. We could not significantly speak of such inadmissibility outside the context provided by our linguistic legislation. And the principle of the ultimately conventional source of logical necessity was extended beyond the area of the relatively formal concerns of the *Tractatus*.

Thus the claim that within the universe of colour there were material exclusions (e.g. the same surface could not simultaneously be coloured red and blue) was fiercely rejected. It was argued that the conventionality of such a posited exclusion did not arise out of a mysterious essence of colour whereby it was differentiated into various mutually exclusive manifestations, but from a conscious or unconscious choice of conceptual organization. And further it was pointed out that recognition of such flexibility allowed one's colour-awareness to take in such phenomena as the fluctuating colour-patterns of shot silk. (I owe this point to the late Dr Friedrich Waismann.)

For Ayer it was such considerations that served to banish necessity from the world of actuality: not of course to substitute a vision of that world as thereby arbitrary (that would be as much metaphysics as absolute idealism) but to expel any sense of the mysteriously ultimate from our understanding of its order. It was not simply that the God of the ontological argument was a conceptual non-sense, if his existence was supposed entailed by his concept; it was also a matter of rejecting the kind of alleged self-authenticating ultimacy of the one allegedly established by that argument. In necessity there was nothing mysterious. And here Wittgenstein's insistence that death was not an event in life comes to mind as if emphasizing that the crossing of the last frontier was at the same time an abandonment of that world of discourse in which alone such formal concepts as necessity and contingency had their place.

In Ayer's criticism of metaphysics we have to reckon with two contrasted but deeply significant strands. There was his rejection as unintelligible non-sense of all that was not verifiable in principle. To affirm the reality of the transcendent was as much non-sensical as to speak of a lion outside this room that disappears without trace whenever anyone looks for it leaving no remotely perceptible hint of its presence. (I owe this example to Professor H. H. Price.) Such a lion is altogether insulated from any sort of conceivable experience; statements that one may make about it, for instance that it is tawny-coated or one-eyed, contribute nothing to evidence of its reality once that total removal from any conceivable experience is posited. Ayer laid weight on the need for positive confirmation unlike Professor Karl Popper who in his *Logik der Forschung* (1935) had drastically modified the emphasis of the *Wiener Kreis* on verifiability, stressing instead the need for the vulnerability of hypotheses, their susceptibility to refutation. But although Ayer emphasized the need for positive evidence (and in particular the evidence of the senses) in making factual claims, and the senseless character of statements in respect of which such evidence was implicitly discounted as irrelevant to their significance, his insistence on the conventional character of so-called necessary truth told in a different direction.

Why for instance (in argument with Sir Isaiah Berlin) did Ayer insist that such propositions: Red is more like purple than green is like scarlet: were true by convention? Berlin insisted that such propositions were universal and necessary, but involving only concepts definable by ostensive definition; they were synthetic, were truths of fact, yet necessary. They were known by the kind of insight that the Cambridge logician W. E. Johnson had called intuitive induction, a rational grasp of universal and necessary relationships between things or events endowed with near-Cartesian characteristics. But although they were very different from Kant's synthetic *a priori*, in that they involved no *a priori* concepts (e.g. substance, causality), to bestow on them the status Berlin claimed for them was to suggest that the kind of freedom conceptually to innovate that had made scientific advance possible was somehow limited by the need to concede fixed, inviolable relationships, grasped by insight of a sort that could not be accommodated by the sort of paradigm suggested in the paper by Einstein mentioned earlier in this lecture.

Had Ayer reflected more deeply on his hostility to Berlin's suggestion, and grasped its implications, he might have seen that he was in fact moving nearer to Popper's position. For what he was seeking to defend was the kind of intellectual inventiveness that he had found menaced by the Cook-Wilsonian emphasis on incorrigible knowledge, with Euclid's axioms the paradigm of authentic certainty in respect of fact. He sought liberation by re-creating a near-Kantian polarity between spontaneous, intellectual creativity and vulnerability at the bar of sense-experience. But wherever by emphasis on the latter, illustrated by the sequel to *Logic, Truth and Language*, in which he sought to make a very powerful case for a phenomenalist view of the external world, he might be thought to be imprisoning intellectual creativity, at the same time he was seeking to emancipate the reach of understanding from the bondage of a philistine, even obscurantist claim to *know*.

This whole story indeed reflects an internal contradiction regularly encountered in the empiricist tradition, a tendency at one and the same to liberate and to confine. Mill gave classical expression in his *Autobiography* (1873) to the internal tensions that the confining element (illustrated in this lecture by mention of Bentham's dismissal of poetry as misrepresentation) may generate in a gifted individual, and later in his eloquent protest against domination by mass standards in his *Essay on Liberty*, went on to show his sensitivity to the world of which his formation had nearly deprived him. Yet in his pamphlet on *Utilitarianism* which followed *Liberty* in time, he showed the depth of the Benthamite influence to which he had been exposed.

Ayer's criticism of metaphysics has been variously indicted not least because of the obvious gusto with which in his early writings their author claimed to topple the gods of more traditional philosophers. Moore, Russell and Wittgenstein, his more obvious immediate ancestors in the English-speaking philosophical world, all in different ways conveyed the impression of a greater reverence. In Moore's case this took the form of a stubborn concern with the sorts of thing there were in the world. The temper of his early lectures on *Some Main Problems of Philosophy* (not published till 1953) remained with him to the end, and his British Academy memorialist, Professor R. B. Braithwaite, insisted that for all his influence on the logico-analytic movement, he was in the end trying to give an account of the different sorts of thing there were in the world. Again Russell not only allowed his famous essay, *A Free Man's Worship*, to be reprinted in his relatively late collection, *Mysticism and Logic* (1917), but in his last years of protest against nuclear armament, spoke of 'cosmic impiety'. And finally Wittgenstein (rightly compared by Professor G. H. von Wright with Pascal), ended the *Tractatus* on a nearly mystical note, counselling silence concerning those things of which we cannot speak, suggesting indeed that such silence was a more powerful form of communication and more appropriate to its subject-matter than any eager speaking concerning the supposed ultimate. Such a silence must dominate any attempt to represent the relation of temporal to eternal. There was a seriousness in Moore's avowed atheism that seemed absent from the young Ayer's enthusiastic dismissal of anything that could not be slotted into the sorts of proposition admitted as valid by the *Wiener Kreis*.

It could indeed be said that it is Popper's work which enables one to see the liberating value of the empiricist treatment of the *a priori*, revealing, *inter alia*, its partially Kantian ancestry. Indeed one of the conclusions of this lecture will be that it is in the area of our understanding of the nature of logical necessity that the work which Ayer presented to the world in his *Logic, Truth and Language* in 1936 made its most important contribution. It was for Wittgenstein (and others) to continue this work, already given a fresh slant by Schlick in his treatment of Henri Poincaré and others; but Ayer compelled notice of its relevance to anyone concerned with the issues raised by alleged human presence to a transcendent reality. For that reality must find its ground of existence in itself.

I mention reverence; for some of the frequently bitter protest brought against Ayer's dismissal of metaphysics is more an indictment of his flippant iconoclasm than of his actual arguments. The latter are sometimes powerful, for instance his criticism of the thesis that all relations are internal to their terms, so fundamental to absolute idealism. This thesis had admittedly been very seriously criticized by G. E. Moore; but his criticism had made use of the Aristotelian distinction between substance and accident; it moved on an ontological plane. Whereas Ayer fastened on the distinction between using a proper name indicatively and descriptively. Thus at first sight one might suppose that the truth of the proposition: Socrates would not have been Socrates if he had not been married to Xantippe, made the existence of Xantippe internal to that of Socrates. But a little attention shows that when we say Socrates *is* Socrates, we are not simply asserting an identical proposition but saying that the man we call by the name Socrates is the man we know as Socrates, with all the characteristics that made him up what he is. And here his marriage is clearly crucial. It is not that he would not still have been called Socrates had his whole life taken a different turn; it is that he would not have been the sort of man he is. The proposition we are asserting is not an identical proposition, but a synthetic proposition, in which we say something new about a named individual that the grammatical form of the sentence used to express it conceals. Moore went deeper to indicate the ontological consequence of rejecting the kind of monism advocated by the idealists; it has therefore a seriousness that Ayer's locating the linguistic confusions that give plausibility to the sort of intellectual interweaving of one thing with another may seem to lack. But a mastery of one's language leading to the banishment of one sort of metaphysical indulgence may be itself a useful propaedentic to a more effective construction.

In ethics Ayer came to rest in the end in a relatively unsophisticated utilitarianism, for all his understandable interest in the style and manner of ethical discourse e.g. the rôle of ought in giving imperative force, of good as expression of approval or commendation. Inevitably the critical attitude to traditional moral restraints appealed to him; Bentham's revisionary spirit was more congenial than e.g. Prichard's fidelity to claims he urged as self-evident to a rational intuition often sharper in the ordinary man than in the so-called intellectual. If Ayer paid lip-service to the thesis that in moral philosophy we sought not new knowledge but a clearer understanding (through constructive analysis) of what we already know, his mood led him to adopt more overtly revisionary styles, seeking only to commend those rules of behaviour that might be seen to advance rather than hinder human satisfaction, increase rather than diminish opportunities of enjoyment.

D. M. MacKinnon

Prichard's claims (in W. D. Ross' works they were called *prima facie* obligations), Moore's intrinsically excellent states of affairs, manifested for what they are to some sort of rational intuition were alike banished from the inventory of the admissible, their epistemic basis wholly questionable. Ethical intuition of any sort had no place in Ayer's scheme; morality was reduced to something not far from a Benthamite system of public advantage.

Such an attitude (and my memory is very far from adequate) has undoubtedly stengthened a tendency to dismiss Ayer's criticism of metaphysics, as something that belonged to a short-lived episode in the history of philosophy, that indeed found its own *coup de grâce* not simply in the later work of Wittgenstein, but even before its dissemination outside a narrow circle, in the writings, for instance of Friedrich Waismann, insistent for instance, on truth that could only be conveyed by such a work as Franz Kafka's *The Castle*, even as Wittgenstein urged the significance not only of Tolstoy's work on the Gospels, but of his novella—*Hadji Murad*. (It should be noted in passing that Ayer's earlier post-war writings included studies of Sartre's *L'Etre et le Néant* (1947), and of the earlier work of Albert Camus in the now defunct periodical—*Horizon*. One might wish that he had also written on Camus' *L'Homme Révolté*.) But the kind of flexibility of mind that in Waismann's work (devoted though he was to Schlick's memory) opened the way to a revaluation of metaphysical speculation remained somehow alien to Ayer, even though it might have been thought that his own concern for the need and right of intellectual innovation (exemplified in his attitude to the *a priori*) might have helped him see that to characterize metaphysics as poetry was a far from dismissive judgment.

Again it is a pity that R. G. Collingwood whose *Autobiography*, published in 1939, carried an attack on the Cook-Wilsonians more bitter than anything Ayer wrote, and whose *Essay on Metaphysics* published the following year included some very illuminating material on the conditions of intellectual innovation (especially in the sciences) did not live to suggest to his younger contemporary the relevance to his pursuits of historical study. And one wonders also whether he might not have found a more deeply sympathetic criticism in Professor R. B. Braithwaite's Eddington Memorial Lecure of 1955, with its quarrying in Matthew Arnold's *Literature and Dogma* in the effort to establish an effective way of treating religious beliefs as a significant and powerful *Als ob*. (I know of no discussion by Ayer of Braithwaite's controversial, but in some ways seminal lecture: seminal not least in the critical discussion it provoked.) That way he might have found the means to present his deep criticisms in a style less offensive and less seemingly contemptuous.

Yet what he offered remains very valuable, not simply by reason of its emphasis on the need to break intellectual fetters, given expression in his conventional theory of the *a priori*, but also by his insistence on the authority of the given. His devotion to sense-experience, the long, painstaking pursuit of the phenomenalist will-of-the-wisp, was in part at least occasioned by a conviction that hard fact was to be found there. If a sense of the vulnerability to criticism of even the most firmly established law together with the elusiveness of hard data encouraged some positivists to move towards a coherence understanding of truth (Carnap's physicalism is the best known example in the period with which this lecture is concerned), Ayer insisted that empirical fact must have the last word.

Where he failed most signally was in his allowing a proper place for the subject to whom that last word had to be spoken. He failed to see that the sort of intellectual self-criticism he practised himself as well as advocated belonged to the biography of a lively, suffering, human being. It is because Kant sought to do justice to this reality that he remains supreme among those who have sought to bring out the splendour and the poverty of the work of those who seek to line the contours of the ultimate. But Ayer by the very temper to which his phenomenalism bears witness offers a permanently valuable corrective to those who would take the often attractive easy road to speculative satisfaction.

Ayer and World Views

FREDERICK COPLESTON

I

As we all know, in Freddie Ayer's famous book *Language, Truth and Logic* metaphysics received short shrift. Metaphysical assertions were dismissed as being all nonsensical (*LTL*, 2nd edn, 41). In the work in question Ayer clearly tended to equate metaphysics with what Professor W. H. Walsh was to describe as 'transcendent' (as distinct from 'immanent') metaphysics (Walsh, 1963). This tendency is also discernible, I think, in the 1949 debate between Ayer and myself on logical positivism. After all, my defence of metaphysics was largely prompted and certainly strengthened by what I believed to be the religious relevance of metaphysical philosophy. A lot of what Aristotle would have described as 'first philosophy' and what some later philosophers would have classified as 'ontology' Ayer would have called 'philosophical analysis'. What he was primarily concerned with undermining was any claim by metaphysicians to be able to extend our knowledge of what exists, of the Absolute or God for example, by metaphysical arguments.

Ayer continued to believe that a claim to possess factual knowledge about reality should not be seriously entertained unless it was possible to mention some observation statement or statements which would be relevant to showing whether the claim was or was not justified. He never renounced an empiricist approach to philosophy. At the same time he came to abandon his initial wholesale condemnation of metaphysics as so much unintelligible nonsense in favour of a more discriminating attitude. I do not think that he was ever much interested in metaphysics. It remained on the periphery of his interests. His change of attitude was doubtless largely due to reflection on what had been said by colleagues whom he respected. For example, in the second volume of his memoirs he refers to Morris Lazerowitz and his wife Alice as having contributed 'to my persuasion that one needed to do something more than merely discard metaphysics as nonsensical' (*MML*, 91). He adds, justifiably I imagine, that 'here the work of John Wisdom may have had a stronger influence upon me' (Ibid.). One can think of other possible influences, Sir Peter Strawson for example.[1] In other words, I see the change of attitude in Ayer's treatment of metaphysics as part of a more general movement in twentieth-century British philosophy to re-examine what is of value in metaphysics and to assess what metaphysicians were about, without, however, committing oneself to the claims that metaphysics can provide us with factual knowledge of what exists, a knowledge which empirical science is unable to provide. If, however, a person adopts a more discriminating or nuanced attitude to metaphysics, it does not follow that the person in question has become a practitioner of metaphysics. This is true of Freddie Ayer.[2]

After the publication of his collection of essays entitled *Metaphysics and Common Sense* Ayer remarked to me that I might be glad to find in the book a somewhat kinder or less unfavourable treatment of metaphysics than was to be found in his earlier writings. To be sure, when a reader of the essay which gives its title to the collection, first comes across the statement that 'metaphysics is nearly always in conflict with common sense' (*MCS*, 64), he may well wonder to what extent Ayer's view of metaphysics has really become more favourable. But if he continues reading, he will find the author asserting that in philosophy nothing should be regarded as sacrosanct, 'not even common sense' (ibid. 81). Indeed, Ayer remarks, even some philosophers 'who wish to dissociate themselves from metaphysics often advance theories which are shocking to common sense' (ibid. 64), such as the theory that everything which exists is constructed out of sense-data, and the claim that nobody ever does anything freely.

The fact of the matter is that even when their theories are very odd, metaphysicians are accustomed to advance reasons or arguments in support of these theories. The reasons given may not convince us of the truth of the relevant theory or claim, but reflection on the reasons may perhaps serve the useful purpose of making us aware of aspects of a situation or of a given concept's peculiarities to which we had not previously adverted. For example, F. H. Bradley's claim that space and time are not really real may seem to be in evident conflict with common sense, but reflection on Bradley's arguments may help us to notice certain peculiar characteristics of the relevant concepts.[3]

[1] I have in mind Strawson's *Individuals. An Essay in Descriptive Metaphysics* (1959).

[2] Unless, of course, one decides to classify as metaphysics some at any rate of what Ayer described as philosophical analysis.

[3] In regard to space and time Bradley argued that each is reducible to relations and at the same time that neither can be reduced to relations. Examination of Bradley's arguments, even if they are not accepted, might serve to throw light on the nature of space and time.

Again, some philosophers have tried to get us to change our ways of seeing the world, and Ayer is not prepared to condemn all such attempts outright. For, as he says in *The Central Questions of Philosophy* 'we cannot safely assume that our existing apparatus of concepts will not eventually be thought in need of radical reform. (*CQ*, 43). In other words, what P. F. Strawson called 'revisionary metaphysics' should not be condemned out of hand. Ayer insists, however, that if a philosopher finds fault with an existing conceptual framework, he or she can be justifiably expected to suggest an alternative framework. On this matter Ayer criticizes F. H. Bradley, on the ground that having depicted all our ordinary categories as riddled with contradictions, Bradley then makes 'a bee line for the Absolute' (*MCS*, 77), which is said to lie beyond our conceptual grasp.

It is hardly necessary to say that concessions of the kind mentioned do not amount to a conversion on Ayer's part to belief in metaphysics as a source of knowledge of reality. They simply give expression to a more nuanced or discriminating view of metaphysics than was to be found in *Language, Truth and Logic*. We can, of course, give credit to Ayer for having adopted a more discriminating attitude. But as I remarked above, its significance should not be exaggerated.

II

In *The Central Questions of Philosophy* Ayer refers to the claim that metaphysics can answer questions which natural science leaves unanswered. What are these questions? he asks. How can metaphysics go beyond natural science? Consider the reply that whereas the special sciences treat of particular parts or aspects of reality, metaphysics is concerned with reality as a whole. How, Ayer asks, could the metaphysician set about depicting reality as a whole except by depicting its various parts successively? The result, however, of this process would be, at best, the creation of an encyclopaedia setting out 'all the theories and hypotheses which were currently accepted in the various branches of science' (*CO*, 13). But while such a work might perhaps be useful, it would be simply a scientific reference-book, not a product of metaphysics.

Ayer is not, of course, blind to the fact that no metaphysician is likely to be satisfied with the idea that his or her job consists in compiling an encyclopaedia of natural science. So he suggests another aim which could be attributed to the metaphysician, namely that of integrating the theories and hypotheses of the particular sciences into one unified world-picture. But though this may seem a more promising view of metaphysics, Ayer is far from finding it acceptable. What form might the desired world-picture be expected to take? It might, Ayer suggests, take the form of a sustained attempt to reduce all the other sciences to one basic science, say physics. If this programme could be fully realized, one might, indeed, claim that a world-picture of world-view had been produced. Ayer suggests, however, that it would be the job of scientists, not of philosophers, to assess the truth-value of the relevant world-picture. Why? Because, Ayer tells us, 'the metaphysican whose theories are not similarly testable by observation would have nothing to contribute' (ibid. 4)[4]. If he were able to make the sort of contribution required, he would be a scientist rather than a metaphysician.

It is possible, I suppose, that when Ayer made the remarks just mentioned, he had in mind the sort of idea of metaphysics proposed by Friedrich Waismann, namely that some metaphysical systems at any rate have embodied visions of the world which have acted as a stimulus to scientists in their work of forming hypotheses and testing them. Given this idea of philosophical world-views as anticipatory visions, stimulating scientific inquiry, it would be clearly implausible to dismiss them as meaningless. For they would have served as valuable contributions to thought and to the advance of scientific knowledge, even if we claimed that the cognitive value of a given anticipatory vision could be established only through a process of empirical verification carried out by scientists.

In addition, however, to the idea of metaphysics as looking forward, so to speak, to the development of empirical science, Ayer briefly mentions another idea, according to which, whereas science treats only of the world of appearance, metaphysics penetrates to a reality underlying the sphere of appearance. Ayer admits that this idea has had a strong appeal for a number of philosophers in both East and West, but one would not expect it to have much attraction for the author of *Language, Truth and Logic*. Nor, indeed, had it. Ayer allows, of course, that there can be a clash between different sets of phenomena, at any rate in the sense that our initial interpretation of a given set of phenomena may clash with a subsequent interpretation. For example, in the dusk I may mistake a tree for a man, an interpretation which is not confirmed by subsequent observation. But, Ayer goes on to ask, 'what possible experience could authorize our making a distinction between appearances as a whole and a quite different reality?' (ibid.). Presumably we can interpret Ayer as implying that neither Śamkara in India nor Bradley in England could reasonably claim to be able to verify any claim to establish a distinction between appearance in general and an

---

[4] In other words, metaphysicians are unable to show that their theories are true, even if they happen to be true.

underlying reality, the Absolute, inasmuch as any alleged verification would belong to the sphere of appearance.

Some people might try to answer Ayer's question by appealing to mystical experience. But while Ayer does not deny either that experiences of the kind commonly described as mystical sometimes occur or that some of them may be worth having, he is not prepared to allow that they possess cognitive value, in the sense that they can justifiably be regarding as increasing our knowledge of what exists. Having already treated of this matter elsewhere,[5] I have no wish to repeat myself here. I simply note in passing that reflection on mystical experience, in so far as its nature can be known from outside, might contribute to the development of a world-view by featuring as one feature or strand in the construction of a general interpretation of reality.

III

Though Ayer may have given up speaking of metaphysics as a mass of nonsense which hardly deserves serious examination, it seems obvious to me that he remained firmly convinced that the only way, besides ordinary observation, of increasing our knowledge of the world is through empirical science, and that the metaphysician is entirely mistaken if he thinks that he is able to achieve this goal by some means of his own. As far as providing genuine knowledge is concerned, metaphysics must give way to science. It is not surprising, therefore, if, in regard to cognitive value at any rate, Ayer took a dim view of efforts by philosophers to produce general interpretations of reality or unified pictures of the world. I am prepared, however, to argue that efforts of this kind are both natural, something to be expected, and justifiable.

It is obviously true to say that human beings exercise or can in principle exercise a variety of activities, such as, for example, scientific inquiry, moral judgment, aesthetic creation and appreciation, religious practices. Further, through exercise of these activities various views of the world are nourished and develop. For example, scientific inquiry leads to a scientific view of the world, not, of course, a static and unchanging view, but none the less one which presupposes scientific inquiry and its results. Again, there are various religious visions of the world, with features which distinguish them from conceptions which rest solely on the theories and hypotheses of empirical science. Similarly, there can be a view of the world in which beauty forms a prominent feature, as well as a view in which the world appears pri-

[5] See, for example, my *Religion and the One: Philosophies East and West* (1982). ch. 9.

marily or at any rate to a marked extent as the field for the human being's moral life, as the stage on which human beings succeed or fail in realizing their ethical ideals. Is it not natural and only to be expected that some reflective minds should examine whatever relations there may be between such various views of the world, with the aim of arriving at a coherent and unified world-view, if this seems to be capable of attainment? If we look at the text of the discussion between Freddie Ayer and the Norwegian philosopher Arne Naess, as reprinted in *The Meaning of Life and Other Essays* (*ML*),[6] we find Arne Naess asserting the need for what he calls a 'total view', a personal philosophy in which one's various convictions about the world and human life more or less cohere (ibid. 120). I do not care much for the phrase 'total view', for our view of the world is necessarily partial and limited and cannot be total in a literal sense. But I certainly agree with Naess's contention that philosophical thought should be regarded as having not only an analysing function but also a synthesizing one. One can see the two functions as complementary.

It may be objected that while no sensible person objects to synthesis as such, the role of synthesis in the formation of world-views has been progressively taken over by science and thereby placed upon a firmer foundation. Though, however, this line of thought has been favoured by a good many philosophers, it stands open to a rather obvious retort, namely that if the scientific outlook on the world is regarded as constituting one factor or element in the varied material which gives rise to the felt need for synthesis, this need can hardly be satisfied in terms of empirical science alone. It is clearly arguable that unless we are prepared to reduce all other phenomena to, for example, those of physics, we cannot avoid leaving room for what can reasonably be described as a form of metaphysics.

To avoid possible misunderstanding, I should perhaps add that it is not my intention to suggest or imply that all philosophers should undertake the construction of world-views. If a given philosopher has a gift for and an inclination towards meticulous analysis in a given area of thought, it is only reasonable that he should use this gift and follow the relevant inclination. To put in a good word for the attempt to develop a coherent and unified interpretation of reality is not the same thing as claiming, for example, that Freddie Ayer should have abandoned the sort of work which interested him and devoted his mental energies to adding to the number of existing world-views. Besides, when I claimed above that analysis and synthesis can be seen as complementary functions of philosophical thought, I meant what I said.

[6] This collection of essays, edited and introduced by Professor Ted Honderich, was published after Ayer's death.

IV

In the Ayer-Naess discussion the former remarks, with reference to Naess's claim that a philosopher should have a total view, that he (Ayer) does not understand 'what the links are supposed to be to make the totality' (ibid. 123). In other words, how does Naess conceive the connections between the component parts of a so-called total view? This sort of question obviously arises whether one talks about a 'total view' or a (limited and partial) world-view or whether one prefers the German word *Weltanschauung*.

Ayer presses Naess to say whether he claims that the connections between different parts of a total view are those of logical entailment. For example, does Naess claim that the account of the body-mind relation defended by Gilbert Ryle in his book *The Concept of Mind* (1949) would logically commit Ryle to any particular moral judgment about the use of violence in human relations? Does Naess believe, in other words, that from statements about what is the case we can deduce statements about what ought to be the case or how people ought to behave?

Naess replies that he does not make the claim in question. He then goes on to say that a book such as *The Concept of Mind* can be interpreted in various ways, and that different interpretations might be more or less coherent with a given moral attitude or stance. Naess does not give any clear explanation of his meaning. But I venture to suggest that he had in mind something like the following line of thought.

Consider a philosopher who denies human freedom, espouses determinism and yet has strong moral convictions, to which he does not hesitate to give forceful expression. Even if we believe that there is no logical contradiction between his picture of the human being and his moral attitudes and judgments, may we not be inclined to think that the possession and expression of strongly held moral convictions would fit in or cohere better with a theory of human nature in which freedom was affirmed than with a theory in which freedom was denied. And we might suggest reasons for thinking this. As Naess refers to views as cohering 'more of less' (ibid. 124), he presumably conceives coherence as admitting degrees. If so, I agree with him. At the same time I am quite prepared to allow that the subject calls for a more thorough exploration than I can claim to have given it or, indeed, that Naess seems to have given it, to judge by what he says in his rather rambling discussion with Freddie Ayer.

V

If Freddie Ayer were in a position to comment on what I have been saying, I can imagine him remarking that up to now at any rate I have studiously avoided tackling the main objection to the construction of world-views, namely that their cognitive value is extremely questionable. If a given thinker is intent on developing a world-view, he is, of course, free to do so. Nobody has the right to stop him or her. But the best that one could hope for as a result of the effort expended is that the relevant world-picture might conceivably stimulate scientific research in a given field, thus contributing to the growth of human knowledge in an indirect manner, by means, that is to say, of pursuing a more reliable path than metaphysical speculation. If we consider world-views simply by themselves, are there any reliable criteria for distinguishing between them in respect of truth-claims?

Philosophers, it may be claimed, are rightly inclined to award poor marks to a metaphysical system which is riddled with contradictions and the various parts of which are logically incompatible. A world-view, considered as a mental construction, should surely exemplify logical coherence rather than incoherence. Perhaps this does not amount to more than saying that a world-view, being a construction by the mind, should manifest the work of thought, which is pretty obvious. At the same time it is reasonable to claim that, other things being equal, a logically coherent world-view can justifiably be preferred to a logically incoherent one. I say 'other things being equal', inasmuch as world-view A, though inferior to world-view B in regard to logical coherence, might possibly express genuine insights which were missing in its competitor.

Though, however, world-views, considered as constructions of thought, can reasonably be judged in terms of their success or failure in standing up to the test of logical coherence, a world-view is offered as a picture of reality or of the world. And is there any guarantee that a logically coherent world-picture is a faithful mirror of reality, unless perhaps we presuppose that the world must be a logically coherent system? To be sure, if someone sets out to develop a coherent and unified world-view, he or she assumes provisionally that the world is a coherent whole. But a provisional assumption, which might admittedly be falsified, is not the same thing as an absolute presupposition. If we wished to argue that the presupposition is theoretically justifiable, we might maintain, with some philosophers, that being is shown to be intelligible in the very act of understanding, and that this implies that reality is coherent rather than incoherent. But I cannot develop this theme now.

In addition to the test of coherence it seems possible to use the criterion of relative comprehensiveness in assessing the respective merits and demerits of different world-views. An absolutely comprehensive world-view is clearly unattainable by the human mind.

None the less, a world-view, by its very nature, can justifiably be expected to aim at covering more rather than less aspects of reality. For example, a world-view which had room for the world as seen by science but which had no room for a moral vision of life or which could accommodate it only by caricaturing or distorting the nature of morality, would, in this respect at least, be inferior to a world-view which did more justice to morality.

Obviously, if we talk about a certain picture of the human being's moral consciousness as being a caricature, we are comparing one interpretation with another and not an interpretation with an uninterpreted datum. Even if, however, we can never get at 'bare facts', in the sense of totally uninterpreted data, most people are convinced that it is often possible to distinguish between conflicting interpretations in regard to truth or falsity, adequacy or inadequacy, and to represent a reasonable case in support of the position taken. It hardly needs saying that in ordinary life we frequently act in accordance with this conviction; and we shall doubtless continue to do so, whatever sceptics may say.

To be sure, the nature of wide-spreading world-views is such that one can hardly give a simple answer to the question whether a given specimen is true or false. If someone does hazard a simple or summary general judgment, he or she probably has in mind some feature of the relevant world-picture which is regarded by the person concerned as the most prominent or the important feature. But one may think that while the general representation is basically acceptable, this or that part of the picture stands in need of a lot of reworking. To say this, however, is to admit that reasoned judgments are possible, judgments, that is, about the truth-claims of different world-views. We are not condemned to unbroken silence.

It must be recognized, I think, that the creation of world-views is none the less a pretty risky procedure. There is, for example, the risk of making unexamined or uncritized presuppositions in a desire to get on with the painting of the picture. Again, there are the risks of over-hastily adopting desired conclusions, and also of allowing one's judgments to be determined by personal prejudices or psychological factors. There is thus no great difficulty in understanding the attitude of philosophers who have carefully steered clear of what they regarded as unprofitable ventures and have focused their attention on what seemed to them sharply defined and manageable questions, admitting, in principle at least, of definitive and final answers. Though, however, this attitude has resulted in a lot of valuable philosophizing, the idea of finally solving philosophical problems one after the other and piling up, so to speak, an increasing number of definitive solutions is certainly open to criticism. I remember once asking Freddie Ayer, in private conversation, whether he could mention any philosophical problem which had been solved in such a way that the solution had won universal acceptance among philosophers and could confidently be expected to escape serious challenge in the future. I was thinking of the way in which, in our own lifetimes, certain philosophical theses had been proclaimed as pretty well unassailable dogmas and then, one fine day, had been called in question, as Professor W. V. Quine called in question the claim that we could justifiably make a rigid distinction between analytic and synthetic propositions. At the moment at any rate Ayer did not seem prepared to cite an example of a philosophical problem which had been solved once and for all. Nor, indeed, was I.

VI

In what I have been saying I have assumed that creators of world-views have been concerned with the attainment of truth, that they have aimed at any rate at giving a true account of the world or of reality as we know it. I did not, however, intend to imply that the creator of a world-picture must necessarily have in view the attainment of objective truth in the relevant sense. A person might conceivably set out to depict reality as he would like it to be. Or he might develop a certain world-view because he believed that thinking of the world in this particular way was especially valuable from a pragmatic point of view, tending to stimulate and encourage lines of conduct which he considered desirable. Creators of world-views, however, are generally philosophers, and we think of philosophers as seeking truth or at any rate as not indifferent to it. A philosopher may, indeed, retain the idea of truth as a desirable goal while giving a pragmatic interpretation to the concept of truth, but the fact that he retains the idea in question shows that he is not indifferent to truth. Introduction of the theme of value for life may express a choice of emphasis rather than complete indifference to the question whether a world-view or a theory is true or false. Consider Nietzsche's theory of the Eternal Recurrence. On the face of it he seems to be telling us what, in his opinion, the world is really like. As, however, every student of Nietzsche knows, he uses the theory as a test of strength, regarding it as having pragmatic value. At the same time he offered some arguments in support of the theory of endless cycles, and the theory has sometimes been interpreted as a scientific hypothesis. I myself would emphasize the pragmatic aspect of Nietzsche's theory, while admitting that mention of arguments suggests that Nietzsche was not entirely indifferent to another aspect. How one interprets the status of the theory is largely a question of where one decides to lay the emphasis.

The foregoing remarks were prompted by the fact that in the discussion between Freddie Ayer and Arne Naess the latter expresses the belief that what he calls a 'total view' has or can have a value for life. Naess suggests tht Ayer would be better off for having such a view, whereas Ayer suggests that Naess would be a better philosopher if he had not got a total view. These personal references were doubtless made humorously. At the same time serious differences were being expressed.

Naess described a 'total view' as being a personal philosophy. It would include, for example, the basic ethical ideals and moral judgments accepted by the adherent of the philosophy in question. In this case it would obviously have implications in regard to conduct and could reasonably be regarded as a guide to life. Ayer, of course, would not deny this, but he presumably thought that the cause of clarity was not well served by mixing up or grouping together factual statements and value-judgments, and he challenged Naess to say whether he really believed, as he appeared to do, that a moral principle of consistently practising a policy of non-violence could be deduced from a belief in, as Naess put it, 'the ultimate unity of all living beings' (ibid. 109). If this is what Naess thought, he was, according to Ayer, mistaken.

In reply Naess maintained that though he did not claim that a moral principle could be logically deduced from a factual or descriptive statement, he rejected any reduction of connections to those of logical entailment or deducibility. The philosopher, as he (Naess) saw him, had the responsibility to connect his views, whether ethical, epistemological or political, in such a way as to form a coherent whole, the connections being possibly 'looser than ordinary scientific connections, looser than deductions' (ibid.) As we have seen, Naess was prepared to speak of parts of a general philosophy as cohering 'more or less'. Perhaps we might regard the philosophy of Schopenhauer as illustrating Naess's point. While Schopenhauer's ethics may not be logically deducible from his metaphysics of the will, considered as an account of how things are, it is arguable that they fit in much better together than would be the case if either were very different from what it actually is. The metaphysics of the Will, as expounded by Schopenhauer, might very well incline a person's mind to consider favourably and accept the ethical part of the philosophy, provided, of course, that he or she had already accepted the metaphysics.

Ayer might retort that this would be a question of a psychological connection, whereas he, as a philosopher, was concerned with logical connections and not with psychology. My sympathies, however, lie with Arne Naess in his claim that the connections between the parts of a 'total view' need not be as strict as that of logical entailment of deducibility. The fact of the matter is, one might suggest, that Naess wanted to find room, in what we might describe as respectable philosophy, for what he called 'total views', of a rather personal nature, whereas Ayer lacked any such desire.

VII

A critic of world-views may very well argue that any such view is likely to reflect some pre-existing belief or conviction, which assumes a dominating and controlling role in the painting of the total picture, and which may remain unsubjected to any rigorous critical examination. Further, once the world-view has been constructed, people will probably be disposed to accept or reject it in so far as it is seen as fitting in with or as contradicting their already formed beliefs, especially when these beliefs are conceived as possessing notable pragmatic importance, a genuine value for life. In other words, so-called 'wishful thinking' is likely to play a determining role not only in the original construction of world-views but also in the attitudes adopted towards them by people other than their creators.

While this line of criticism has, of course, to be borne in mind, I should like to add that there is nothing objectionable in principle in the sustained attempt to make an already held belief fully articulate, to explore its implications, and to develop a coherent world-view in the light of it. For example, world-views of a religious nature have sometimes been developed within the womb, so to speak, of an already existing set of religious beliefs, traditions and practices. A development of this kind can be regarded as a natural enough process of a religion becoming intellectually self-conscious. It is, or course, likely to involve the making of presuppositions. After all, the process must start from some base. But there is no absolute bar to critical examination of the relevant presuppositions being set in train by the process of reflection. To be sure, one might try to avoid setting out on this road, out of fear of where it might lead. But I do not think that this is necessarily the case.

VIII

In the course of this talk I have tended to refer to world-views and metaphysical systems as though they were the same sort of thing, and I dare say that this practice is open to adverse criticism on several grounds. For example, one might wish to speak of some wide-spreading hypothesis advanced by a physicist as providing us with a world-view, even though 'metaphysical system' would reasonably be regarded as a highly inappropriate descriptive term. Again, one might reasonably refer to a given poet or novelist as suggesting the outlines of a world-view, even though it would be very misleading to describe the writer in question as a metaphysician. Further, some philosophers would probably be prepared to claim that the genuine metaphysician is concerned with displaying the basic structure of reality, which underlies and is presupposed by the various different kinds of phenomena, whereas the author of a world-view is concerned with constructing a coherent and unified picture of changing aspects of the world and human life, a picture which, by the nature of the case, is itself subject to change.

While, however, I admit the justice of such criticism, I feel inclined to excuse my rather loose way of speaking by remarking that many of the mental constructions which are commonly described as metaphysical systems in histories of philosophy might quite well be called 'world-views'. For they certainly do provide pictures of the world, even though formal arguments, which one would hardly expect to find in poems or novels, are advanced in support of claims that given pictures are more or less faithful representation of reality.

IX

To conclude. At a time when I was a good deal engaged in attacking logical positivism, a reviewer commented that, for me, philosophizing seemed to be pretty well equivalent to carrying on a dialogue with A. J. Ayer. This was something of an exaggeration. But one could do much worse than carry on a dialogue with Ayer, and I certainly wanted to contribute to the defence of metaphysics against the battering which it had received in *Language, Truth and Logic*. Anyway, if Freddie Ayer came to adopt (I do not claim that anything I said had much to do with it) a more nuanced or discriminating attitude to metaphysics, I in my turn became progressively more conscious of the limitations of philosophy. Though, however, I find myself attracted by the idea of philosophy as a set of second-order disciplines, such as philosophy of science, philosophy of history and so on, I continue to believe that any blanket condemnation of metaphysics and the creation of world-views is unjustified. As I have explained, the endeavour to form a coherent and unified interpretation of reality as known seems to me natural and something to be expected. As for this contribution to the series of lectures in memory of Freddie Ayer, I regard it not so much as an attack on Ayer as an opening up on various lines of thought in response to some brief and, it seems to me, over-simplified remarks which he happened to make about world-views. With Freddie Ayer self-defence tended to take the form of challenge and attack, and I regret that circumstances have deprived me of hearing his comments and criticism.

Language, Newspeak and Logic

S. R. SUTHERLAND

Some books are like parents, grandparents or old friends. They have been with us from our earliest days and one treats them almost with familiarity. They belong to one's youth and the recognition that they have been around for months and years keeps company with surprise. For philosophers such a book is A. J. Ayer's *Language, Truth and Logic*, first published over fifty years ago in 1936. There is a sense in which a similar point may be made about some individuals, but discretion and good manners should deter us from succumbing to the philosophical disease of pressing an analogy too far. Suffice it to say that over a period during which most English speaking philosophers were content (or perhaps constrained) to work within a context which was significantly influenced by Ayer's clear and cajoling formulation of a twentieth century of empiricism, F. C. Copleston provided one of the few distinctive alternative philosophical perspectives on major metaphysical questions. This essay will reflect upon the influence of Ayer's *Language, Truth and Logic* some fifty years after its publication, upon the philosophical discussion of religion and theological questions.

The impact of the book at the time of its publication was quite dramatic and of equal interest was its continuing success in sales terms. Ayer admits, however, that the book 'can be accused of sacrificing depth to clarity', (*PL*, 154) but in terms of wide and lasting impact clarity is a decided asset. The thoughts in the book, as Ayer agree, were not original and, 'Reviewing this work at a distance of more than forty years, I have many faults to find with it . . .' (ibid. 155). None the less Ayer still finds himself 'in sympathy with the spirit of the book' and still 'broadly adheres to what may be called the verification approach' (p. 156). Responses at the time of first publication were quite divided and Collingwood is reported to have spent time in his lectures attacking the book philosophically and to have remarked, 'If I thought that Mr Ayer was right, I would give up philosophy'.

Perhaps we are now at the outer extremities of the eddies and ripples set in motion by the book, but we cannot but marvel at its impact, and as authors, envy sales in the hundreds of thousands—quite remarkable for a work of philosophy.

My focus in this essay however is the narrower question of the significance of the book for religion and theology. His critique of theology is offered in the chapter of the book which Ayer described as 'peripheral to the main tenor of the book', but which none the less 'was the one which arouses the greatest animosity'.

I

Let me begin, however, by a coat-trailing piece of the first order which will focus upon the second word in the title of the paper—'Newspeak'. As an addendum to the main text of his novel *Nineteen Eighty-Four*, George Orwell offers an account of 'The Principles of Newspeak'. From these pages which repay general consideration I wish to focus upon two or three short extracts:

(i) In the year 1984 there is not as yet anyone who uses Newspeak as his sole means of communication either in speech or in writing.

(ii) The purpose of Newspeak is not only to provide a modicum of expression for the world-view and mental habits proper to the devotees of Ingsoc, but to make all the other modes of thought impossible. It was intended that when Newspeak had been adopted once and for all, and Oldspeak forgotten, a heretical thought—that is a thought deviating from the principles of Ingsoc—should be literally unthinkable, at least as far as thought is dependent on words.

(iii) Its vocabulary was so constructed as to give exact and often very subtle expression to every meaning that a Party member could properly wish to express, while excluding all other meanings and also the possibility of arriving at them by indirect methods. This was done partly by the invention of new words, but chiefly by eliminating undesirable words and by stripping such words as remained of unorthodox meanings, and so far as possible of all secondary meanings whatever.

(iv) Newspeak is designed not to extend but to *diminish* the range of thought.

My charge against *Language, Truth and Logic* is that there are just enough points of similarity, just enough bells were rung by Orwell's words, to justify a *prima facie* case against *Language, Truth and Logic* that, whatever the intent of the author, the book is conceptually restrictive and, indeed, intellectually imperialistic in its character.

[In parenthesis I am not making a historical or literary point, nor in any way suggesting that Orwell was influenced by Ayer's book. We do know that Orwell and Ayer became friends in the 1940s, and both

Ayer's *Part of My Life* and Crick's biography of Orwell (1981) give accounts of this. Crick hints that Orwell might 'have picked something up from Freddie Ayer in Paris or London about the verification principle' (op. cit. 521), but the passage in Crick implies that either Orwell, or more probably Crick, did not then understand how the terms 'verify' and 'falsify' were being used philosophically. The passage quoted from *1984* uses the word 'falsify' in the sense of 'making false' as in 'falsifying a record' rather than as in 'showing a record to be false'. Better not to try to even hint at influence of Ayer on Orwell on such evidence.]

I shall make one or two general points about *Language, Truth and Logic* and Newspeak, which shall be the context for my remarks on theology and religion. Perhaps without being too fanciful one can, by making appropriate substitution, use the above quotations as lenses through which to inspect *Language, Truth and Logic*.

(is) In the year 1936 there is not as yet anyone who uses the language of logical positivism as his sole means of communication.

The point here is quite clear. *Language, Truth and Logic* is not describing a natural language, it is prescribing how we ought to talk. Of course, it differs from Newspeak in that the prescription is not politically or ideologically grounded in order to coerce—to reinforce a power structure—but is based upon a particular pattern of analysis intended to persuade. It is, however, intended to supersede not just certain types of philosophical and metaphysical argument and talk, but, as the examples from morality and religion show, also what non-philosophers do say and want to say.

(iis) The purpose of *Language, Truth and Logic* is not only to provide a medium of expression for the world-view and mental habits proper to the devotees of Logical Positivism, but to make all other modes of thought impossible. It was intended that when verificationism had been adopted once and for all, and Metaphysics forgotten, a heretical thought—that is a thought deviating from the principles of Logical Positivism—should be literally unthinkable, at least so far as thought is dependent on words.

And so one is enjoined to bid farewell to metaphysics and theology. This quotation from Orwell may be used helpfully to distinguish between Kant's philosophical conclusions, and those of the Logical Positivists. In one sense Newspeak is less radical than the recommendations of *Language, Truth and Logic*. Newspeak rules out, as unthinkable, thoughts, '. . . at least as far as thought is dependent on words'. The implication that thought may be subdivided into what is dependent on words, does not sit easily alongside Ayer's insistence that beyond what

79

can be said (as sanctioned by his theory of meaning) lies quite literally 'nonsense'. Ayer's thesis is a matter of logic, not psychology, and there is no hint of possible thoughts not 'dependent on words' in the sense suggested. Kant none the less, who also was not concerned with psychology, and who was equally concerned with the bounds of the intelligible and meaningful, was rather less radical than Ayer in this conclusion. Beyond the phenomenal describable world there lies the noumenal world, not equally perspicuous, but none the less real and none the less significant for our understanding of the phenomenal world. Most obviously for this paper this shows in Kant's willingness to see some use for the term 'God' which fits neither with Ayer's stricture that the relevant sentences be either analytic, or verifiable in principle on the one hand, or susceptible to non-cognitive or emotive analysis on the other.

Here my sympathy lies firmly with Kant.

(iiis) *Language, Truth and Logic*'s vocabulary was so constructed as to give exact and often very subtle expression to every meaning that a Logical Positivist could properly wish to express, while excluding all other meanings and also the possibility of arriving at them by indirect methods. This was done partly by the invention of new words, but chiefly by eliminating undesirable words and by stripping such words as remained of unorthodox meanings, and so far as possible of all secondary meanings whatever.

Effectively this is what Ayer proposes for the vocabulary of religion. The word 'God' is not allowed to function as either a name or a description for 'If one allows that it is impossible to define God in intelligible terms, then one is allowing that it is impossible for a sentence to be both significant and to be about God'. (*LTL*, 2nd edn, 118).

(ivs) Logical Positivism is designed not to extend but to *diminish* the range of thoughts.

Tongue-in-cheek analogies apart this, of course, is the major charge to be made against *Language, Truth and Logic*: that ultimately it diminishes the range of thought. In giving consideration to this charge, I shall restrict my attention in this essay to the areas of religion and theology.

'Language, Truth and Logic', and the responses to it

(1) The position which Ayer adopts is quite straightforward. The classic affirmations of theology (theistic religion) are in the end

non-sense because they aspire to affirm truths about God without being able to specify how we could verify, or in principle show to be true, such claims. [I shall not in this essay comment on the problems which arose in formulating the verification principle, nor its more deadly son, the falsification principle.]

Now there is no doubt that this is a radical proposal. Ayer is asserting, on the basis of his theory of meaning, that what Paul, Augustine, Mohammet, Anselm, Aquinas, Luther, Calvin etc. hoped to say was unsayable—indeed that in their attempts to say the unsayable they produced only non-sense.

I must confess to a sneaking regard for such baldness. Of course those who came after *Language, Truth and Logic* did allow that perhaps when we say 'God is love', we were saying something, but it was not something true or false, it was rather something at best about ourselves. The classic and much debated example in the subsequent literature was such a claim as 'God is love', or 'God loves each one of his creatures'. Let us consider

(a) God loves each one of his creatures.

If that is to be factually or literally significant we should, according to *Language, Truth and Logic*, be able to specify experiences appropriate to establishing its truth or falsehood. In fact an attempt to do this tends to leave the believer in the position of Job—having lost all; family, fortune, friends, health, sitting in a dung-heap scraping his boils—still affirming,

(b) I know that my redeemer liveth

—a magnificent riposte, but hardly a statement for which there exists any empirical evidence. It is a claim, as the Book of Job makes plain, about a transcendent God whose ways are beyond comprehension. As such Ayer argues, it is non-sense. Such utterances (a) or (b) may tell us much about the psychology of the believer: whereas—

> The point which we wish to establish is that there cannot be any transcendent truths of religion. For the sentences which the theist uses to express such 'truths' are not literally significant (*LTL*, 2nd edn, 117–8).

That is a radical way of correcting our 'world-view and mental habits'. Does it *diminish* our range of thought, or does it simply clarify the boundaries of thought which we had failed to recognize?

(2) There followed an elaborate series of responses to Ayer's critique of theology. A massive, and, I must say, largely arid and boring literature developed amongst philosophers of religion and theologians. Some of the best of it—for example Basil Mitchell in the Oxford

collection *Faith and Logic* (1957)—was good and stimulating; but much that was quite tawdry—including some of the pieces in the famed *News Essays in Philosophical Theology* (Flew and MacIntyre, 1900) gained considerable currency and undue influence.

(3) Ayer, and what followed had the effect of a good purgative. Of course there was much to be questioned in the language of religion and theology, but over-indulgence in a good purgative brought in some quarters the inevitable consequence—verbal diarrhoea (following, as one wag put it, 'constipation of thought').

For decades after the publication of *Language, Truth and Logic* philosophers of religion in the UK, and also largely in the USA, had an almost obsessive interest in verification and falsification. That attention should have been given to the issues raised in *Language, Truth and Logic*, and after, is quite right, but surely those who had read Kant, or Hume, should not have been caught unawares?

The answer there is 'Yes and No': 'No, they should not', because the substantive issues about the possibility of theology *had* been raised with great care and subtlety by Kant; 'Yes' because of course Ayer based his critique of theology on a very radical form of empiricism (rejected in earlier terms by Kant, as equally misguided), which had as its *dual foundation a theory of meaning and commitment to a particular form of philosophical analysis applied to language.*

Those who responded to *Language, Truth and Logic*, and after, fell into two main types: (a) Those who accepted the broadly empirical theory of language but tried to show that this did not rule out theological utterance (e.g. John Hick). (b) Those who rejected either the theory of meaning or the empiricism, or both (this type comprises many different approaches—e.g. Wittgensteinian, Barthian—a strange, and by and large unco-operative group of 'allies').

I must confess to a sense of relief that these are no longer the sole or even main thoroughfares of philosophy of religion. However, it would be shoddy simply to indicate that the debate has moved on, to give a muted cheer or two, but not to express an opinion on the substantive question of the significance of *Language, Truth and Logic* for theology and religion. It is to this that I now turn.

Critique of *Language, Truth and Logic*

I return to our starting point, and the comparison with Newspeak: My charge is that *Language, Truth and Logic* was imperialistic and did aim, and succeeded, for a generation of philosophers of religion, at *diminishing* thought.

The nub of the matter is whether what occurred was a diminishing of thought, or simply the exclusion of the nonsense of religion and theology from the domain of significant thoughts and discourse.

My critique of Ayer's position will be centred on three examples of patterns of thought which run counter to the tenor of *Language, Truth and Logic*, and which, if legitimate, are counter-examples to the universal applicability of its theory of meaning. What I shall not offer in this lecture is a critique of his account of the language of morality, but if that were accepted then much of what I now offer could be undermined.

Much of the attention given to *Language, Truth and Logic* has focused on verification/falsification as a criterion of meaning. What has been less closely discussed, but is equally central to Ayer's enterprise, is the ease with which he *analyses the meaning* of prepositions into *cognitive* and *non-cognitive* elements. Yet this is quite central to the practice and the plausibility of the enterprise.

For example, it is implausible to say that 'God is love', or 'God loves us', has *no* meaning, for many people do seem to have a use for such expressions. A verificationalist or positivist, however, does not have to be quite so implausible for he, so to speak, 'first slice analyses the utterance' into two elements. *The first* is the claim that it is *literally true that God loves us*, and *the second* is that *we rather approve of God for this because we attach a very high value to love.*

The first element is, on Ayer's account, a monumental error, because the test for literal or for actual status is failed by such statements. They are not literal statements with a status of True or False, they are nonsense.

However, the implausibility of this as a conclusion is mitigated by the allowance that the *second* element has meaning, but only of a non-cognitive kind—either that we approve of love, or that we fear the implication of a world with no God. In either case we are giving expression to emotions, but NOT making sensible factual claims about a transcendent order. The sentence is, in Ayer's phrase, 'emotionally significant'. My argument is that this is not evidence of the fine scalpel of analysis at work, bringing health to our diseased and disordered thoughts, but rather the blunt instrument of intellectual prescription, laying down what we may or may not say and think.

Example I

I believe in God the Father Almighty, Maker of Heaven and Earth. By application of the methods and conclusions of *Language, Truth and Logic*, the meaning of the relevant sections of this line of the Creed could be said to have two elements: (a) the belief that certain factual claims about God and his relation to the world are true; and (b) the expression of certain emotions of awe and reverence.

The claims implicit in (a) about the relationship between God and the world fail the tests of factual meaningfulness proposed by Ayer, whereas a claim of apparently similar form would not:

> I believe in the wisdom of President Reagan, winner of three Presidential elections.

With appropriate conditions specified there is implicit in this empirically testable (and therefore actually meaningful), albeit false, claim about President Reagan's electoral success. According to Ayer, however, the claim implicit in the first line of the Apostles' Creed is not even false, it is literally meaningless. In both cases according to Ayer's analysis, the second element of meaning remains—the expression and indeed encouragement of certain emotions. An important point for Ayer is that the two types or elements of meaning are contingently related. Even if one fails, the other (the emotionally significant) might as a matter of fact be retained.

My question here must be, 'What is the point of this analysis?' It cannot be to understand what the believer means when she utters the first line of the Apostle's Creed. What she means is not

> I believe that there are empirically testable truths about God, which, as it so happens, elicit feelings of awe and reverence in me

What the believer means is very complex and includes many elements of which the following are quite crucial,

> (a) an interpretation of the nature of the world in which we live,
> (b) a commitment to live in certain ways,
> (c) an expression of the emotions of awe and reverence,
> (d) a hope for the future.

However, it is not simply the complexity which resists Ayer's account of the meaning of such an affirmation, it is the fact that the various relations between the various elements are not contingent or causal in character. This is not to imply that the reading of the nature of the world or the hope for the future are legitimated solely by the emotion of awe, or by the commitment to live in a certain way, but more modestly that the emotion, the commitment and the hope are not 'caused' by the reading of the world, but the possibility of such a reading makes the emotion more rather than less appropriate.

There are complex issues here about the non-contingent relations between some emotions and their objects which I have examined elsewhere, *via* an analysis of Cook Wilson's most stimulating suggestion: 'That the conception of God cannot be realized without certain emotions is an essential feature of the conception' (Wilson, 1962; Sutherland, 1977, chs. III & IV).

My point is this: to begin to understand what the believer is saying, to attempt to understand what she means, is to begin to hold together a variety of elements—to begin to appreciate their inter-dependence. Ayer's prescription for understanding seems to be quite the reverse. It is to pull the elements asunder. The implication is that it is not an attempt to understand, it is a prescription for what may be thought or believed. To see his procedure in this way, is to see *prima facie* grounds for the suggestion that it '. . . diminishes thoughts'.

Example II

One central feature of the language of religion and theology in that such language spells out the possibility of a view of human life as a life lived *sub specie aeternitatis*. Whether or not such a view is sustainable is perhaps a question near the heart of the debate between atheists and believers. The point here at issue is whether or not Ayer's account of religious language and thought can equip us to explore such a question. The natural direction of a verificationist approach is to argue that either there is such a view of human affairs (and by implication such a viewpoint) or there is not. If there is such a view and appropriate viewpoint, then we ought to be able to give an account of the experiences relevant to verifying or falsifying such a claim. However, I do not believe that any sensible theologian philosopher who has read his Kant would make such a bold claim. At best rather, one might make the attempt to show that such a view is possible, in the sense of intelligible, and that if it is, this is of immense importance for us. The focus of the claim that there is a view of human affairs, *sub specie aeternitatis*, is then upon this world and possible interpretation of it, rather than upon justifying the claim that there is a possible experience described as 'seeing the world from the standpoint of eternity'.

The importance of such an idea is hard to over-estimate. Most importantly, the possibility of a view of human affairs *sub specie aeternitatis* reminds us of our particularity—our historicity and our limitations as spatio-temporal beings. This leads to a genuine recognition of what is relative about our individual or even collective viewpoints without giving way to a crippling relativism which refuses to rank or order different viewpoints. Even if we never attain to 'the' viewpoint which gives us 'the' view *sub specie aeternitatis*, the possibility that there is such a view provides a context for enquiry into the world in which we live, and for the criticism or evaluation of the beliefs about that world and our place in it, which both recognizes the relativity of our stance, but refuses to equate that with radical relativism. There is much more which follows from the possibility of such a viewpoint. Unless *Language, Truth and Logic* includes the means of handling such matters with some subtlety and depth, then once again there is at least *prima facie* evidence for the constriction of thought. My intention here is simply to expose an important area of theological and philosophical discussion which I do not believe can be properly contemplated within the principles of *Language, Truth and Logic*. The proper pursuit of that area of discussion belongs elsewhere (Sutherland, 1984).

Example III

The last example which I wish to discuss is the concept of hope.

There is no direct clue given in *Language, Truth and Logic* about how the concept of hope would be dealt with; but minimally, and in line with the approach taken by most philosophers since then in the empiricist tradition (Price, 1969; Day, 1986), two different traditions would be identified. For example, the hope that the weather might improve or that the stock-market will rise would be analysed into two elements:

(a) the belief that it is at least possible, causally as well as logically that these things will happen; and

(b) the wish or desire that these things should happen.

There are even stronger versions than this. For example J. P. Day (op. cit.) argues that one must believe not only that it is causally possible that these things might happen, but that it is probable that they should. However, we need here to confront the difficulties which that analysis raises.

The difficulty which a verificationist or even falsificationist account of meaning would encounter in the discussion of hope, is as follows. In order to satisfy the claim that the belief element in hope is meaningful or intelligible, one would have to be able to specify what would verify that belief element. In the case of changes in the weather or stock-market this is fairly straightforward, and on the basis of moderate understanding one can specify what would count as a causal sequence with the appropriate changes as its conclusion.

Consider, however, rather different cases; for example, the religious hope that there is a heaven, or the secular counterpart, the hope for utopia. Now there are two difficulties here, both of which are well signposted in the history of thought and writing in these topics. The first is that no account of heaven or utopia is, upon examination, adequate. The content of the object of hope is, in these examples, not easily specified other than in the most abstract or general terms—'the presence of God', or 'ultimate happiness'. The consequences for the verificationist are severe, for if we cannot specify what these objects of hope are like—religious or secular—then we cannot specify what would verify having attained them, nor therefore give a meaningful account of the claim that they are possible. The obvious implication to draw is that hope for these things is no more than desire—no more than Freud's 'illusions'.

Consider a further case—suggested by Gabriel Marcel (1951)—the example of a mother who knows full well that her son has been killed in battle but who still hopes that one day he will return. Again there is no specification which can be given—or would be offered—of how that might come to be, of whatever, therefore, the mother in that strict sense 'means' when she utters such a hope. Do we therefore reject such 'hopes', classify them as 'merely' the expression of emotion or desire. In Marcel's words, that would be to 'translate (the language of hope) into the language of provision or of judgement based on probabilities' (1951, 66). Such of course, is precisely what such hopes are not. A judgment that they are is a misconstruing, a distorting, and ultimately, in Orwell's term a 'diminishing' of thought, and therefore of the possibilities of life.

Conclusion

This essay has pursued an admittedly slightly fanciful literary analogy between the programmes of George Orwell's Newspeak, and A. J. Ayer's *Language, Truth and Logic*. This was a device to give focus to the question of whether the duality of verification and analysis offered by Ayer had inevitably exceeded its useful purgative rôle in such a way as to clearly constrict our understanding and to thereby 'diminish thought'.

Three examples were briefly outlined whose subtlety seems to elude the rather crude treatment which would be given by the application of the principles of *Language, Truth and Logic*, and if the implicit suggestions are correct then there is a case that conceptual possibilities are diminished, and that 1936 might in this sense lead to 1984.

On the Relation Between Commonsense, Science and Metaphysics

STEPHAN KÖRNER

Among A. J. Ayer's many influential contributions to philosophy are the accounts of the nature of metaphysics which he propounded at various stages of his philosophical development. Whereas his early position is a clear version of the antimetaphysical attitude of the Viennese circle and, more generally, of logical positivism, his later position is, as he generously emphasized, in some crucial respects indebted to Peirce's pragmatism and to Ramsey's analysis of the structure of theories. His later views on the nature of metaphysics are contained in his book *Central Questions of Philosophy* and in his reply to my criticisms in a *Festschrift*, published on the occasion of his retirement from the Wykeham Chair of Philosophy at Oxford University (Macdonald, 1979). Although in this reply he describes his later account of metaphysics as 'much too perfunctory', it does constitute an important attempt at answering one of the central questions of philosophy.

The following essay has two main aims. One is to take a fresh look at Ayer's later view of metaphysics in the light of his reply to my criticisms, in particular at his thesis that metaphysical propositions are not assertive, but express policy-decisions the nature of which is best understood with the help of Peirce's distinction between facts and the arrangement of facts and Ramsey's distinction between primary and secondary systems. The other aim of the essay is to defend my own account of the nature of metaphysics and to exemplify its usefulness by exhibiting the relations between commonsense, science and metaphysics. Certain minor terminological differences between the present essay and its predecessor will—it is hoped—help to emphasize the empirical or, more precisely, the anthropological character of my approach. The essay is divided into two parts. Part I contains a brief consideration of those views of Peirce and Ramsey to which Ayer expresses his indebtedness (§1) and a discussion of Ayer's views, especially those expressed in his reply to my early criticisms (§2). Part II contains a brief analysis of the notions of a supreme (cognitive) principle, a categorial framework and a speculative metaphysics (§3) and of their rôle in commonsense and scientific thinking (§4)

Stephan Körner

I

1. On Peirce's and Ramsey's views of the relation between facts and their arrangement

A characterization of our thinking about the world in which we find ourselves and in which we act might well start by pointing out that its aims include not only the discovery of facts but also their arrangement in ways which serve our various purposes. Yet the distinction between facts and their arrangement is far from being clear or generally agreed. Indeed in a wide sense of the terms there is no difference between facts and their arrangement since any such arrangement itself constitutes a fact. That the distinction can be drawn in a variety of ways, is shown by Peirce, who regarded it as central to his early pragmatism, as well as to his late pragmaticism. The following example which illustrates his change of mind is due to Peirce himself.

The example concerns the difference between hard and soft bodies, in particular the correct answer to the question as to 'what prevents us from saying that all hard bodies remain perfectly soft until they are touched, when their hardness increases with the pressure until they are scratched'.[1] His original reply was that 'there would be no *falsity* in such modes of speech' since they 'would involve a modification of our present usage of speech with regards to the words hard and soft but not their meaning'. For the words in their new usage 'represent no fact to be different from what it is' but only involve 'arrangements of facts which would be exceedingly maladroit'. (loc. cit.) In other words, the difference between a hard thing and a soft thing and any other difference between things must be based on actual, as opposed to merely possible, tests.

This analysis is later strongly rejected on the ground that a person's conduct depends on what the person believes *would* happen under various circumstances i.e. on the person's 'conceived conditional resolutions'; and that 'the conditional propositions, with their hypothetical antecendents' in 'which such resolutions consist' are 'of the ultimate nature of meaning'. (*CSP*, 5.453). Peirce moreover has come to hold that 'these conditional propositions with their hypothetical antecedents' or, briefly, these subjunctive conditionals, 'must be capable of being true' (loc. cit.). In other words, the subjunctive conditional on the basis of which we decide, for example, whether an object is hard or soft, expresses neither a mere arrangement of facts nor a mere logical possibility, but a kind of fact, which Peirce characterizes as a possibility 'of a real kind' (loc. cit). In order to appreciate why Peirce regards

[1] See Peirce, 1960, Vol. V section 40, §3 (briefly *CSP*, 5.403).

90

subjunctive conditionals which express real possibilities as facts and not as arrangements of facts, it may be useful to recall that laws of nature, e.g. the laws of Newtonian dynamics, have the form of subjunctive conditionals. While laws of nature would normally not be classified as either facts or as (more or less suitable) arrangements of facts, one would, if forced to choose between either classification, very likely prefer the former to the latter.

Peirce's later view still leaves room for a distinction between facts and their more or less suitable arrangement. It is, however, far removed from restricting the task of philosophy to the arrangement of facts or, in Wittgenstein's terminology, to 'perspicuous representation' (*übersichtliche Darstellung*) which can be compared to 'arranging the books of a library' rather than adding new books to it.[2] For one of Peirce's philosophical aims was to propound and defend a 'scientific metaphysics'. He 'liked to call' it 'synechism, because it rests on the study of continuity' (*CSP*, 6.202) which, like Leibniz, he regarded as an all-pervasive feature of reality and, hence, as 'a regulative principle of logic, prescribing what sort of hypothesis is fit to be entertained and examined' (*CSP*, 6.173). His regret that 'logicians have too much neglected the study of *vagueness*' (*CSP*, 5.505) is, among other things, based on the conviction that 'whenever degree or any other possibility of continuous variation subsists absolute precision is impossible' (*CSP*, 5.506).

The distinction between empirical facts and their explanatory arrangement, which is central to Peirce's pragmatism, closely resembles Ramsey's distinction between the 'meaning or content' of a theory and 'its symbolic form' and between primary and secondary systems.[3] Indeed Ramsey's view of theories can be—and has been—regarded as a version of an important aspect of pragmatism. For our present purpose the following brief summary of Ramsey's view of the nature of theories will, it is hoped, be sufficient.

A theory is regarded as a language serving the explanation of facts which occur in a universe of discourse called 'the primary system'. This system is supposed to be 'in some way given to us, so that we have a notation capable of expressing every proposition in it' (op. cit. 101). The facts of the primary system are represented by atomic propositions and truth-functions formed from names of a finite domain of individuals and from functions, i.e. functors (such as '$x+y$') and predicates (such as 'x is red'). A simple example of a primary system, given by Ramsey, contains atomic propositions 'such as $A(n)$, $B(m, n)$,

---

[2] See Wittgenstein, 1953, §122; Wittgenstein (1958) 44.
[3] See his 'Theories' in Ramsey (1978), 121 and *passim*. For a helpful exegesis see *The Anatomy of Inquiry* by Israel Scheffler (1963), 203f.

where m, n take positive or negative integral values, subject to any restrictions, e.g. that in (m, n) m may only take the values 1, 2' (op. cit. 103).

The secondary system is created by the introduction of 'new propositional functions $\alpha(n)$, $\beta(n)$, $\gamma(m, n)$ etc. . . . Its propositions are any truth-functions of the values of α, β, γ etc.' The axioms of the system are propositions laid down about these values. Its theorems are the propositions which are deducible from the axioms. The primary and the secondary system are linked by a '*dictionary* which takes the form of a series of definitions of the functions of the primary system A, B, C . . . in terms of those of the secondary system α, β, γ, e.g. $A(n) = \alpha(n)$ v $\gamma(0, n^2)$' (op. cit. 104). From these definitions, taken as equivalences, together with the axioms of the secondary system, it is possible to deduce propositions of the primary system 'which are called *laws* if they are general propositions and *consequences* if they are singular' (loc. cit.). It is, as Ramsey points out, possible to eliminate the propositional functions of the secondary system, say α, β, γ, from the axioms and the dictionary and, hence, from the totality of laws and consequences. This is done by means of existential quantification. Schematically the transition proceeds from 'Dictionary & Axioms (α, β, γ)' to '$(\exists \alpha, \ell, g)$: Dictionary & Axioms (α, ℓ, g)' where the functional variables α, ℓ, g replace the functional constants α, β, γ. Ramsey calls the totality of laws and consequences following from the existentially quantified conjunction of dictionary and axioms the 'eliminant' of the theory. It is this totality which according to him the theory 'asserts to be true' (op. cit. 104), i.e. factually or empirically true. By means of the existentially quantified sentence, now known as the Ramsey sentence, it can be shown that whatever can be asserted in the language of the theory can also asserted without it, i.e. that the empirical content of the theory can be separated from its theoretical arrangement. It follows that the logical relations between different theories, e.g. their logical compatibility or incompatibility, coincide with the logical relations between their empirical contents.

In preparation for the critical discussion of Ayer's view of metaphysics it is useful to draw attention to the following features of Ramsey's account of theories. First, the primary and secondary system, as well as the dictionary of any theory are all embedded in classical predicate logic, which neglects the inexactness of some commonsense concepts. Second, Ramsey does not consider the difference between metaphysical and scientific theories. Third, he consequently does not consider the problem of the nature of the conflict between metaphysical theories which, at least, *prima facie* differs from the logical incompatibility of their empirical contents, if any.

2. On Ayer's later views of metaphysics and his indebtedness to Peirce and Ramsey

According to Ayer commonsense thinking includes a primary system in Ramsey's sense. The system includes 'purely factual propositions' representing 'what is actually observable' (*CQ*, 33). Yet, 'since the distinction between fact and theory is only relative we have' according to him 'some choice as to where to draw the line'. The secondary system 'goes beyond the primary in that it legislates for possible as well as actual cases and can also contain terms which are not related to anything observable'. It is 'concerned with what Peirce called the arrangement of facts' (loc. cit.). Since metaphysical propositions are located in the secondary system, the primary system must—however the line between facts and their arrangement is drawn—be free from metaphysics. Yet Ayer's way of drawing the line fails to exclude metaphysics from his primary system and, hence, from commonsense thinking. This can be shown *inter alia* by considering his account of the relation between percepts and physical objects, both of which are regarded as belonging to the primary system (*CQ*, 110).

Ayer agrees with Hume and other philosophers that, for example, the percept of a chair, that is to say a person's experience of a certain ordered set of perceptual data (or 'qualia') differs from a physical chair in that the latter, but not the former enjoys 'a continued and distinct existence' (*CQ*, 72) He also acknowledges that this difference raises the question, as to what is involved in our making the transition from judging something to be a chair-percept to judging it to be a physical chair and, more generally, what is involved in 'making the passage from percepts to physical objects'. His answer to the question is that this passage has to be treated 'not strictly as a process of logical construction, but rather, in Hume's way, as an exercise of the imagination'. In other words 'the continued and distinct existence, not of percepts, but of the objects into which they are transmuted, is simply posited' (*CQ*, 107).

Now, whether or not the positing of the continued and distinct existence of physical objects, as opposed to percepts, is merely a matter of imagination or also a matter of evaluating various kinds of evidence, it does in any case amount to applying and, hence, to assuming the applicability of a member of a family of concepts, the critical analysis of which has been a central concern of traditional metaphysics. The concepts in question are in particular various concepts of substance (or of being part of a substance). That the use of such a concept or concepts forms part of commonsense thinking is an anthropological fact which throws serious doubt on Ayer's claim that this primary system is free from metaphysical assumptions. Indeed any history of the ideas employed in Western culture shows how the commonsense concept of substance has changed under the influence of popularized theology, philosophy and science. And philosophers from the pre-Socratics to Kant and beyond have paid critical attention to the concept or concepts of substance which they found in the commonsense thinking of their day. Ayer not only holds that the primary system being 'limited to the domain of actual fact' is free from metaphysics, but he also seems to hold that—apart from the possible addition of new factual propositions—it is not subject to change. This view which is inconsistent with the history of ideas, is also among others, strongly rejected by Peirce whose 'critical commonsensism' implies the changeability of even those beliefs which 'acritical commonsense' considers indubitable (see *CSP*, 5.44).

Ayer's primary system of commonsense thinking is embedded in a logic which satisfies the Fregean requirement that the definition of every concept determine for every object whether or not it falls under it. This requirement of exactness is accepted by Ramsey for all primary and secondary systems and is rejected by Peirce as inconsistent with his synechism (see §1). It is also rejected by Wittgenstein. A convincing proof of the inexactness of commonsense thinking follows from an inquiry into legal rules, which must, if the law of the land is to be obeyed, be understood by all citizens and, hence, be expressible in ordinary language. The occurrence of border-line cases is a commonplace among lawyers. It follows from the fact that the meaning of some legal concepts is partly determined in the course of their application by the following steps: the judge's acknowledgment that the case to be judged is a border-line case of a concept, used in the formulation of a law; the judge's decision to turn it into a positive or negative case of the concept; and—in many cases—the treatment of this decision as a precedent for future decisions by the same judge or other judges.[4]

As has been pointed out earlier, Ayer holds that subjunctive conditionals, as opposed to truthfunctional implications, do not express facts and that they consequently have to be assigned to a secondary system. This view conforms to Peirce's early pragmatism and is opposed to his later pragmaticism, which implies that the laws of nature, expressed by subjunctive conditionals, represent real possibilities and not mere arrangements of facts (see §1). Yet if Ayer had not excluded subjunctive conditionals from the realm of fact, he might have found it difficult to defend the thesis that e.g. the principle of continuity cannot be regarded as a true or false factual proposition. For the principle—whether regarded as metaphysical or scientific—has the

[4] For details see my 'Über Sprachspiele und rechtliche Institutionen' (1981).

form of a subjunctive conditional to the effect that if an aspect of nature involves a change, then the change is necessarily continuous.

In his book *The Central Questions of Philosophy* Ayer discusses the views of other philosophers on the nature of metaphysics. But, like Ramsey, he does not distinguish between the scientific and the metaphysical contributions to a secondary system. He does, however, indicate such a distinction in his reply to my criticisms. (See Macdonald, 1979, 332). In it he makes the following statement (my italics): '. . . *if I were to make a distinction* between the scientific and metaphysical contributions to a secondary system, I should locate the metaphysical elements in the choice of the entities which the system countenanced and the conventions to which they are made subject' ibid. 332). The conventions are, like all propositions of a secondary system, not 'assertive', but 'acceptable or unacceptable arrangements of facts' (loc. cit.). This characterization of metaphysical propositions can be supplemented by Ayer's remark on a specific example of a metaphysical proposition, namely the principle of continuity. In it he characterizes 'the disagreement between those who accept and those who reject it . . . as a disagreement of policy' (ibid. 330), as opposed to a disagreement about facts, expressed by true or false factual propositions.

Ayer's account gives rise to two difficulties. One arises from the fact that a person may accept more than one secondary system, for example *inter alia* a biological and a physical theory. Such a person is faced with the question, whether the entities of all his secondary systems should be countenanced by him or whether and, if so, why the entities of one of the secondary systems should be regarded as more fundamental. The question is particularly serious for anybody who hopes that eventually one of the theories, say the biological, will be reduced to another, say the physical. It is perhaps even more serious for anybody who rightly holds that the two theories are incompatible, because one of them, say the biological theory, implies a principle (e.g. the principle of continuity) the negation of which is implied by the other, say the physical theory. The question is not answered in Ayer's account of the metaphysical contribution to secondary systems.

The second difficulty arises from Ayer's thesis that the disagreement between the acceptor and the rejector of a metaphysical principle is a disagreement of policy, i.e. a disagreement between opposing policy-decisions. A policy-decision, as normally understood, is a decision to adopt a course of action in order to achieve a certain purpose. Now there can be little doubt that the acceptance of a metaphysical principle, e.g. of the principle of continuity or its negation, can be a policy-decision. Thus it may be that a scientist uses a theory for the purpose of prediction, even though he rejects the theory because of its inconsistency with a metaphysical principle which he judges to be true and though he expects or hopes that the theory will in due course be falsified. A famous, recent example is Einstein's position regarding orthodox Quantum Mechanics, to the development of which he has made important contributions. Einstein, on the one hand, rejected the theory as lacking in explanatory power because of, among other things, its inconsistency with the principle of continuity; but, on the other hand, he made the policy-decision nevertheless to apply it because of its predictive usefulness. His judgment or conjecture of the principle's truth was one of his motives for trying to produce a new theory which would match the orthodox theory in predictive power and would be consistent with the principle.

Einstein's example and similar examples, found in the history of science, do not, of course, amount to a refutation of Ayer's pragmatist account of metaphysical principles as expressing policy-decisions. For it might be argued that Einstein misunderstood his own scientific thinking by wrongly interpreting a policy-decision as an assertion or conjecture of a factual truth. Yet a case study of Einstein's and similar positions does throw sufficient doubt on Ayer's thesis, to justify the proposal and defence of an alternative analysis of the content and function of metaphysics which would not only imply a refutation of that thesis, but would in addition also support the other objections, made earlier, to his position. These include in particular objections to the theses that the primary system, contained in commonsense thinking, is free of metaphysics (and, *it seems*, not subject to change); that a person's primary system and the person's secondary system or systems are embedded in an exact logic; and that all subjunctive conditionals are non-factual propositions, expressing arrangements of facts. The proposal and defence of the required alternative analysis is the next and final task of the present essay.

II

3. On supreme principles, categorial frameworks and speculative metaphysics

It is an anthropological fact that—with very few exceptions—human beings acquire at an early stage of their development the ability to make in one way or another certain distinctions which involve the acceptance and application of a logic. They acquire *inter alia* the ability to distinguish in their experience between particulars and attributes or, as Frege put it, between objects and concepts, as well as to distinguish between cases where a certain particular (or ordered set of particulars) is a positive, a negative or a borderline case of a certain attribute, i.e. where the particular is with equal correctness judged a positive or a negative case of the attribute—though not jointly a positive and a negative case of it. In making these distinctions one accepts a weak principle of non-contradiction or inconsistency to the effect that for every attribute and every particular, the attribute is not jointly applicable and inapplicable to the particular. If one restricts oneself to the consideration of exact concepts, i.e. concepts without borderline cases, the weak principle of non-contradiction can be replaced by the principle of non-contradiction, as formulated e.g. by Aristotle, Frege and Brouwer. The weak principle of non-contradiction constitutes the core of different logics, e.g. of various versions of classical and intuitionist logical theory.[5]

By means of any of these logical systems one can define the notion of a person's supreme principle, which is central to the understanding of the role of metaphysics in commonsense and scientific thinking. A general proposition is a person's supreme principle if, and only if, the person accepts the requirement that any proposition which is inconsistent with the principle has to be rejected as incorrect. Although a person's set of supreme principles may be internally inconsistent, it is in the present context sufficient to consider only internally consistent sets of such principles. For our purpose it is of special importance to consider those supreme principles which form a fundamental and indispensable part of a person's general thinking about the public world or, briefly, of a person's 'categorial framework'.

These fundamental framework-principles include principles of logic, without which one could not think correctly about a public world or anything else; principles of intersubjective interpretation or objectification, without which there would be no acknowledgment of public objects, as opposed to mere subjective appearances; and principles determining the constitution of the maximal kinds (of public objects) and the individuation of their members, without which there would be no public universe of discourse. As regards logic it is important to distinguish between, on the one hand, the logic (or logics) underlying commonsense thinking and the ordinary languages which are common to all members of a society and, on the other hand, the logic (or logics) underlying the specialist thinking in mathematics and the sciences which depend on the application of mathematics. The main difference between the two types of thinking is that the former admits the use of inexact concepts while the latter forbids it. This difference has, in one way or another, been acknowledged by philosophers as different in their philosophical approaches as Plato, Frege, Peirce and Wittgenstein, as well as practising and theoretical lawyers (see §2).

[5] For details on this and the other topics of §3 see *Metaphysics Its Structure and Function*, (1984) (briefly *MSF*).

Stephan Körner

The fundamental framework-principles of intersubjective inter-pretation or objectification determine which subjective appearances are also intersubjectively or objectively given entities, by governing the use of concepts the applicability of which to an appearance implies its intersubjective or objective character. Examples are the concepts of substance and of causality in various senses of the terms. The specific content of these framework-principles may differ from one group of persons to another. The same applies to the framework-principles which determine the constitution of maximal kinds and the individua-tion of their members. Examples are the principles that all objects belonging to the public world are physical objects, which are individu-ated by their spatio-temporal location; or the principle that all objects belonging to the public world are either inanimate physical objects or living beings, which are individuated with the help of the Leibnizian principle of the identity of indiscernibles.

From the fundamental framework-principles one must distinguish auxiliary framework-principles, which facilitate the application of the former. For our present purpose auxiliary principles of idealization will prove of particular importance. (See *MSF*, chs. 1, 6, 7). In any idealization, which will concern us here, one can distinguish between its basis, its result and the conditional identification of the basis with the result. In the simplest case the basis and the result are two different concepts. Their conditional identification consists in treating them in certain contexts and for certain purposes *as if* they were one and the same concept, for example when an engineer conditionally identifies the concepts of an empirical and of an Euclidean triangle, or a lawyer the concepts of a group of persons and of an individual person. What applies to the idealization of single concepts applies *mutatis mutandis* also to their instances, to propositions in which the concepts are applied to their instances, as well as to sets of such concepts, instances and propositions. Idealizations may be more or less comprehensive. A highly comprehensive type of idealization, which is particularly rele-vant to the present topic, involves the idealizing transition from a whole area of commonsense thinking to a mathematical or scientific theory (see §4).

From fundamental supreme principles which are indispensable to thinking about a public world and auxiliary supreme principles, which facilitate the use of the former, one must distinguish 'external' supreme principles, which are wholly dispensable to such thinking. An extreme example would be a person's acceptance of the proposition that by walking under a ladder one brings misfortune upon oneself as supreme principle. Another example would be the acceptance of the supreme belief that there exists a just and omnipotent deity. Yet while the superstitious and the religious belief are both dispensable to human

98

thinking about a public world, they differ in important ways. Thus, to put it very briefly, it could be reasonably argued that just as the acceptance of some auxiliary framework-principles may facilitate one's conformity to the fundamental principles of one's categorial framework, so the external, supreme belief in a just and omnipotent deity—but not the external, supreme belief about walking under ladders—may facilitate one's conformity to the fundamental principles of one's morality.

The supreme principles which constitute a person's categorial framework must be distinguished from the person's speculative metaphysics, if any. For speculative metaphysics is not concerned with thinking about a public world, but with thinking about 'reality' or 'the world in itself'. Speculative metaphysics is often contrasted with science and regarded as a poor substitute for it. Yet some outstanding scientists did not only regard them as compatible, but found speculative metaphysics helpful in their scientific work. Thus according to Schrödinger 'only metaphysics', i.e. as is clear from the context of the quotation, speculative metaphysics, 'can inspire the hard work of physics' (see Moore, 1989, 386). It is in this connection worth recalling that some originally speculative metaphysics has become part of widely accepted categorial frameworks of commonsense and scientific thinking, as is exemplified by the Democritean atomic theory. In this respect it resembles some branches of pure mathematics, such as non-commutative algebra, which, though developed without regard to any practical use, have become essential to science and technology.

4. From commonsense to metaphysics without and with the mediation of science

Of the many views which are held about the relation between metaphysics and science two views seem to be particularly popular among scientific experts and laymen. According to one, which goes back at least to Comte, metaphysics is the predecessor of science, which after the emergence of scientific thinking has been or, at least, should be replaced by it. According to the other view, which goes back at least to Kant, true metaphysics is implicit or as Kant puts it, immanent in science (see Kant, 1968, 161f.). A more moderate version of this view is the assumption that the metaphysics implicit in science is nearer to the truth than the metaphysics implicit in commonsense thinking. Both these views are based on arguments which ignore the relation between commonsense thinking and scientific theories. They particularly ignore that neither commonsense nor scientific thinking is free from metaphysics and provide no conclusive reasons for preferring a commonsense-based to a science-based metaphysics.

The transition from commonsense thinking to scientific theories is brought about by idealizations. Their basis is the conceptual net of commonsense thinking, expressed in ordinary language or, more precisely, in some part of it. Thus Newtonian dynamics is the result of an idealization the basis of which are the concepts and propositions of commonsense thinking about ordinary physical objects. The modifications which result in a mathematically formulated theory necessarily involve the replacement of a logic of inexact concepts by an exact logic, as well as the replacement of empirical by mathematical concepts—for example, a concept of empirical continuity by a concept of mathematical continuity. The modifications may also affect the commonsense conceptual net in other ways, for example, by replacing the commonsense concept of substance by a concept defined with the help of a conservation law, or—as is the case in Newtonian dynamics—by replacing the concept of ordinary physical objects by a concept of particles the only properties of which are their mass and spatiotemporal location and their being subject to certain laws of motion. The changes of the commonsense conceptual net which are not logical or mathematical, consist either in deductive abstractions or in theoretical innovations, i.e.—roughly speaking—in the removal of certain strands of the conceptual net or in the addition of new strands to it.[6]

The result of the mentioned changes in the commonsense conceptual net also involves *ipso facto* a replacement of its maximal kinds and its criteria for the individuation of their members. It may in particular also happen that, as has been mentioned earlier (in §2), different theories involve the assumption of different maximal kinds. A case in point are the contemporary theories in biology, physics and chemistry, which do not imply whether, if at all, the maximal kinds of one or two of these theories are 'ultimately' or 'really' maximal and which leave this question open. At present there is no consensus among the scientific experts about the correct answer. Thus Francis Crick not only holds that 'the ultimate aim of the modern movement in biology is in fact to explain *all* biology in terms of physics and chemistry' but also argues that this aim is likely to be achieved. This optimism is, however, not generally shared by his colleagues (see Crick, 1966, 10).

In order to understand the possible influence of a new scientific theory on the members of the society in which it has been discovered, it is useful to consider its application for the purpose of prediction by a team, consisting of scientific experts and laymen. Before doing so, it is advisable, for the sake of brevity, to distinguish between 'commonsense statements', expressed in the language common to experts and laymen, and 'theoretical statements', expressed in the language of the theory,

---

[6] For details see my *Experience and Theory* (1966) ch. XI.

shared by the experts only. (The former statements refer to the basis, the latter to the result of an idealization.) The co-operative application of a theory falls into the following phases: (1) observation or production of an initial state, described by an initial commonsense statement; (2) commonsense statement that the conditions for the conditional identifiability of the initial commonsense statement with an initial theoretical statement are satisfied; (3) (mixed) statement of the conditional identifiability of the initial commonsense with the initial theoretical statement; (4) logical deduction of a final theoretical statement from the conjunction of the initial theoretical statement and the axioms of the theory; (5) 'deidealization' of the final theoretical statement, resulting in a final commonsense statement; (6) commonsense statement to the effect that the initial commonsense statement together with the commonsense statement of the satisfaction of the identifiability-conditions imply the commonsense final statement. It is important to note that the last commonsense statement can be correctly made by a layman, who refers to the existence of a theory, which though known to experts, is not known to him. (In this respect it resembles the Ramsey sentence (see §1) from which it, however, radically differs in other respects, for example, by replacing the equivalences of Ramsey's dictionary by conditional identifiabilities.)

A layman's categorial framework is clearly not affected by any specific scientific theory, if he merely knows that there exists a scientific theory, the application of which can be interpolated between the commonsense descriptions of certain initial and certain final states. Yet even a person who is fully acquainted with such a theory might regard it as no more than a useful fiction, i.e. a conjunction of propositions which, though lacking any factual content, can for the purpose of increasing our factual information be treated as if they were factual propositions. He might point out that just as the employment of various sorts of legal fictions does not alter the nature of commonsense thinking, so the use of scientific idealizations also does not change it. This view of scientific theories and idealizations closely resembles Wittgenstein's early view that ordinary language 'is in order as it is' and his later variations of it. It also recalls Ayer's view that all propositions of a secondary system and, hence, all meaningful scientific and metaphysical principles are 'not assertive' but express 'arrangements of facts' or 'policy decisions' (see §2). If a scientific expert considers the idealizing transition from commonsense, concepts, particulars and propositions to their idealized counterparts as mere aids to commonsense thinking, then the fundamental, as opposed to the auxiliary, supreme principles of his categorial framework will be unaffected by the adoption of a new scientific theory.

Stephan Körner

The view that the content of scientific theories is, in spite of their practical value, 'less real' than the content of commonsense thinking is compatible with the preceding analysis of idealization, but is not implied by it. The same applies to the opposite view that scientific theories, far from involving an ontological downgrading of commonsense thinking, involve an ontological upgrading of it. This view goes back to Plato's theory of Forms, in particular to his account of the relation between empirical and mathematical entities. If one accepts the view that the idealizing transition from commonsense to science amounts to a transition from 'less real' to 'more real' or, to use a Platonic term, 'really real' entities, then any inconsistency between science and commonsense must be resolved in favour of science. That is to say, that in so far as a person's categorial framework is based on commonsense and is inconsistent with science, it must be replaced by a categorial framework consistent with science or, more precisely, with those scientific theories which at the time are judged most adequate.

Its supreme logical principles will depend on the logic in which the accepted scientific theories are embedded, which normally amounts to replacing a logic admitting inexact concepts by a logic conforming to the Fregean requirement of exactness. There may have to be a change of intersubjectivity-principles, but no fresh introduction of such principles, since such principles are already implicit in commonsense thinking. The determination of the maximal kinds, i.e. of the principles of their constitution and of the individuation of their members, will depend on the objects and attributes used in the accepted scientific theories. The categorial framework may also contain auxiliary supreme principles, in particular principles of idealization or, more precisely, principles of second-order idealization, i.e. idealization of idealized commonsense entities. A person may for a variety of reasons, for example because of logical inconsistencies or other conflicts between the accepted theories, find it difficult or impossible to decide which supreme principles should properly be accepted. The occurrence of such uncertainties does not reduce the usefulness of the notion of a categorial framework in analysing the relations between commonsense, science and metaphysics. Indeed any analysis which ignored these uncertainties and the vacillations which may be caused by them, would be highly unrealistic.

A brief statement of some of the theses included in, or implied by, the preceding analysis of the relation between commonsense, science and metaphysics may help to underline the main differences between this analysis and the views of Ayer and other philosophers: The distinction between particulars and attributes in the experience of a public world involves the more or less explicit acceptance of a categorial framework, consisting of logical and non-logical supreme principles. The notion of a categorial framework is a generic concept which allows for differences between various specific categorial frameworks. Such differences may exist between their logical principles (i.e. their peripheral logical principles, as opposed to the weak principle of non-contradiction); between their non-logical, fundamental principles (i.e. their intersubjectivity principles, the principles defining the constitution of a framework's maximal kinds and the individuation of their members); and between their auxiliary principles (especially the principles of idealization).

The same non-logical, general proposition, such as the principle that all change is continuous, may play different roles with respect to the categorial frameworks of different persons. It may be that the proposition is a fundamental supreme principle for one person, that its negation is such a principle for another and that it is neither for a third. It may be, to use Ayer's term, 'assertive' for one person and purely regulative for another, in the sense that this person has made a 'policy-decision' to act in certain contexts *as if* the propositions were true, although he judges it to be false or is uncertain as to its truth or falsehood. If the proposition can be formulated in a commonsense or in a scientific language, its commonsense version may be supreme for one person and its idealized scientific version supreme for another. It may be a categorial framework-principle for one person and a proposition of speculative metaphysics for another, who may or may not believe that it could eventually become a framework principle. The predictive usefulness of scientific laws is independent of their consistency with the categorial frameworks of their users. However, the consistency of a scientific law (or any other proposition) with a person's categorial framework is a necessary condition of the proposition's having some explanatory value for the person.

Logical Positivism and Intentionality

HILARY PUTNAM

When 'Freddy' Ayer asked me to contribute to his volume in the Library of Living Philosophers series (which, regrettably, has *still* not been published), I was delighted, and while the main topic of my contribution[1] was the sense (if any) in which it can be a 'necessary' truth that water is H_2O, I devoted a section of that essay to problems that I saw with Ayer's account of the paradigm intentional notion, the notion of reference. Ayer ended his reply by saying that he could not satisfactorily meet my objections, and with characteristic modesty and good humour he added that it was only small consolation that, in his opinion, no one else could satisfactorily account for reference either. The thoughtfulness, fairness, and responsiveness of Ayer's entire reply reminded me of the way in which the same qualities were displayed in Carnap's reply to my contribution to his volume in the same series. These two replies—Carnap's and Ayer's—display the virtues of the philosopher who searches for truth, and who genuinely welcomes serious criticism, in a truly exemplary way. I treasure both of them, and they are bound up with my memories of those two wonderful philosophers.

In today's lecture, I shall not review the difficulties I laid out in 'Is Water Necessarily H_2O', because those difficulties had to do with Ayer's own account of reference to mental particulars, an account which is closer to Russell's than it is to the main doctrines of logical positivism. Instead, I shall consider the treatment of intentional notions by the two principal leaders of the movement, namely, Carnap and Reichenbach.[2]

First, a word as to what I shall mean today by 'intentionality'. It has been said with justice that it is characteristic of analytic philosophy as a movement (and not just of logical positivism) to make the relation between thought and language (or between language and the understanding of language) a central—sometimes *the* central—ques-

---

[1] 'Is Water Necessarily H_2O' is included in my *Realism with a Human Face* (1990) by permission of the Open Court Publishing Company, which will publish *The Philosophy of Alfred Jules Ayer*, when that volume appears.

[2] It should be noted, however, that Reichenbach disliked the label 'positivism', and always referred to the movement to which he and Carnap belonged as 'logical empiricism'.

tion of philosophy. But, to pre-philosophical common sense at least, it would seem that any account of the relation between language and the understanding of language has to include some account of the relation between language and the world; and, taken in this way, the relation to be accounted for is just what Brentano and Husserl understood by intentionality. Moreover, this problem was known to Carnap, at least, before Carnap became a positivist; for in Carnap's doctoral dissertation, *Der Raum* (Space), there are admiring references to Husserl. Yet Brentano and Husserl believed that it was impossible to give a naturalistic account of intentionality, and logical positivism is avowedly naturalistic. So, how did Carnap come to think (and how did Reichenbach think) that a naturalistic answer to this problem (often called 'Brentano's Problem', nowadays) had been given by logical positivism?

The general lines of the reply are well known: while the problem of the relation between language and our understanding of language remains a reasonable question for the positivists, and one to which they proposed answers, the idea that a part of the question is 'the relation of language to the world' is rejected as a confusion. Brentano's Problem is one of the problems that Carnap would surely have dismissed as a 'pseudo-problem'. Whether it is or is not a pseudo-problem is a larger question than I can deal with today, except for some very brief remarks at the end; for the most part, what I wish to study is the more restricted question, do the reasons that the positivists gave for dismissing this question, or this family of questions, really work? And if they fail, just *how* do they fail?

Carnap and Solipsism

One way of seeing how these questions might seem to arise for the positivists, and how they attempted to dismiss them, is to consider the charge of 'solipsism' that was often brought against Carnap's celebrated *Logische Aufbau der Welt*. On the face of it, such a charge might seem fully justified. For the 'ontology' of the Aufbau, the domain over which the bound variables of the ideal language are intended to range, is *the reconstructor's past and present 'elementary experiences'*. When Carnap writes out an arbitrary synthetic statement in the ideal language, all it speaks about is Carnap's 'elementary experiences'. So, according to Carnap, the world consists of Carnap's 'elementary experiences'—what is wrong with this argument?

According to Carnap, what is wrong is the following: it is true (Carnap thought at that time), that every cognitively meaningful statement is either a tautology or is expressible as a synthetic statement about 'my' elementary experiences. (The idea—later to become explicit, and still later (in Carnap, 1936, 1937) to be given up by Carnap—that any meaningful synthetic statement can be conclusively verified, and that its meaning is given by a description of the verifying experiences, is already implicit in this doctrine). But, Carnap argued in the Aufbau, the 'language of science' (i.e. the cognitively meaningful) can be rationally reconstructed in alternative and equally legitimate ways. (The 'Principle of Tolerance' was already implicit in this claim.) If, in one reconstruction of the language, the 'ontology' is 'my' experiences, in another, equally admissible, reconstruction, the 'ontology' might be physical objects. The adoption of one reconstruction or another is not a commitment to the noumenal existence of either elementary experiences or physical objects. Indeed, to know what the nominatum of a sign is is only to know how the sentences containing that sign receive truth values, and this can be displayed equally well by different rational reconstructions. The very term 'ontology' is misleading, Carnap told me years later, and he was extremely critical of Quine for introducing it into analytic philosophy.

On Carnap's view, there are only two sorts of meaningful statements: one can make ordinary scientific statements within the ideal language (years later, when Carnap wrote 'Empiricism, Semantics, Ontology', these become the 'internal statements', the answers to the 'internal questions', distinguished in that essay from both the senseless 'external questions' of metaphysics, and the meaningful 'external questions' of pragmatics and syntax) and one can make syntactic statements about the various rational reconstructions, for example, 'In the system of the Aufbau, the only primitive predicate is *Elementary experience X is remembered as similar to elementary experience Y*'. Confusing the latter sort of statement with statements of transcendent metaphysics, e.g. 'only my elementary experiences really exist' is what gives rise to the charges of solipsism, idealism, materialism, etc., that are constantly being brought against logical positivists on the basis of the character of their various (alternative) reconstructions of the language of science. Carnap's 'solipsism' is a harmless 'methodological solipsism' (i.e. the adoption of one particular basis for the reconstruction from among a number of possible choices), not a bit of transcendent metaphysics.

The upshot is that the question, how all or any of these reconstructions relate to 'the world', is a pseudo-question. For example, if I adopt the Aufbau system, it is quite wrong to charge me with believing that only my own elementary experiences exist. For, if the question as to the existence of other people's experiences is meant as an ordinary internal question, then the answer is that other people, physical objects, and the experiences of other people all exist as a question of empirical fact (since these are all identified with various logical constructions out of my experiences, and the sentences about these constructions which translate 'there are other people', 'there are material bodies', and 'there are experiences of other people' correctly state empirical facts in the system). On the other hand, if it is meant as an external question, then either the question is a syntactic question, answered by saying what the primitives of the system are, or it is a meaningless pseudo-question. The radical idea that the questions of classical philosophy are all illegitimate attempts to transcend the bounds of the language, is present in the Aufbau, as it was, of course, already in Wittgenstein's *Tractatus*, even if the Aufbau does not explicitly state a theory of meaning.

However, there is a major problem with all this—one which Carnap did not have the resources to deal in the Aufbau itself. The difficulty is the following: Carnap's reply to the charge of solipsism turns on the notion of 'equally possible' (i.e. equally correct) reconstructions of the language. But *what does 'equally possible' mean*?

The problem is one with which Quine has wrestled in recent years (and one with respect to which he 'vacillates' between different attitudes[3], Quine tells us), namely can one say that there are in some sense equally true descriptions of the world which are incompatible when taken at face value? If I reconstruct the language of science in the Aufbau way and then reconstruct it again on a physicalist basis, the two reconstructions will not simply be equivalent in the sense in which 'equivalent' is used in standard logic.[4] Indeed, if we simply conjoin them, we may get *contradictions*.

To see the problem, suppose, *per impossibile*, that the programme of 'methodological solipsism' could really be carried out, and thing sentences could be translated into sentences about (my) elementary experiences. It is hard to believe that this could be done without employing explicit definition at any point; but if I do employ explicit definition and define a physical object as a logical construction (in the sense of *Principia*, which served as Carnap's model of rational reconstruction), and also (when I take physical objects as basic, in my 'alternative' physicalistic reconstruction of the language of science) define my elementary experiences as logical constructions in the physicalist language, what will happen? In the 'methodological solipsist' conceptual scheme, a physical object, say this rostrum, is a set of sets of sets of sets . . . whose ultimate members are certain of my own elementary

---

[3] Cf. Quine's 'Reply to Roger F. Gibson, Jr; Translation, Physics and Facts of the Matter', in Hahn and Schilpp, 1986.

[4] For a discussion of philosophical uses of the notion of equivalence, see Chapter 2, 'Equivalence,' in my *Realism and Reason: Philosophical Papers*, Vol. 3 (1983), 26–45.

experiences. In the physicalist conceptual scheme, my elementary experiences are sets of sets of sets . . . whose ultimate members are certain physical objects. Given the axiom of foundation of set theory, conjoining the two schemes will lead to a contradictory set of statements. So the pressing question is: in what sense can two *incompatible* theories be 'equally possible' reconstructions of the same language and the same science?

Even if one could somehow carry out the two constructions, the phenomenalist and the physicalist one, without using any explicit definitions, and the two resulting schemes were compatible, a problem would still remain. For, if we regard the 'definitions' of the terms as mere conventions of abbreviation and not as parts of the systems, then the one system, *taken in unabbreviated notation*, and the other system, *likewise taken in unabbreviated notation*, simply speak about different things. One is a collection of truths about my experiences and the other is a collection of truths about physical objects. So in what sense are they both correct reconstructions of the same (unformalized) theory? And if the 'definitions' are parts of the system, and not mere conventions of abbreviation, what does it mean to say they are 'definitions'? *Exactly what* status is being claimed for them?

After the Aufbau, Carnap did develop the famous 'verifiability theory of meaning' (which he always credited to Wittgenstein). In one way this does answer the foregoing questions: two reconstructions are equally correct,[5] assuming the verifiability theory of meaning, if they lead to the same predictions. (More precisely, for each sentence of the one, there must be a sentence of the other, which is equivalent to exactly the same set of elementary experience sentences.) But—ignoring the fact that the demand for conclusive verification turned out to be too restrictive, and ignoring the fact that the programme of phenomenalist reduction could not really be carried through—this solution only moves the difficulty to the metalanguage. For, if 'prediction' means prediction of *my* elementary experiences, then reference to 'my elementary experiences' enters into the whole system twice over. It enters once in one of the alternative rational reconstructions (the 'methodological solipsist' one), and again, at the meta-level, in the criterion for the adequacy of rational reconstructions.

Can Carnap make the same moves as before at the meta-level? Can he say, 'to be sure there is a methodological solipsist criterion for the

---

[5] Strictly speaking this is only a criterion of *equal correctness* of reconstructions, and we also need a criterion of correctness. But Carnap would certainly say that a reconstruction is correct if (it is reasonable to suppose, given the imprecision and vagueness of ordinary unformalized scientific language, that) the reconstruction and what is reconstructed (unformalized scientific language) are equally correct in exactly the same sense.

adequacy of rational reconstructions, but there is an equally good physicalist criterion'? (Say, that two reconstructions are equally adequate[6] if they predict the same observation sentences in thing language.)

Doubtless Carnap *would* say this. But let us go more slowly.

Suppose that Carnap had chosen to be a phenomenalist, but *not* a methodological solipsist in the Aufbau. Suppose, that is, that the 'ontology' of the Aufbau had been the elementary experiences of *all* people, not just my elementary experiences. Then, whatever the virtues of the Aufbau, it would not have addressed the problem of intentionality that we described at the outset. For the assumption that we can *understand* the Aufbau would have presupposed that we can *refer to the experiences of other people. How* this is possible would not have been illuminated.[7]

Similarly, if the sense in which the various alternative reconstructions are 'equally possible' or equally adequate is expressed physicalistically, say by saying that they are all equally good devices for making predictions about observable things, then again the problem will arise: *how are predictions about observable things understood?* How can statements about external objects so much as make sense? Again Brentano's Problem rears its ugly head. And it is here that we remember that Carnap does not *only* say that there are alternative, equally possible, reconstructions of the language; he also says that the methodological solipsist one has *epistemic priority*.

What this means, if it means anything, is that the methodological solipsist one is the one we can *understand*; that it is *by* seeing that they are in some sense 'equivalent' to the methodological solipsist one that we understand the others. But at this point all illusion that the various ontologies are completely on a par vanishes. At bottom, the answer to Brentano's problem is that we *don't*, in any substantive sense, refer to anything 'external'; language is just a device for anticipating *my* experiences. To almost all present day philosophers, of whatever persuasion, this will seem like retreating to solipsism—or solipsism plus the view that the real existence of the experiences of others is a 'pseudo-question'—to avoid admitting that Brentano's problem has not been either solved nor dissolved.

---

[6] Here see note 7.

[7] I do not mean to suggest that avoiding this problem was Carnap's motive for methodological solipsism; rather (possible under the influence of Frege) he was moved to methodological solipsism by the belief that elementary experiences are 'private' in a sense which implies that I *cannot* refer to the elementary experiences of other people—a view whose incoherence becomes obvious as soon as one tries to communicate it to another person.

Reichenbachian 'Realism'

Although Reichenbach does not produce a book wholly devoted to epistemology until *Experience and Prediction* in 1938, the views laid out in that book had been sketched in a whole series of articles in the course of the preceding decade.[8] On the surface, those views look very 'realist'. Reichenbach insists that we observe physical things, not sense data, that unobserved physical things are not logical constructions out of observed things, that unobservables such as electrons and atoms are inferred entities, not logical constructions, etc. And at times Reichenbach likes to contrast his 'realism' with Carnap's 'positivism' (Reichenbach, 1936) and with what he sees as John Dewey's anti-realism with respect to theoretical entities (Reichenbach, 1939). But things are not so simple.

They are not so simple, because the claim that 'we observe physical things, not impressions' has surprisingly little conceptual content for Reichenbach. For example, in *Experience and Prediction* Reichenbach holds open the possibility of constructing two languages:[9] a more 'positivist' (in his sense) language, in which physical things (e.g. the tables and chairs that we see) exist only when I observe them and have only the properties that I observe them to have, and a language in which unobserved physical things exist (and I may decide that some of my observations about the physical things I observed were incorrect). Taking 'physical thing' in the way the first language requires us to take it, physical things are virtually identical with the empiricist's 'impressions', and, indeed, Reichenbach does sometimes call this first language 'the language of impressions' or 'the egocentric language'. (Apparently my taking the thing that I see as a chair does not entail that it could exist unperceived, for Reichenbach, if my adoption of 'the egocentric language' is a real possibility for me.) But even Reichenbach's notion of 'realist language' is somewhat strange.

What Reichenbach holds is that, while I can construct my language so that inductive inferences to the existence and behaviour of unobserved things are permissible (Carnap, after giving up phenomenalism, makes the same move at the very end of *Testability and Meaning*

[8] For example, 'Ziele und Wege der physikalischen Erkenntnis', *Handbuch der Physik,* Vol. 4: *Allgemeine Grudlagen der Physik* (Springer, 1929), 1–80; 'Die philosophische Bedeutung der modernen Physik,' *Erkenntnis* 1, no. 1, 49–71 (1930), *Ziele und Wege der heutigen Naturphilosophie* (Leipzig, Felix Meiner, 1931), 64 pp., a review of Carnap's *Logische Aufbau der Welt* in *Kantstudien* 38, 199–201 (1933): translations of all of these are included in Reichenbach and Cohen, 1978.

[9] Reichenbach calls these 'Egocentric language' and 'Usual language'. See Reichenbach, 1938, 135–145.

(1936)), doing so requires the postulate that 'unobserved things obey the same laws as observed things', and this postulate is a *convention*.[10] It is not an analytic sentence, to be sure, because certain empirical conditions have to be fulfilled or this postulate will lead to contradictions, but that *unobserved objects exist and obey the same laws as the observed objects **provided that** the observed objects behave in such a way that this assumption leads to no contradictions* is a pure stipulation. It is hard to see how someone who holds *this* view is entitled to berate Dewey, as Reichenbach does, for (allegedly) denying the 'independent existence' of the theoretical entities of science! (Although Reichenbach says that this view—that the inductive inference to unobservables depends on such a stipulation—was added after *Experience and Prediction*, it is, in fact, clearly foreshadowed in that work (see Reichenbach, 1938, 145f).

The impression that Reichenbach's 'realism' is hardly substantial is reinforced when one considers Reichenbach's view of truth. Briefly, he rejects the notion of truth as metaphysical. (He never considers a purely disquotational view, as far as I know, but I believe he would have found such a view uninteresting, as not providing us with any substantial notion we can use to *appraise* the sentences we utter and write for cognitive success.) The notion he proposes in place of the notion of truth, the only notion he has for measuring the cognitive success of an assertion, is the notion of *weight*, where the weight of a sentence is my estimate of the relative frequency of successful assertions in some appropriate reference class containing the sentence whose weight it is. (Weight is not itself a relative frequency, but a betting-quotient with respect to an unknown relative frequency, and, indeed, the reference class to be used in estimating the weight in question depends not just on the sentence whose weight I am assessing, but also on my total cognitive situation. Weight is, in effect, Reichenbach's frequentist substitute for Carnap's notion of 'degree of confirmation'.) Sentences are not true or false: it is just that I am justified in 'betting' with them.

But what is all this 'betting' for? Here Reichenbach is quite unambiguous: the whole purpose of inquiry is the prediction of experiences[11] (described, however, in thing language). But whose experiences? Is science concerned with finding strategies for predicting the experiences of other people? (In which case some ability to *refer* to the experiences of other people seems to be presupposed in the very notion of 'science'.)

[10] The conventional character of 'extension rules' is stressed by Reichenbach in Reichenbach, 1951, 266–267.

[11] For example, in *Experience and Prediction,* (1938), 'truth' is eventually rejected as a mere idealization of 'weight', and 'weight' is identified with *predictional value* (190–191).

Or does my understanding of *my* language consist in my ability to successfully predict *my* experiences?

The fact is, that Reichenbach never really faces this question. On the one hand, he does (cf. Reichenbach, 1953) advocate choosing the narrowest possible basis for epistemology, which he considers to be the observable things available to one person at one single time, and this might seem to support the view that, in the last analysis, Reichenbach too has no notion of intentionality beyond the use of language to anticipate one's own experiences. But such a reading does not square with the following argument for rejecting 'the strictly positivistic language':

> Its insufficiency is revealed as soon as we try to use it for the rational reconstruction of the thought processes underlying actions concerning events after our death, such as expressed in the example of the life insurance policies.' (op. cit. p. 150).

What Reichenbach simply does not face is this: if the 'convention' that *there are times after my death, and events which occur at those times* (subject to the proviso mentioned above), is just a *stipulation*, and making such a stipulation is to be justified as a practical action, in terms of the 'entailed decisions', as Reichenbach repeatedly tells us, then we are pushed back to the question of the character of the metalanguage in which these entailed decisions are to be discussed and evaluated. Is the metalanguage *already* a realist language? If it is, how, without an infinite regress, did I justify the choice of a realist metalanguage? If it is not, then how can I justify the choice of a realist object language, except purely as a means for more elegantly or economically (recall Mach's 'economy of thought') making predictions about what I will experience while I am alive? If *that* is my justification for the choice of realist language, then I am in the same position as the positivist: I can *say* that I am buying the insurance policy for the sake of people who will live after I am dead, but that is itself a way of talking which is for *my* sake while I am alive. On the other hand, if my justification for the choice of realist language, the one I give in the metalanguage, is that it enables me to do things for the sake of people who will live after I am dead more efficiently, and that is the 'bottom line', then my metalanguage must clearly be a realist one.

The upshot of all this, I fear, is rather sad: I do see that either Carnap or Reichenbach really thought through the problems involved in viewing language simply as a tool for the prediction of experiences. Perhaps the 'problem of intentionality' *is* in some sense a 'pseudo-problem', but if so, that is not something that the positivists succeeded in making clear.

Hilary Putnam

Perception and Intentionality

Yet one should not leap to the conclusion that there is nothing 'fishy' about questions like 'how can we refer to things that are external to the mind?' For one thing, this question is suspiciously similar to that old stumper, 'how can we know that there *exist* things external to the mind?' If I am asked, for example, how I know that this rostrum exists, and I do not immediately take the question to be a philosophical one, I will reply that I *see* it (or that I *saw* it, if the question should be put to me in the future). To get me to take the question as a philosophical one is, in part, to get me to conceive of the 'possibility' that I might be mistaken, not just on the present occasion, but on all occasions, or on such a large number of occasions that the 'general reliability of perception' is called into doubt. After such careful instruction, it will—if I am a normal philosophy student—seem flagrantly 'question begging' to answer the sceptical doubt of the existence of external things by saying 'I see the rostrum'. (Of course, if I am not a normal philosophy student but G. E. Moore, it may not seem question begging, but that is another story.)

Once having been persuaded that there is a real question here, the philosopher (for that is what philosophy students are supposed to become) may try many different moves—too many to be listed here. He may—to cite just one possibility—produce a theory according to which perception is just a matter of the 'existence of causal chains of the appropriate type' and a theory according to which knowledge is just a matter of having true beliefs which are caused in appropriate ways, and say that the sceptic has not *shown* that causal chains of the appropriate type for perception, and for knowledge of what I am perceiving, do not exist, and that this means that the sceptic has not shown that I do not *know* that I am seeing a rostrum. If the sceptic asks how I am supposed to even be able to *refer* to the rostrum in order to form true beliefs about it, the philosopher may try to produce a causal theory of reference as well. In this way a number of philosophical industries have gotten started, and all of them are extremely busy today.

In my last few sentences I indicated that the sceptic may well broaden the field of his scepticism from perception to intentionality, and indeed the two sceptical problems are closely linked, both logically and in the history of philosophy. For example, just as there is a common sense 'pre-philosophical' answer to 'how do you know there is a rostrum there' ('I see it'), so there is a common senses 'pre-philosophical' answer to 'how can you refer to external things such as the rostrum ('What's your problem? If I can see rostrums and handle them, surely I can learn what they are called.') And, as a matter of fact, the philosophers who discovered there was a 'problem about intentionality' already knew, or took it as a matter of course that they knew, that there was a 'problem of perception'. And if the problem is not about reference to 'external' things, in the funny sense of 'external' in which everything except my own mind is supposed to be 'external', but about reference to my own present, or past, or future experiences, there are similar pre-philosophical answers ('You mean there is a problem about how I can *expect* to have an experience?'), which we must somehow come to distrust as 'question begging' before we can 'see the problem' of intentionality.

I have argued elsewhere (Putnam, 1989) that attempts to define reference in terms of patterns of efficient causation do not succeed, and that, in addition, the notion of a 'cause' employed in such theories presupposes structures of causal explanation which themselves use many intentional notions.[12] There is not time today to even state these views of mine properly, let alone defend them, but for someone like myself, who sees the currently fashionable return to some mixture of materialism and empiricism as a dead end, it is natural to entertain the thought that there is a way around the problems we have been discussing which is not a matter of a straight forward 'answer' to certain 'questions'. In a nutshell, the suggestion is, what if the common sense pre-philosophical answer is the only answer? What if being convinced that it is not an answer to both questions (how do you know the rostrum exists? how can you so much as refer to the rostrum?) to say 'I see the darn thing' is not coming to 'see the problem' but falling into a deep confusion?

One way to try to show this would be to try to show that such 'possibilities' as the possibility that I alone exist, and I am a brain in a vat, are not real possibilities at all.[13] Another—one thinks of Wittgenstein's Private Language Argument—would be to try to show that the possibility of thinking about anything (let alone about 'the nature of reference') presupposes the existence of public objects and public language. A philosopher who takes this line need not hold that the common sense answers *are* 'answers' to the philosopher's questions, as Moore did, or that they pre-empt the possibility of empirical scientific study of either perception or reference. Rather, what he should say is that the philosopher's questions gain their very sense from the supposition that certain possibilities make sense, and that once we see that we cannot consistently suppose that they do, we should also see that the enterprise of a 'theory of the nature of intentionality' or of 'the nature of perception' is an enterprise of answering questions we cannot under-

[12] See 'Is the Causal Structure of the Physical Itself Something Physical', Chapter 5 of Putnam, 1990, 80–95.

[13] Cf. the opening chapter of my *Reason, Truth and History* (1981) for an attempt along these lines.

stand we-know-not-how. Note that if saying this is saying that the questions are 'pseudo-questions', it is in a very different sense of 'pseudo-question' than any that Carnap or Reichenbach had in mind. Their notion of a pseudo-question derived from the Machian (they called it 'empiricist') idea that the whole purpose of cognition is prediction; the dissolution of the question of intentionality just suggested derives instead from an exploration of what Strawson called 'the bounds of sense'. Strawson was, of course, referring to Kant, and to the possibility of carrying on the Kantian enterprise of *exploring the presuppositions of cognition* without giving that enterprise a metaphysical interpretation.

Ludwig Wittgenstein was a philosopher who had a lifelong involvement with that task. His *Tractatus* excludes any 'problem of how language relates to the world' by excluding the very idea of a metalanguage. This has been criticized from two directions. On the one hand, Carnap criticized it in his *Introduction to Semantics* (1942) on the grounds that one could add a disquotational definition of truth (in the style of Tarski) to *any* formal language. Whatever the merits of this criticism, it does not speak to our issue; for a purely disquotational definition of truth and reference does not speak to the problem of 'the relation of the language to the world', as is shown by the thorough compatibility of such a view with Carnap's own 'methodological solipsism'. On the other hand, it would also be criticized by those who think (as Hartry Field (1972) once did) that a definition of 'primitive reference' can be given in terms of efficient causation. Here it may seem that Wittgenstein simply ignored a possibility; but in fact we know from his notebooks that he (like Kant) regarded it as absurd to think that we can understand how language connects with the world in terms of causal chains of appropriate kinds.[14] My purpose today is not to argue that he was right (although I have already said that I believe he was); it is to point out that, if I understand his views correctly, then the *Tractatus* already regarded the idea that there is a 'problem of intentionality' as a confusion, but *not* for reasons which were anything like Carnap's and Reichenbach's.

---

[14] I believe that one reason for this, in Wittgenstein's case as in my own, was the recognition that causal chains do not simply identify themselves as being causally explanatory, 'of the appropriate type', etc., or, indeed, as consisting of 'causes'. Only when a language is already in place can we think of certain events as forming 'causal chains of the appropriate type'.

Probability and the Evidence of our Senses

D. H. MELLOR

Our knowledge of the world comes to us, one way or another, through our senses. I know there's a table here, because I see it, and that there's traffic outside, because I hear it. And similarly for our other senses. I know when it's cold, because I feel it; when there's sugar in my tea, because I taste it; smoke in the air, because I smell it; and so on.

The knowledge we get directly from our senses in this way is of course only a small part of what we know about the world. Most of our knowledge depends also on memory. It is not my senses that are now telling me what I saw yesterday: my knowledge of that comes from my memory of what I saw then. Then again there are many things I know—about Queen Victoria, for example—not because I am seeing, hearing or remembering them, but because I have been told about them. Most of our knowledge of history comes not from our own observation of historical events, but from professional historians; just as most of our knowledge of science, whether of microphysics, biology or cosmology, comes from professional scientists.

But all this knowledge still comes in the end through people's senses. My second-hand knowledge of history and science comes through my senses: through my hearing what historians and scientists say or seeing what they write. And their first-hand knowledge comes through their senses: from what they see written in historical documents, or by means of scientific instruments such as microscopes and telescopes.

This is not to say that our knowledge of the world depends only on our senses. To see things through a microscope, for example, it is not enough to have good eyesight. One needs to know what to look for and how to recognize it, skills that are not easily acquired, as all microscopists know (Hacking, 1983, ch. 11). And history, as everyone knows, is harder still: our knowledge of history depends not only on the skilled observation of historical data, but on its availability, selection and interpretation.

Indeed all our knowledge depends on interpretation in the sense of depending on our concepts. To see that it is raining we need the concept of rain; historians of the French Revolution need the concept of a revolution; and astronomers need the concept of a star. Where these concepts come from is a contentious question, whose answer will no doubt vary from concept to concept. Most, I suppose, come from our language and our society, although some basic ones may come from our senses, and others from our genes. But wherever they come from, our knowledge of the world will still depend on our senses. To know that it is raining you need more than the concept of rain: you need to see, hear or feel—or be told by someone who sees, hears or feels—that it is raining. So our theory of knowledge, whatever else it does, must answer the question: how do our senses give us our first-hand knowledge of the world? That is undoubtedly one of the central questions of philosophy, and one that occupied Ayer throughout his philosophical career.

But why should it have occupied him? Why is it a philosophical question, as opposed to a question in the physiology, psychology or sociology of perception? What more needs saying about how our senses give us knowledge than how (once we have the relevant concepts) our eyes, ears and other senses do in fact let us know that it is raining, that there was a French revolution, the Big Bang, and so on? Those are not philosophical questions, and even if answering them presents practical or even theoretical problems, it is not immediately obvious why it should present conceptual ones.

But it notoriously does, and the source of these problems lies in our concept of knowledge, or rather in what philosophers take this concept to entail. Different philosophers of course hold different views about that, which I shall not even try to survey. But since the same problems arise on almost all of them, we may as well discuss them in terms of Ayer's view of knowledge—much of which I anyway accept—and that is what I shall do.

Ayer (*PK*, ch. 1) rejects the view that knowing something is being in a special state of mind distinct from believing it. That view was quite widely held when Ayer wrote, and it still has some adherents; but not many, and since most philosophers today agree with Ayer, I shall not argue that point again here. It is however worth repeating that knowing need not be a special state of mind for there to be more to my knowing something than my believing it. The difference between knowing and believing need not lie in my state of mind: it can, and does, lie in other facts about it. Specifically, for a belief of mine to be knowledge, the proposition I believe must be true, and my belief in it must be warranted in some way—something must entitle me to believe it. Or, as Ayer (*PK*, 35) put it,

> the necessary and sufficient conditions for knowing that something is the case are first that what one is said to know be true, secondly that one be sure of it [i.e. fully believe it], and thirdly that one should have the right to be sure.

Not everyone who agrees with Ayer that knowledge is belief plus something extra agrees with him about what the extra something is. But I do, and I shall take his two extra conditions—truth and entitlement—for granted. However, these two conditions themselves raise contentious conceptual questions. First, there is controversy about what it is for a belief to be true. But that is not what I want to discuss, and for present purposes we can take the concept of truth for granted. What I want to discuss is the other, entitlement, condition: what it is to 'have the right to be sure' of something, or—as I shall put it—to be warranted in believing it. This is the condition which makes the fact that our senses give us first-hand knowledge of the world appear to pose a serious conceptual problem.

To see why, we must ask how our senses warrant our beliefs about the world. Apparently, they do it by giving us evidence for them, as the familiar phrase in my title, 'the evidence of our senses', indicates. For example, what any eye-witness says he saw at the scene of a crime provides evidence for the jury's beliefs about what happened there. What historians see in the documents they decipher provides evidence for their beliefs about the French Revolution. What astronomers see through telescopes, directly or *via* (e.g.) photographs, provides evidence for their beliefs about remote parts of the universe.

But what beliefs do our senses give us evidence for, and what makes what they give us evidence for those beliefs? Let us take these questions in turn. First, the beliefs for which our senses give us evidence are, on the whole, the ones they cause us to get. Suppose for example that our eye-witness's testimony causes our jury to believe that the defendant was indeed at the scene of the crime: then that is the belief for which what the eye-witness saw is their evidence. Similarly, if seeing a jocular entry in Queen Victoria's diary convinces a historian that she was amused after all, then that again is the belief for which his seeing that entry is his evidence. And the beliefs which seeing the results of experiments causes scientists to get are likewise the very beliefs for which those results are their evidence.

This is not of course to say that our senses only, or always, give us evidence for the beliefs they cause. Our historian might, for example, have believed that Queen Victoria was amused before he ever saw her diary: the fact that his seeing it was not the cause of his belief does not stop it being evidence for it. But usually the beliefs for which our senses give us evidence are the ones they cause; and since these are the paradigm cases, on which all the others depend, they are the ones I shall discuss.

Now for my second question. Even when our senses do cause the beliefs for which they give us evidence, that may still not be how they give us evidence for them. The question remains: how do our senses give us evidence?—a question whose answer will naturally depend on what evidence is. Now I am assuming, of course, that having evidence for a belief is one way of satisfying Ayer's third condition for making the belief knowledge. It is a way of warranting the belief, i.e. of warranting its truth: that is, the truth of the proposition believed. And what makes being warranted a virtue in a belief is the fact that, although not all beliefs are true, truth is what all beliefs aim at. Why, and in what sense, they do so are questions I cannot go into here—except to say that one good reason for wanting true beliefs is that our beliefs need to be true to ensure that the actions they combine with our desires to cause will succeed in fulfilling those desires (Whyte, 1990).

At any rate, the fact that, for whatever reason, belief always aims at truth is what underlies Ayer's first condition for knowledge: it is why, in order for a belief to achieve the status of knowledge, it must be true. And this in turn provides the point of Ayer's third condition, that the belief be warranted. For what warranting a belief is supposed to ensure is that the proposition believed is true. So this in particular is what evidence is supposed to do: ensure the truth of the belief for which it is evidence.

Or at least that's what evidence is supposed to do when it is conclusive. But of course evidence is not always conclusive. What our eyewitness saw may not prove that the defendant was at the scene of the crime: it may not entail the truth of that proposition. But it may still warrant it to some degree. So evidence for the truth of a belief can come by degrees, not only in amount (how much evidence there is) but also in how *probable* the evidence makes it that the belief is true. A good look at a well-lit politician, for example, makes it far more probable that he is whom he appears to be than a quick glimpse of a dimly lit one does.

Providing a measure of how strongly beliefs are warranted is not of course the only use of probability; but it is an important one, and it is the one I want to discuss. In particular, how should probability be understood when used in this way? For probability has several very different interpretations, and which of them we should apply here is a seriously disputed question. And this dispute matters because, as we shall see, applying the wrong interpretation generates intractable conceptual problems about how our senses give us our first-hand knowledge of the world. And that, I shall argue, is why Ayer and many others have found these problems so intractable: they have not applied the right interpretation of probability. That is what I propose to show: how applying wrong interpretations generates these conceptual problems, and how applying the right one dissolves them.

First, therefore, I must say something about the relevant interpretations of probability; though I need not say much, and nothing very technical. There is of course a mathematical calculus of probabilities

(Howson and Urbach, 1989, ch. 2) which—for example—makes a proposition's probability of being false 1 minus the probability of its being true. But the details of this calculus do not matter here. What matters here is not the mathematics of probability, but how that mathematics, whatever it is, should be interpreted when used as a measure of how strongly evidence warrants a belief: that is, as what we may call 'evidential probability'.

One influential interpretation of probability, which Ayer unaccountably overlooks, is the subjective one (e.g. de Finetti, 1931). This takes the probability calculus to measure the strength of our beliefs. That is, it takes belief to come by degrees—we can believe things more or less strongly—and uses the calculus to measure those degrees as so-called 'subjective probabilities'. Of course what matters here are degrees of warrant rather than degrees of belief, but the two are connected. For suppose my evidence for the proposition that it is raining gives it a probability 0·8 of being true. Should I not then believe this proposition to that very degree: in other words, give it a subjective probability of 0·8? Arguably I should, since arguably we should believe any proposition to just the degree to which our evidence warrants its truth.

But this connection on its own does not justify a subjective interpretation of evidential probability. We still need an interpretation of probability to make sense of degrees of warrant as well as degrees of belief. But subjectivists do offer to make sense of degrees of warrant by saying, not how strongly I should believe a proposition given my present evidence for it, but how I should *change* my degree of belief in it if I get more evidence (Jeffrey, 1983, ch. 11). The adequacy of this so-called Bayesian theory of evidence is indeed a moot point (Kyburg, 1978), but not one we need discuss. For the trouble I want to discuss is caused by another feature of subjectivism which it shares with the two quite different interpretations of probability that Ayer (e.g. *CQ*, ch. VIII.B) does consider.

The first of these is the logical interpretation, which takes evidential probability to measure a logical relation between a proposition and the evidence for it (Carnap, 1962). This relation is not of course deductive: it does not make evidence *entail* the proposition it is evidence for, i.e. make it impossible for that proposition to be false if the evidence is true. Evidence which does that (as for example the evidence that you are reading this entails that you are reading something) is indeed conclusive; but it is also very rare. Most evidence, as we have seen, does not entail what it is evidence for. Hence the idea of a weaker logical relation of 'partial entailment' which can make the truth of one proposition warrant the truth of another more or less strongly.

The most obvious and basic objection to this idea is that there really is no such logical relation (Ramsey, 1926, §1). If one proposition's being true makes it more or else probable that another one is, that is a matter not of logic but of contingent fact. It is not logic that makes what an eye-witness sees good evidence that the defendant was at the scene of the crime: it is facts about the light, the witness's eyesight, what the defendant looks like, and so on. If the strength of logically inconclusive evidence is to be measured by probabilities at all, they must surely be contingent probabilities, not logical ones.

I think this is indeed a fatal objection to any logical theory of evidential probability. But it is not the only objection, and not the one I want to press. For it certainly does not apply to the Bayesian theory, nor to the other interpretation of probability Ayer considers, the frequency interpretation. This identifies probabilities with so-called relative frequencies: i.e., in simple cases, with fractions (see Russell, 1948, pt V, chs. III–IV). For example, it identifies the probability of a smoker's getting cancer with the fraction of similar smokers who do get cancer. The frequency interpretation faces objections too; but at least, unlike the logical interpretation, it makes evidential probabilities contingent. Its problem with them is simply that evidential probabilities look nothing like frequencies. With what frequency, for example, could we identify the probability that the defendant was at the scene of the crime, given what our eye-witness saw? The best candidate, I suppose, is the frequency among similar scenes (where a similar eye-witness sees something similar) of scenes at which someone who looks like the defendant was present. But even that is most implausible; and in general it is so hard to find credible frequencies for evidential probabilities to be that few philosophers take the frequency interpretation of them seriously.

But I want to press a different objection, related to one which Ayer himself pressed against the logical and frequency theories, and which applies also to the Bayesian theory: namely, that they all interpret evidential probability as a relation between evidence and what it is evidence for. They differ of course in what they say the relation is. The logical theory says it is logical, whereas the other two say it is contingent: either on some frequency, or on how strong our beliefs were to start with. But one way or another, all three theories take evidential probability to be a relation between propositions: the one that states our evidence, and the one for whose truth this is our evidence. And this is the feature, that all these theories take for granted, which makes it so hard to say how our senses can give us first-hand knowledge of the world.

Why so? Why cannot evidential probability be a relation, logical or contingent, between one proposition, P, which we believe and another one, Q, which states our evidence for P? The reason Ayer (*CQ*, ch. VIII.B.3) gives is that P will have many different but equally good probability relations to other propositions we believe: Q_1, Q_2, and so on. Which of these should we adopt? For what we really want to know, about any proposition P that we believe, is how probable, given our evidence for it, is its truth? And that question cannot be answered just by the relational facts that P is very probable relative to Q_1, most improbable relative to Q_2, fairly probable relative to Q_3, and so on. The answer to that question must come from something else, that will fix the right Q for P's evidential probability to be relative to.

The standard solution to this problem is to say that the right Q is the conjunction of all our relevant beliefs: Q_1 *and* Q_2 *and* Q_3 *and* . . . so on. In other words, P's evidential probability is its probability relative to all the evidence we have for or against it. And that seems roughly right, although it does present more problems. One is that, as it stands, it makes evidential probabilities subjective, since P can have one probability relative to my evidence, and a quite different one relative to yours. Yet if we discovered this we should certainly think that one of us was wrong: we do not really think that evidential probability is subjective. So perhaps it is relative not to the evidence we actually have, but to the evidence available to us: which then poses the further problem of saying what it is for evidence to be 'available'.

However, since this is still not the problem I want to press, I will waive it, and suppose for simplicity that, for me, P's evidential probability is relative to the totality Q of my evidence for or against it. But what is Q? It cannot just be the conjunction of all the propositions I believe. For one thing, that will include P; and P's probability relative to itself, or to any conjunction including it, is 1. In other words, if our beliefs could be evidence for themselves, they would all be conclusively warranted. But of course they cannot be: no belief can be evidence for itself. But what then distinguishes the beliefs that are our evidence from the other beliefs for which they are evidence?

Well, one might think that nothing does and nothing needs to, on the grounds that even if our beliefs cannot be evidence for themselves, they can at least be evidence for each other. So collectively, if not individually, they can bootstrap themselves, so to speak, into evidential respectability. But this so-called 'coherence' theory of evidence and hence of knowledge (see Armstrong, 1973, 155) seems to me so absurd that I propose (like Ayer) to say no more about it. For at least so far as our senses are concerned, there is a fairly clear *prima facie* distinction between the evidence, Q, which they give us about how things look, sound, feel, taste and smell, and other beliefs, P, for which Q is our evidence. The distinction between P and Q, moreover, need not be either universal or absolute, since we can obviously have different evidence for different beliefs. In particular, therefore, our beliefs can form evidential hierarchies: that is, one belief for which our senses give us evidence can thereby become evidence for another belief. For example, the blurred view I see through a window may give me evidence for believing it has water on it, which may in turn be my evidence for believing it is raining; and so on. And where, in such hierarchies, our evidence stops being the evidence of our senses is not a question to which we need a general answer.

The question we do need an answer to is not where our hierarchies of sensory evidence stop, but where, and how, they start. I have said that our beliefs cannot be evidence for themselves. But surely some of them must be: for how, unless they are, can they provide evidence for our other beliefs? The whole object of evidence is, after all, to warrant the belief it is evidence for: in other words, to ensure its truth. But if my believing Q never ensures that even Q is true, how can it ensure that anything else I believe is true? Our hierarchies of sensory evidence must therefore surely start with beliefs which do warrant themselves in this way. And so, according to Ayer (*FEK*, ch. I) and many others, they do: with beliefs in 'sense data'. Sense data are items like pains, sounds, patches of colour in our visual fields: items so given to us in experience that we can only believe in them if they are really there, so that our beliefs about them really do warrant themselves in the sense of ensuring their own truth. This is the essential feature of sense data, the feature which enables them to be the starting points of our evidential hierarchies: to be, in other words, as the name 'sense data' implies, the ultimate evidence of our senses.

Unfortunately, the idea of sense data poses notoriously intractable problems. It is not even clear that there are any, i.e. that our senses give us infallibly true beliefs even about our own experiences. And even if they do, it is even less clear how such beliefs could give us enough evidence to warrant all the other beliefs our senses give us. How can all our knowledge of our present surroundings, never mind all our knowledge of history and science, be warranted by a handful of visual and other experiences? I, like many others, cannot see how anything could meet both the conditions that sense data need to satisfy: that beliefs about them must (i) be self-warranting and (ii) provide enough evidence to warrant all the other beliefs about the world that we get through our senses. This is the dilemma with which the concept of sensory evidence confronts the theory of knowledge, and it seems to me quite intolerable.

How can we escape this dilemma? Not by pretending that the problem it poses is unreal because in everyday life we play a 'language game' in which we all talk as if our senses were trustworthy. So we do, but that does not explain why they are, i.e. why our trust in our senses is so often rewarded with true beliefs and hence successful actions and predictions. Nor, on the other hand, can we honestly escape the dilemma by pretending to be sceptics, by claiming that after all we do not really know most of the things which we can all see and hear to be going on around us. No one believes that, and philosophers should not say things they do not believe: philosophy is not a branch of fiction.

To escape our dilemma what we need to realize is that our senses need not warrant our beliefs by giving us *evidence* for them. In particular, my senses need not give me sense data in order to give me evidence for the other beliefs they give me, since they can warrant my beliefs without giving me any evidence for them at all. That they can do this is really undeniable—especially by those who believe in sense data. For as we have just seen, our beliefs about our own sense data are by definition warranted, not by any other beliefs of ours, but by the sense data themselves. My belief that I am in pain is not warranted by anything else I believe, but simply by the fact that I am in pain and that, pain being what it is, we believe we are in pain when and only when we are in pain. There is a link between being in pain and believing one is in pain which makes our beliefs about whether or not we are in pain very probably if not certainly true. This is what warrants those beliefs and makes them knowledge. And this is why we need no evidence to warrant the belief that we are in pain, or that we are not in pain—or that we are having, or not having, experiences of any other kind: sounds in our ears, colour patches in our visual field, sensations of touch, taste, smell, feelings of joy, grief, and so on. Beliefs about all these things are warranted—made at least very probably true—not by any evidence but simply by the fact that these experiences are self-intimating: that what causes us to believe we are having them is that we *are* having them. This is precisely what enables our hierarchies of sensory evidence to start with beliefs about our present experiences: this is what makes them sense *data*.

But if beliefs about experiences can be warranted in this way, so can other beliefs; and so in particular can the beliefs which constitute our first-hand knowledge of the world. Our senses can easily warrant the beliefs they give us about the things and events we perceive without giving us evidence for those beliefs. They can simply make those things and events intimate themselves to us, just as our experiences do, by making us generally believe they are there if and only if they really are there. And that is precisely what our senses do, by providing causal links between us and our surroundings which make the fact that something is present be what causes us to believe that it is. That is how my eyes tell me there is a table here: by so linking me to it causally that the fact that it is here causes me to believe that it is here.

The causal link between the table and me may of course go *via* a visual experience, but that's not what warrants my belief. My belief is not warranted by any self-warranting belief about my visual experience, as Ayer ('Knowledge, belief and evidence', in *MCS*) eventually realized. But this is not, as Ayer thought, because experiences can warrant beliefs about other things directly, so that, as he put it (121),

> in certain cases one acquires the right to be sure of a proposition not through holding any other beliefs, but simply because one is having or has had certain experiences.

That is true only of propositions about one's experiences, not propositions about tables. My belief about my table is not warranted by any experience I am having, but by its being so caused by the table—whether *via* an experience or not—that it is very probably true.

In other words, the data of our senses are by no means restricted to our experiences. They include all the perceptible features of things and events which cause us, by means of our senses, to get beliefs about them only when those beliefs are at least very probably true. Such beliefs are just as well warranted by this fact about them as our beliefs about our experiences are, and are therefore just as able to start off the hierarchies of evidence which in turn warrant our other beliefs about the world.

Recognizing this fact, that our senses can warrant the beliefs they give us without giving us evidence for them, rescues us immediately from the dilemma facing the traditional concept of sensory evidence. For if our senses need not *give* us evidence for the beliefs they give us, then those beliefs can simply *be* the evidence of our senses—which is, after all, just what we all naturally think they are.

This account of the evidence of our senses does however face a couple of specious objections, to which I can here only sketch my replies. One is that to be sense data, things must logically guarantee the truth of our beliefs about them, which ordinary perceptible objects do not. For even if my eyes give my belief that there's a table here a probability 1 of being true, that probability is still contingent on facts about my eyesight, the lighting, and so on. So this belief, unlike my beliefs about my present experiences, might have been false; and this allegedly stops it being warranted. But that simply does not follow, any more than the fact that my table might not have been here stops my belief that it is here being warranted. Warrants can be real, and conclusive, without being necessarily so.

The other objection to this account is that it allows our beliefs to be warranted without our knowing they are, which to many people seems absurd. But is it? Imagine for example someone who does not know that he is colour-blind, perhaps because he has never heard of colour-blindness. But in fact he is not colour-blind, and his eyes can make his belief that something is red very probably true even though he does not know that they do. Does this really mean that that belief of his is not warranted, just because he does not know it is? Surely not. For if it did, our eyes could not have warranted *any* of the beliefs they gave us about the colours of things before colour-blindness was discovered: and that really is absurd (see Mellor, 1988b, §5).

I conclude therefore, despite these objections, that our senses can and do warrant the beliefs they give us without giving us evidence for them. But what, finally, does that tell us about the probabilities involved? It certainly tells us something. For although on this view our senses still warrant the beliefs they give us by making them very probably true, these high probabilities are no longer *evidential*. They no longer measure a relation between one proposition that I believe and another one that states my evidence for it. Indeed the probabilities here are not relational at all. They are simply a sub-species of the non-relational probabilities which causes give their effects. For as I remarked at the beginning, the beliefs our senses warrant first are the beliefs they cause us to get: or more precisely, as we now see, the beliefs which they make the facts that make those beliefs true cause us to get. In other words, our senses warrant the beliefs they give us by making them effects of the very facts that make them true. Making my belief that there is a table here an effect of there being a table here is what makes that belief of mine very probably true and therefore warranted.

But how, and in what sense of probability, does the causation which links my belief to the fact that makes it true make it also very probably true? Where does this high probability come from? The answer is that it comes from the causation. Causes always give their effects probabilities (Mellor, 1988a): 1 if the causation is deterministic, less if it is not—but still, in the cases that concern us, high. And these causal probabilities, I have argued elsewhere (Mellor, 1982, 1988a), are neither logical relations nor degrees of belief nor relative frequencies. They are what Popper (1957) first called propensities and what I (Mellor, 1971) mean by 'chances': namely, objective non-relational properties, as real as lengths or temperatures, and present in every single case of causation, including the causation of our beliefs. The fact that there is a table here can only cause me to believe there is by giving me a significant chance of acquiring that belief. And then, if that chance is high enough, that belief will be warranted. For that chance, the chance of my believing there is a table here when there is, just *is* the probability that that belief of mine is true. And as we have seen, giving a belief a high enough probability of being true is precisely what it takes to warrant it.

That is how our senses warrant the beliefs they give us: by making the facts which make our beliefs true cause us to get them and thereby give them a high chance of being true. Why did not Ayer see this? I think the reason is that he simply overlooked this so-called propensity interpretation of probability, which is what this account of how our senses warrant our beliefs needs. He should not have overlooked it, since he not only attended the 1957 Bristol symposium at which Popper's (1957) version of this interpretation was first presented, he took part in the discussion of it (Körner, 1957, 78–89). But after that he never mentioned it, just as he never mentioned the subjective interpretation of probability. But that lapse mattered less, because a subjective interpretation can only give us a theory of evidential probability. And however natural it may be to think, as Ayer did, and many still do, that this is what we need, because our senses warrant our beliefs by giving us experiential evidence for them, it really is not, because they do not. Only by seeing that, and by applying the right non-evidential interpretation of probability, can we account, as Ayer could not, for the evidence of our senses.[1]

[1] This lecture has been somewhat revised for publication. The final version has been improved by comments made by Robert Nola (who drew my attention to Ayer, 'Knowledge, belief and evidence', MCS) and Jamie Whyte.

Seeing Qualia and Positing the World

TED HONDERICH

1 Qualia and Ayer's Use of Them

It is the business of philosophy to deal without presupposition with the question of the general nature of the world and with the question of how or indeed whether we can know that nature. These are questions to which answers are given in the realism of ordinary belief, as it can be called, the phenomenalism of Berkeley, the pragmatism and the scientism of Quine, and the varieties of scepticism. The ontological and the epistemological questions are bound up with another, that of the nature of perception—the question of what it is, in general, that happens when we perceive. What is called naive realism is an answer, as are representation theories, and phenomenalism again. If the question might be better defined, so as to distinguish it from the related scientific question, it is no matter of mere conceptual analysis. Let us start with this question of the nature of perception.[1]

When Jane and Selina see the table, two things other than persons are part of the story. If Jane shuts her eyes, one of these ceases to exist. Of course, you may say, there are two of *something* other than persons, since there are two neural processes. However, the fact relevant to our question is different. It is that there are two things in the sense of being two perceptions or perceptual experiences, Jane's seeing the table and Selina's.

Is it still necessary to struggle against the idea that the neural processes, or parts of them, are identical with the perceptions? I shall not do that here.[2] Nor shall I struggle with functionalism as a supposedly

[1] I am most grateful for good comments on an earlier draft of this paper to Tim Crane, Marcus Giaquinto, Griff Phillips Griffiths, Bill Hart, Robert Heinaman, Goran Hermeren, Christopher Hookway, Paul Noordhof, Jane O'Grady, Christopher Peacocke, Ingmar Persson, Gabriel Segal, Barry Smith, Timothy Sprigge, Peter Strawson, Jerry Valberg, and Arnold Zuboff. With respect to the three questions in my first paragraph, it seems to me that Donald Davidson's suggestion, despite the reasons he gives, that the epistemological question can be treated quite independently of the question of the nature of perception, is optimistic (Davidson, 1989, 165–166).

[2] See my *A Theory of Determinism: The Mind, Neuroscience, and Life-Hopes* (Honderich, 1988), Ch. 2, or *Mind and Brain* (Honderich, 1990), Ch. 2.

complete or basic account of the perceptual experiences. Functionalism so conceived is following true identity theories and of course behaviourism into the honourable past of the Philosophy of Mind.[3] Rather, let us proceed in terms of what very nearly unites the human race, and has been called Mental Realism. It is a conviction to the effect that conscious episodes generally, including perceptual experiences, have a character different from that of neural processes. This character, which may be physical despite not being neural, is not merely a matter of the causal or logical relations of these episodes to other such episodes and to stimulation and action. Mental Realism, differently described, consists in attempts to specify this real character rather than look elsewhere.[4]

There has been a *great* tradition in philosophy, as Ayer rightly insists, which says something more precise than that two perceptual experiences realistically conceived are part of the story when Jane and Selina see the table. There are, says Locke, two simple ideas of sensation. Neither idea, in this use of the term, is or could be the table or any other physical object. Berkeley speaks similarly of ideas, and Hume, with the same intent, has it that there are two impressions. Mill offers sensations, Moore and Russell sense-data or sense contents, C. D. Broad sensa, C. I. Lewis, Nelson Goodman and Ayer qualia and percepts. Farewells to this tradition have often been made, recently by Donald Davidson, but so far they have always been premature.[5]

It is fundamental to the tradition that there do exist *qualia*, as I shall henceforth call them in accordance with one of several recent usages, although the term *percept* would do as well. These are entities taken as standing in some relation to ordinary physical objects. Thus they are distinct from qualia when those are taken to be similarly related to general properties of such physical objects—universals. There are said to be qualia of my sort, for example, which may be described as visual cat-patterns. Qualia in this sense—my concern is *only* with them—are said to have two general characters. First, they are said to be objects of perception, the objects of what is in a sense the only real perception. They are entities we perceive and in particular see, or anyway of which we are aware. I am unsure whether they are what other philosophers have in mind when they speak of *properties* of experience, awareness or perceptions. Second, either they are said by definition not to be objective but rather to be subjective—that is what is usually said—or it is *not* said that they *are* objective.

[3] For Hilary Putnam's own rejection of functionalism, see his *Representation and Reality* (Boston, 1988). By true identity theories I mean, roughly, eliminative materialisms, and thus not such theories as Davidson's Anomalous Monism, which appears to call for the label Property-Dualism.

[4] For my Mental Realism, see Honderich, op. cit., 76–89.

[5] Ayer, *CQ*, 70–71, 58ff., Davidson, 1986.

If they were in this somewhat special sense objective, which is to say ordinary and macroscopic physical objects, they would have three properties among others. They would be (a) perceivable by more than one person, (b) open to more than one sense, and (c) capable of existing when not perceived.[6] If they are subjective, whatever else is true of them, they lack these three features. Ayer, in his last accounts of perception, in the books *The Origins of Pragmatism* and *The Central Questions of Philosophy*[7], was perhaps influenced by William James's idea of a neutral 'primal stuff', and begins a certain sequence of reflections by taking some version of the second option just mentioned. That is, in place of stating qualia to be non-objective, he does by intention not state them to be objective, but takes them as neutral. That, as I say, is how he begins.

It is one of my intentions to try to say something new of the claim that there are qualia, in either sense. But let us now see how Ayer makes use of qualia to arrive at the rest of his answer to the question of the nature of perception and also his answer to the ontological question of the nature of the world and the epistemological question of our knowledge of it. By the world, as already implied, I mean less than usual—just what is objective in the sense of having at least the features of being commonly perceivable, and perceivable by more than one sense, and of existing unperceived. This common world does not include particles, shadows, conscious episodes even if they are physical, and no doubt other things.

His claims, put one way, are that perception and the world are both a matter of *qualia statements*, each recording the existence of a quale (*CQ*, 106). This is not his earlier phenomenalism, for two reasons. He does not now suppose, in connection with the ontological question, that physical-object statements can be translated into qualia statements—that qualia statements set out logically necessary and sufficient conditions for physical-object statements. Rather, physical-object statements are in a different way to be analysed into or based on qualia statements. The analysis involves exercises of the imagination. Secondly, whatever the nature of the looser relation between qualia statements and physical-object statements, we do end up with both qualia and physical objects, and the objects do not in the phenomenalist way consist of the qualia.

To throw into stronger relief the role of qualia statements, Ayer gives the analysis as a process of *construction*. Physical-object statements are

[6] In *The Origins of Pragmatism*, 305, Ayer adds some secondary characteristics of such physical objects. They have parts not visible to the perceiver, etc.

[7] *CQ*, Chs. 4, 5; *OP*, 298–336. With respect to the matter of the subjectivity of qualia, see *CQ*, 93ff., and *OP*, 311ff., 298. Cf. *FEK*, 243–263.

constructed from, in part, qualia statements. Because this is not strictly a matter of *logical* construction, as already noted, and, quite as important, because we do not stay, so to speak, at the level of the materials of the construction, no light is shed on it by familiar talk of the construction of numbers and so on in the work of Russell, Carnap and others (Russell, 1914, 1917; Carnap, 1928). Nor does Ayer intend an account of how young children do or even might come to have physical-object beliefs, although he does in fact put what he says in some such terms. What he does, as he says, is to follow James and others and give us a *fictive* construction (*CQ*, 106; *OP*, 321, 329; Macdonald, 1979, 'Replies', 289).

We are informed of the intellectual progress of an observer, or perhaps better an experiencer, which progress is perhaps in part as follows. If we put aside a yet earlier stage having to do with qualia differently conceived, as related to general properties rather than ordinary physical objects, the observer's experience initially consists of qualia in our sense, and of Ayer's neutral sort. The observer thinks of it that minimal and secure way. Where you and I would have, so to speak, the cat going behind the sofa and coming out the other side, he has one earlier and one later cat quale, or more precisely, two visual cat-patterns. But the fact that there is this type-recurrence, and the fact that his visual and his tactual experiences in ways coincide, issue in his imagining or coming to think instead of what are called *visuo-tactual continuants*. Two or more qualia are replaced by one visuo-tactual continuant. Such items are thought of as existing between times when he is having experience of them. Such items are *posited*, which is to say that they are decided on in order to allow for an account of things that has the virtue, above all, of simplicity.[8] One visuo-tactual continuant attracts special attention. It is what, if the observer had arrived at our conception of physical objects strictly speaking, would be known by him to be his own body. Partly by way of his interactions with other such visuo-tactual continuants, and what they say, he makes further progress, and comes to a certain end-state.

Visuo-tactual continuants are now replaced in his thinking by entities which have the possibility of existing without *ever* being perceived (as distinct from existing between times of being perceived) and indeed the possibility of existing in the absence of any observers at all. They are also in a way within the possible experience of a number of observers, and of course are in a way open to more than one sense. They are *objective or physical objects*. Again this is a matter of positing.

[8] For a brief and excellent account of simplicity in this connection, see Mackie, 1976, 66–67.

Ayer takes the term 'posit' from Quine. As I have implied, he mostly subscribes to something like what goes with it for Quine, at least in 'On What There Is', and is also part of James's thought and perhaps of pragmatism generally.[9] What he says or implies is that no enterprise of positing, no conceptual scheme assigning existence to a class of entities, is better than any other from the point of view of truth. To speak differently, our observer *takes a decision* or *chooses* as to the existence of physical objects, or *opts* for them, which is not to say he is pronouncing on a question of fact. There is no fact of the matter. In making his choice he is guided by convenience, mainly simplicity.[10]

This end result of the observer's progress also includes something else. Physical objects are now conceived as causes of the qualia with which the story began, and, still more important, qualia *are* now regarded not as neutral but as subjective entities. The progress and the end result are said to stand in some analogy to the process whereby common sense gives rise to physics, and the world of common sense is then interpreted or revised in terms of physics. It is also said to be true of the culminating stage that we now have objects of perception in two senses, or two orders of objects of perception: physical objects and qualia.

To say so may be misleading. It cannot be, despite the talk of perceiving physical objects, that the observer has what it is natural to call real perception of such objects, that he does, in the most ordinary sense of the word, *see* them. That is, he does not have sensory awareness of them. He does not, to remark on one reasonably clear feature of this sensory perception, have what can be called *non-inferential* awareness of them. There is an irresistible reason for saying this. If this *were* the observer's situation, Ayer's doctrine would include within it what is distinguished from it, naive realism as it is called, which is to the effect that we have non-inferential awareness of exactly physical objects. Further, the rest of his doctrine would be otiose. The whole thing would be rebarbative, involving a particular kind of double perception or seeing-double that is unthinkable.

Thus to say that the observer perceives or experiences physical objects—as earlier it was said he perceived visuo-tactual continuants—must indeed be to say that he posits them in the course of sensorily perceiving or being aware of qualia. This is confirmed by Ayer's saying that his doctrine is a variant of what he calls the scientific approach.

---

[9] *OP*, 303. See Hookway, 1988, for a survey of the development of Quine's views in this connection. James's view is expounded by Ayer in *OP*. Quine's 'On What There Is' is in Quine, 1953.

[10] *OP*, 329–336; *CQ*, 107–108, 110. The passages are perhaps not wholly consistent, some being realist rather than pragmatist in tenor.

That is a kind of representative theory in which, as he says, the existence of physical objects is represented as a probable hypothesis we are justified in accepting because of the way it accounts for our experience.[11]

I am not wholly confident of the import of Ayer's last accounts of perception and the world, his answers to the question of the nature of perception and the questions of the nature of the world and our knowledge of it. My uncertainty is partly but not wholly a matter of the relation between the end-state of the fictive construction as against the fictive construction proper.

The perception question, I take it, is answered only by way of the end-state, not the fictive construction itself. Ayer does not suppose that we go through those various stages of the construction—visuo-tactual continuants and so on—in an ordinary experience of perception, say seeing the table. Further, it is not be forgotten that the end-state does indeed appear to be the result of *progress*, a *better* view. It is where the reflective experiencer ends up. It is how he, and we, are to characterize his experience, and of course ours. We are to do that, in part, in terms of qualia taken as subjective, not neutral.

As for the question of the world and our knowledge of it, that is plainly supposed to be answered by the fictive construction—however we may be diverted by the end-state. What we are given in the construction, it may seem, is an account of how we could or might come to a kind of acceptance of physical objects, and the proposal that this route would provide a kind of basis for the acceptance (cf. Strawson, 1979, 42). The modal proposition about a route we could in some sense follow, the tale of what could happen, is evidently just a way of putting the argument about the physical objects—an argument that can be separated from the fiction. It is that if we accept the existence of neutral qualia, which we can, we can move from this not by deductive steps but by essentially empirical inferences to the acceptance of physical objects.

These are an inference to the existence of persistent entities (visuo-tactual continuants in place of various momentary qualia in two sense modes), an inference to physical objects, and an inference to their causal powers. But the middle inference so-called is complicated, to say the least, by the intrusion of the doctrine of positing. When we have got to physical objects we have not got to a matter of fact.

I am not confident that certain propositions about perception and the world are those which are best taken from the fictive construction and

[11] *CQ*, 66, 108. Cf. 72–3, where Ayer writes of the qualia philosophers with whom he associates himself that they suggest 'that when I look, or at any rate believe myself to be looking, at the table in front of me, what I primarily see is not the table at all but something else, which has the impermanence and also the subjectivity of a mental image.

the end-state, those that can best be wrenched out of them. Still, I shall without further ado take it as the first of my four conclusions, a tentative one, that certain propositions are a best choice as to summing up Ayer's answers to the questions, and then go on to consider them. At least most of them have been held by many philosophers. They are as follows.

> In perceptual experiences we perceive or are aware of subjective entities, qualia. These issue in our positing or inferring objective entities, the world. This is a matter not of truth but essentially of simplicity. We perceive the objective entities in the sense that they are posited by us in the course of our perceiving or being aware of qualia. We take the objective entities to be causes of the subjective entities.

2 Arguments for Qualia

In the dispute about the nature of perception, qualia continue to have friends—Christopher Peacocke in speaking of the sensational properties of perceptions has been taken to raise the question of whether he is one[12]—but many philosophers desire to escape them. I am in the latter group. A first thing to be said of qualia is that they cannot properly be conceived as objects we *perceive*, indeed *see*. It is plain that we cannot perceive qualia in the sense that we see tables. The ungrammaticality of saying that we see qualia has to do with the fact that the seeing of tables is in part our being in a causal relation, of which much is known, to exactly a physical object. There can be no standard seeing of subjective entities. What must be said, then, is that qualia are things we see in another sense, or, as it may help to say, things of which we are aware. they are objects of awareness.

Does the relative elusiveness of this conception of awareness make uselessly unclear the notion of qualia, which are partly defined as objects of such awareness? One might seek to show this, but I shall not. Rather, I shall consider whether qualia exist, thereby presupposing a sufficiently clear idea of them.

The traditional method by which philosophers have attempted to establish their existence is the argument from illusion. It consists, in fact, of four arguments. These have as true premises (i) that we sometimes perceive a physical object as other than it is, as when a person who gets behind the ropes in Madame Tussaud's is mistaken for

---

[12] Peacocke, 1983, Ch. 1, 52–53. I am reassured that while he takes qualia or sense-data theories to have a core of correctness, he does not suppose that there are subjective entities which we perceive. (Letter).

a waxworks dummy, (ii) that we are subject to hallucinations, as in the case of mirages, phantom limbs, and the pink rats of delirium tremens, (iii) that things look different under different conditions, as with the coin that looks elliptical and the seemingly bent stick in water, and (iv) that our own bodily natures always contribute to our perceivings—this last premise is essentially the neuroscience of perception. Ayer, to my mind rightly, agrees with a number of recent philosophers—Michael Tye for one[13]—that so much is unpersuasive in these arguments that they do not establish awareness of qualia in ordinary perception (*CQ*, 73–88; *OP*, 304–305, 307–308).

However, he does advance what he takes as a simpler, more effective and indeed highly persuasive reason for awareness of qualia—awareness, as he alternatively says, of no more than what can be included in a strict account of experience, awareness of that content which gives us a premise for an inference or a positing.

(i) The given reason depends on a physical object's having at least the three properties or features noticed earlier, and I shall quote it fully.

> Can my present view of the table, considered purely in itself as a fleeting visual experience, conceivably guarantee that I am seeing something that is also tangible, or visible to other observers? Can it guarantee even that I am seeing something which exists at any other time than this . . .? I think it evident that it cannot. But if these conclusions are not logically guaranteed by the content of my present visual experience, one is surely entitled to say that they go beyond it, and just this is what I take to be meant by saying that my judgment that this is a table embodies an inference. It embodies an inference, not in the sense that it results from any conscious process of reasoning, but just in the sense that it affirms more than can logically be entailed by any strict account of the experience on which it is based. What I mean here by a strict account is one that is tailored to the experience, in that it describes the quality of what is sensibly presented, without carrying any further implication of any sort (*CQ*, 80–81; cf. *OP*, 304–305, 307–308).

This argument, not all of it as explicit as it might be, begins with the proposition that I do not see that what I see is what I touch—I do not really or sensorily perceive in any way that what I see is what I touch. Again, the truth of the proposition about something's being open to several senses is not something that I really perceive. Nor do I really perceive, secondly, that what I see is seen by others, or, thirdly, that it can exist at other times unperceived. Rather, it is a matter of inference or positing that what I see is what I touch, that it is seen by you, and that

[13] Michael Tye, 'Visual Qualia and Visual Content', forthcoming.

it can exist unseen. So much for the first premises of the argument. From them, it appears, Ayer concludes that I do not really perceive what has the three properties. But there is the further indubitable premise that I do somehow perceive or that I am somehow aware of *something*. We must therefore conclude that what we really are aware of is something less than what has the three properties. That is an experience strictly described, the content of an experience, a quale.

What is to be said of this argument? One thing is that it operates, as I myself have been operating, with a science-free conception of real perceiving or awareness. The main thing here is that this perceiving itself involves interpretation. That proposition sums up a good deal of research in the psychology of perception (Marr, 1982). Still, facts of the given kind, which complicate our idea of real perceiving, can hardly put in question, to take the strongest point of Ayer's argument, that I do not now or at any time *see* that the table goes on existing unperceived. The seeing of what I do really see may involve or give rise to close or distant relatives of inference, but I do not in this way see that tables exist unperceived. The case is perhaps obscure and less strong with the other two features of physical objects, but perhaps still strong enough. Let us not linger over this, partly because the fact by itself that I do not really see that the table can exist unperceived might be thought to give Ayer what he wants, which is that what I am aware of is a quale.

In fact, although the argument has taken philosophers back,[14] I cannot myself think that it is an improvement on the argument from illusion. What is to be said about it allows or concedes that we do not really see the truth of the three propositions. Let is be granted that we infer it. To speak differently, let it be granted that we do not see but rather infer or posit these three general properties of physical objects. Does it follow that we do not really see the physical objects and so must be regarded as being aware of qualia? It does not.

In fact, what is left perfectly possible is that, although I do not really see the three properties in question, I do really see exactly and no less than what has them. It remains possible that I have sensory awareness of exactly what does in fact exist unperceived, and is also touched, and is also perceived by you. That I *do* infer or posit, as we may suppose, that it has certain properties, does not entail that inference enters at all into my *seeing it*. To speak more precisely, that I do infer that it has certain properties does not entail that inference enters into my seeing of *others* of its properties. The argument, on reflection, does not damage naive realism. There can be no reason to fasten onto this realism the idea that in really seeing a thing I really see *all* its general properties,

---

[14] At any rate it did for a while take me aback. (See Honderich and Burnyeat, 1979, 312).

any more than there is reason to fasten on it the idea that when I see the front of a thing I also see its back or its weight.

As it seems to me, then, this argument as it has been presented depends on confusing inferences or posits that I may choose to grant with an inference or posit that I am inclined to deny, and whose denial is destructive of the doctrine we have been considering. *No argument at all is given for the existence of an inference of the required kind, and hence for entities entering into a premise.* It will be thought at this stage, however, that there is more to be said by a defender of qualia. He will put aside the bad argument but persist in his cause.

(ii) What he will say is that what I have called really seeing other properties of the physical object—other than the mentioned three properties—must *itself* be regarded as a matter of awareness of a quale and an inference or posit with respect to these other properties of the object. What are these other properties? Well, cannot I say that I see at least the relative size of the table, its shape from a particular angle, the position of the table vis-à-vis other things, including its want of movement? I have no reason, at least as yet, to take these photographable things as subjective, as other than properties of the table. Their very description, certainly, does not commit me to their being anything other than such properties.

The defender of qualia, however, will find a quale and an inference here. According to him I am aware of the quale or part of a quale which is of the shape of the table from a particular angle. As a consequence of this I infer or posit the property of the table which is its shape from a particular angle. But of course I am conscious of no such act of inferring or positing. This is not likely to be disputed by the defender of qualia. He will necessarily follow something like Ayer's supposition and say, to remember Ayer's words, that none the less I go beyond the content of my experience, affirm more of the table than is given me by my experience strictly described.

This ascription of a quale to me involves various difficulties, one of them having to do with the last bit. This is the difficulty of making effective use of the idea of an inference that is not conscious. That is not to say that there is no general sense that can be attached to the idea of an unconscious inference.

There is no difficulty in supposing that each of us has many neural dispositions. That is, we are so constituted neurally that a certain triggering event, perhaps a stimulus in the ordinary sense, completes a causal circumstance for a certain effect. The disposition constitutes most of the circumstance, and the triggering event the remainder. There is good reason to think that we are the possessors of myriad dispositions, and there can be no serious objection to speaking of very many of the associated episodes, some of them computational, as unconscious inferences. This will be most natural when what I have called the triggering cause and also the effect are *somehow* within experience, although of course not a matter of what Ayer speaks of as a conscious process of reasoning.

The difficulty for the defender of qualia, or one difficulty, lies not in this general idea but rather in the actual or possible *pervasiveness* of these dispositional episodes. No doubt they are part of the story of dreams. There can be no barrier to supposing, in particular, that one or more of these episodes are involved within exactly the kind of awareness which the defender of qualia takes to be in no sense inferential—that is, awareness of qualia. There can be no obstacle established in advance to *its* including dispositional episodes of the kind in question. Here one can think in particular of episodes specified in the theory of vision which have to do with supposed qualia which are in some sense three-dimensional (Marr, 1982). But then, evidently, *we lack any distinct idea of exactly a sort of inference which, for the defender of qualia, enters into the perceptual story later, at the right place.* We cannot by this means locate and establish certain distinctive entities, qualia, which enter into the premise of a particular sort of inference.

(iii) Is it possible to do better in giving sense and persuasion to talk of a distinctive sort of unconsious inference or the like in only the right place? Well, it comes to mind to suppose that the defender of qualia has a certain possibility. As remarked before, he will say of my seeing the shape of the table from a particular angle that I *go beyond* the content of my experience, *affirm more* of the table than is given me by my experience strictly described. A certain question arises here. What is that *more*? Given that my supposed quale is of the shape of the table from a particular angle, what is the additional thing that I affirm of the table in the conclusion of my inference or in my posit? Once we have put aside the whole matter of three properties of the table which I do not now see in any sense, and which we are allowing to be inferred, what is the additional thing?

In one important sense, there can be no such addition, and hence meaning cannot be given in a certain clear way to talk of inference or positing. That is, all that I can be said to infer or posit in so far as what is naturally called *content* is concerned, and as already assumed above, is the shape of the table from this angle. But that is exactly the content of my supposed object of awareness, the quale. There can be no real inference here in the way that there may be an inference from what I see to the fact of the table's existing when unperceived. There, we have a lot of distinct content in the conclusion. *Here we lack what is absolutely necessary, a distinction between a supposed premise and a supposed conclusion.*

Ted Honderich

(iv) Is there another sense in which I can be said to go beyond or affirm more than something which I am said to be given in my experience strictly described? What may come to mind, roughly speaking, is that what I go beyond to or affirm is that the table *really* has a certain shape from this angle. Again a question arises.

What is it that I go beyond? It cannot be said to be an experience to the effect that the table *appears* to have that shape from this angle, or that I *appear* to see such-and-such a shape, or whatever. If this were said, the defender of qualia would be engaged in a form of circular argument, *petitio principii*. He would be assuming qualia in his argument for them. A glance back will make this clear. We are engaged in the attempt to answer the question of whether qualia exist. We have latterly been considering whether we can succeed by distinguishing something given in experience strictly described, distinct from something more which we affirm. We have just supposed that what we go beyond to is the affirmation that the table does have a certain shape from this angle. What is it that we go beyond? The answer given is in effect that it is a quale. That is disastrous.[15] *We are assuming what we are supposed to be proving.*

(v) Let us finish here by glancing at a further supposition that may come to mind as a result of remembering Ayer's original argument. It is the supposition that in seeing the shape of the table from this angle I can be said to go beyond the experience to the propositions that that shape can also be touched by me, can be perceived by you, and persists unperceived. Might that do the trick?

It cannot, for the same reason as in the case of Ayer's original argument. Let it be granted that I do somehow infer or posit the three facts about not the table itself, as originally, but the shape of the table from this angle. *That does not entail that my actual seeing of the shape of the table from this angle involves any inference in any sense.* The supposition rests on confusing inferences that may be granted with the inference that is needed, and whose absence appears to stand in the way of the progress of the defender of qualia.[16]

It is my second conclusion in this paper, then, that Ayer's principal argument for the proposition that we are in fact aware of qualia, and also related arguments for the proposition, are not more compelling than their antecedents. The conclusion leads to a question and a difficulty, my third subject.

[15] Here and elsewhere in this paper, I do not disagree, as may seem possible, with pp. 42–44 of Strawson's admirable essay, 'Perception and Its Objects' (1979), where it is allowed that we can give a certain restricted description of our perceptual experience. Strawson does not in fact allow the existence of private objects of perception.

[16] There is at least a suggestion of this error in Mackie, 1976, 48–49.

3 Mental Realism and Distinctiveness of Perceptions

As noticed earlier, some of the greatest of philosophers have taken us to be aware of qualia. Hume and the others mentioned can have added to them, arguably, Descartes and Kant (*CQ*, 70). In the face of this agreement, and the likelihood of more of it to come, it might behove us to look again at the arguments from illusion, and perhaps at the argument by Ayer just questioned. Perhaps so, but something else comes to mind. Is there a greater source of commitment to qualia? There does seem to me to be such a greater source, indeed two of them, and therefore a difficulty in the way of scepticism about qualia.

It was said at the beginning that when Jane and Selina see the table, two perceptual experiences, two seeings, are part of the story. We took it that these are not truly identical with neural processes, and also not at all adequately conceived in the functionalist way as merely the terms of causal or logical relations. Like all conscious episodes, they have a different general character, known to all of us. There is reason to suppose that this conviction, Mental Realism, was shared by all of the quale philosophers. Does the very nature of Mental Realism lead in the direction of qualia? Is there the same tendency when it is asked how perceptual experiences adequately conceived are to be distinguished from other conscious episodes or mental events? What can be said of them particularly?

It is my suggestion that the philosophers in question were led to qualia, at least in part, by the very nature of Mental Realism. They were also led to qualia by the assumption that the only account of perceptual experiences adequately conceived is in terms of qualia.[17] What distinguishes really seeing a table from thinking about one that is not being perceived, and from desiring a missing table, and from imagining one, and so on, is exactly a quale. What other account can be given of perceptual experiences?

I am reassured in these ideas by the fact that at least one philosopher of perception takes a theory of qualia to be nothing other than a half of a particular theory of the mind which involves Mental Realism (Hirst, 1967; cf. Hirst, 1957, 182). The theory is interactionism, an affront to Occam whose peculiar burden is that some free-floating conscious episodes are effects of environment and some are causal with respect to it. The first half of that theory, we are to suppose, is necessarily to the effect that the environment gives rise to qualia. More generally, it is supposed that *any* theory of the mind which involves Mental Realism— any theory of the mind which however contentiously can be called a

---

[17] I see that this supposition is at least implicit in John Foster, *A. J. Ayer* (London, 1985), 161–177.

dualism[18]—is committed to qualia. It is, we are told, saddled with them.

This line of thought needs to be made clearer, as it can be by glancing at several versions of Mental Realism. One is Brentano's, later turned into something different by Roderick Chisholm. It is to the effect that every conscious episode involves activity directed upon or with reference to an intentional object, which is to say an object that does not exist in the ordinary way, but has existence in the understanding (Brentano, 1973; cf. Chisholm, 1957). Putting aside difficulties in this view, it is clear, first, that its nature, by which I mean its structure and language, suggests the doctrine of qualia. That is, what the view suggests is that consciousness consists in the awareness of objects which are subjective. Secondly, the view raises a certain question. Both thinking of an absent table and seeing a table, on this view, involve an inexistent object. How is the seeing to be distinguished from the thinking? The natural answer is to try to assign distinctive characteristics to the object in the case of the seeing—to try to take it as a quale.

G. E. Moore, in his version of Mental Realism, took each conscious episode to have two elements, one of them being consciousness itself, the other being an object. Here, still more strongly, the structure and language of the view suggests that conscious episodes involve what might be called an internal relation of awareness, as distinct from such a relation to a physical object. Here too, further, the question arises of what distinguishes the objects in the case of perceptual experiences as against others. The natural answer, to which Moore was strongly inclined, is that they have certain special characteristics, those of qualia (Moore, 1922).

What is it that is so unacceptable about the doctrine of qualia? Answering this question will prepare the way for what may be possible, an alternative account of perceptual experiences and of their distinctiveness.

The doctrine of qualia, as has been said often enough, places me behind a screen or veil. It would be better to say a wall, since, for one thing, what comes between me and ordinary physical objects consists itself in objects having certain sorts of properties. There is, we seem to be informed, the visual quale that is cat-shaped, the tomato-related quale that is red, and so on. The objects which are qualia, we are informed, in fact have all of the sensory properties that we unreflectively assign assign to physical objects as perceived. This cannot be right as it stands, however, since the property of shape and perhaps that

---

[18] On the point of whether a Mental Realist theory of mind and brain more arguable than interactionism is rightly called dualist, see Honderich, op. cit., 110–111.

of colour, as we unreflectively understand them in assigning them to physical objects, are observable by others and persist when unperceived. What *can* be said is that qualia have properties somewhat differently conceived, which are counterparts of all sensory properties ordinarily conceived. Qualia are simulacra, indeed images (cf. Tye, op. cit.).

It is proper to speak of the doctrine of qualia putting me behind a wall of qualia, further, since the qualia are *all* that I am sensorily aware of. I may infer or posit ordinary physical objects beyond the wall, and take those physical objects to be causal with respect to the wall, but I do not in the ordinary sense see or otherwise perceive them. Thirdly, with respect to the wall, I am the only one who is behind it. It is the wall of *my* qualia. Each of us is in solitary confinement. It is never the case that anything of which I am sensorily aware is numerically identical with anything of which you are sensorily aware.

The doctrine of qualia, then, assigns to me sensory awareness of simulacra of ordinary physical objects, by which I mean items with something like sensory properties, and it allows me sensory awareness of only such simulacra, and these simulacra are private to me. The sensory properties are not the only properties of the objects to which I am confined by the doctrine of qualia, but they are enough for the moment.

We have noticed that two versions of Mental Realism, in their structure and language, at least make it natural to take up and struggle with the doctrine of qualia in connection with perceptual experiences. Both suggest that conscious episodes involve an internal relation of awareness. There is another version of Mental Realism, less colourful than Brentano's, more contentful than Moore's and, not that the matter is important in the present context, consistent with at least one clear physicalism (Honderich, op cit., 71–86).

Here the distinctive nature of a particular or token conscious episode or mental event is characterized in terms of a duality within it: such an episode or event consists in what can be called an interdependent subject and content—interdependent in the sense that neither could exist in the absence of the other. The subject is not a person, not the possessor, container or locale of a conscious episode or mental event, or in any other way external to it. (On this view a person, by contrast, is importantly a matter of a certain sequence or history of conscious episodes or mental events.)

A subject is no more than a discernible element of and within a conscious episode or mental event. What else is to be said of the subject is only that it is of a kind such that each of my conscious episodes contains another instance of the kind. The content is not in this sense of a single kind. What it is most natural to say of contents is that typically they differ. They are diverse. More important, a content in this particular sense is not an abstract object, but rather, as some philosophers say, a psychological entity. Further, a content of this sort may or may not be representative. Such a content, if representative, would itself be regarded by many philosophers as itself a matter of attitude and proposition—or attitude and, in another smaller sense, content. This version of Mental Realism, like the others, is by certain comparisons neither literal nor precise. All versions have the glory, as against most identity theories, and also behaviourism, functionalism and so on, of sticking to the subject, the subject of consciousness.

What is important about this view for our present purposes is that it does not assert, and has no need to assert, that the relation between subject and content is one of awareness. The view is in this way akin to Davidson's finely-argued denial of private objects of thought generally.[19] The subject, so-called, does not *perceive* the content and is not to be described as *aware of* it. An awareness relation is at least natural in views which have far grander conceptions of a subject, as a person conceived differently than as a sequence or history of mental events. In the present view, what is said of the relation is that it is one of interdependence—neither subject nor content could exist without the other. That can be enlarged upon, but not in such a way as to turn the relation into what needs to be avoided.

This Mental Realism has among others the recommendation that it is not vulnerable to suspicions of vicious regress. The qualia doctrine, in contrast, when it inserts a quale into what we unreflectively take to be awareness of a physical object, and makes the quale necessary to that awareness, invites the suspicion that in consistency it needs another intermediate object of awareness, one which stands to the quale in some such way as the quale stands to the physical object, and so on.

However, the principal reason for taking up this Mental Realism, in so far as its conception of the internal relation is concerned, is simply that it does not falsify what we can discern, and more particularly recollect, and specify by way of past-tense demonstratives, which is conscious episodes themselves. It does not falsify by speculatively enriching what we can discern. In now thinking of what occurred a moment ago, my registering the trees out the window, I go beyond what I can be confident of recalling if I venture to speak of the conscious episode as involving not only a duality of a certain kind but also an internal awareness relation.

[19] Davidson, 1986, 1989, 1990. Davidson is also opposed to what was mentioned above, but not considered, the common discovery of an object of awareness along with an attitude within what I call a representative content.

That is not all. Suppose we came first to this minimal version of Mental Realism by reflecting on conscious episodes of other than the perceptual kind. Suppose we *were* at this stage tempted to conceive of the internal relation between subject and content as one of awareness. Suppose we then turned our attention to perceptual experiences, and realized that giving in to the awareness temptation had a certain upshot: the unacceptable doctrine of qualia, solitary confinement. That consequence in itself would or should for good reason stiffen us up, rescue us from temptation. The consideration that Mental Realism without an internal awareness relation does not commit us to qualia is one fact. That it is recommended by helping to save us from them is another.

So much for the structure and language of Mental Realism and the doctrine of qualia. There remains the second matter, that of giving an account, within Mental Realism, of perceptual experience in its distinctiveness. Certainly there *is* distinctiveness about the content of my seeing the table, as against the content of my just thinking of it. This has led philosophers to assign something like properties of shape, colour and so on to the content of the seeing—which assignment of properties is fundamental to the doctrine of qualia. The perceptual content has a character which has given rise to talk of properties, and the content of the thinking does not.

It is this character which is one large thing that stands in the way of what will come to mind, an account of perceptual experiences which takes them to be just beliefs (Armstrong, 1961, 1968). Any such account must be weakened in order to deal with certain objections—I do not believe that the stick in water *is* bent, and I do not believe one line *is* shorter in the Muller-Lyer illusion—and there are also objections to the weakened account, notably by Tim Crane.[20] Even if these objections can be somehow accommodated, there remains the simple fact that there is a great difference between my now seeing the table and my believing, as I leave the room, that it is there behind me, or that it is brown or whatever. The idea that perceiving *is* a kind of believing is hard to resist, but it is impossible to think no more needs to be said.

What *is* the distinctive character of perceptual experience? It may be true, as argued by Crane and others, that it is in some particular sense not conceptual. What stands in the way of my having full confidence in a general view of this kind is the fact of the many and diverse ideas of a concept, some of them roughly to the effect that any experience which is discriminatory or uses or gives rise to recognitional capacities is conceptual. Still, the doubt that perceptions are conceptual contributes

[20] Crane, 1988; 'The Non-Conceptual Content of Perception', forthcoming.

to the problem in hand. So does something else, which perhaps is clearer.

Seeing the table against just believing it is behind me seems not to be statemental or propositional. It seems not to have statemental or propositional content. Statemental content can be clarified in a traditional way. A statement or proposition is the sort of thing of which there is but one involved in all utterances which say the same thing of the same thing—that is, affirm the same property or status or whatever of the same referent (Lemmon, 1966). Hence, anything that has statemental content must be an utterance or have an utterance somehow integral to it, perhaps in such a way that just the utterance issues from it. Further, if this is a further step at all, anything that has statemental content must be or involve a determinate utterance. In effect, I think, this requirement of determinacy includes a requirement of limit. Consider a thing which is or involves what we may be tempted to speak or as a disjunction or conjunction of statements where the disjuncts or conjuncts are infinite or indefinitely many, and they are not subject to some organizing rule which makes for comprehension, say a rule of counting. Such a thing, as it is at least reasonable to say, is not an utterance. It lacks what was called limit. In any case, I so use the term 'utterance'.

A perceptual experience, whatever is to be said of conceptual content, evidently does not have statemental content in this sense—my seeing the table cannot be regarded as having integral to it an utterance as just conceived. What it gives rise to is at least an indefinitely large number of utterances, an indefinitely largely number of what many philosophers, including Ayer, have called basic statements. Here we have a further source of the doctrine of qualia. If a perceptual experience has respresentative content, as seems undeniable, and it does not have statemental content, or, at least in a sense, conceptual content, what possibility is left to us but to conceive of this content as an entity related to a physical object in that it is a simulacrum of it? If a perceptual experience has representative and non-statemental content, how can that content be other than a quale? If we are stuck with subjective entities having certain sensory properties, further, we are dragged back to conceiving of the relation between subject and content as awareness.

In trying to reply to this, what can be said first is that if the demand placed upon us is only and precisely to *distinguish* perceptual experiences from other conscious episodes, to mark off a species within a genus, then we have obvious things to say.

(i) The contents of perceptual experiences fall into categories, one category for each mode of perception. That is, contents with respect to each mode of perception have to do with a particular range of properties of physical objects. I see some set of properties, touch another set, and so on, despite the fact that some sets have members in common. In contrast, non-perceptual experience or much of it ranges over all properties.

(ii) As implied already, in connection with the matter of statemental content, the content of a perceptual experience is rich. I may, in seeing the table, attend to parts of it, but I see more than I attend to, much more. There are many complexities here, but none that can destroy this distinction between seeing and what is ordinarily called thinking of the table. What I get, in seeing the table from this angle, is a lot more than I have in thinking of it in any way.[21]

(iii) It is a related but different fact that the content of a perceptual experience is in a sense not selected or discriminated. I think of the table in a certain way, but I do not, in the same sense, see it in a certain way. I cannot choose to see less than I do, as I may choose to think of a corner of it. Again there are complexities.

(iv) Also related but different is the fact that seeing in itself is never active in a way which is common with non-perceptual experience. That is, it is not purposive or goal-directed, a matter of desire. I may indeed have a purpose in looking at something. My seeing itself is not purposive in the way that my trying to answer a question is purposive.

(v) Perceptual content somehow *gives* me a bit of the world, as thinking of it does not. To say that annoying thing is to report, very unsatisfactorily, a fact. The Given, of which philosophers used to talk, is wholly a matter of perceptual experience. Perceptual experience, to remember Russell, allows me knowledge by acquaintance, not description.

Much more might be said of each of these five considerations, and perhaps of others, but it is clear that we can satisfactorily *distinguish* perceptual from other experience. Alas, that fact cannot give us philosophical tranquility. This is so since it seems to be one thing to make the given distinction and another to *give the nature of the content of perceptual experience*, to conceive of it or provide an account of it. One way of succeeding in this second enterprise, if not the only way, would be to give, in a certain sense of the word, an acceptable *analysis* of this content. The doctrine of qualia gives such an analysis, but an unacceptable one.

Michael Tye, another sceptic about qualia, has suggested that we characterize perceptual experience functionally, but, as remarked earlier, the programme of functionalism seems to me futile (Tye, op. cit.). Further, we are looking for something open to introspection, or at

---

[21] Cf. Fred Dretske's distinction between analogue and digital coding of information in Dretske, 1981, Ch. 6.

any rate what might be called introspective recollection, and it is at least uncertain that functional role is of this kind.

I know of no acceptable analysis of perceptual experience, and, to confess, have struggled in vain to come to one. No doubt the best place to look is the dark neighbourhood of the last distinction, having to do with the Given and acquaintance. I am tempted by the idea that perceptual experience involves our having a certain unique guarantee—the idea that it is such as to deliver truths to us in a certain way. This, of course, runs up against at least the objection that it threatens to rule out what cannot be *ruled out*, which is scepticism about the world.

To be tempted towards an analysis is not to have one. How serious is this lack? To ask a better question, what are the consequences of this lack? In particular, should we reluctantly join those who can enthusiastically struggle with the doctrine of qualia? My own response to this, not tranquil, is a certain resoluteness. We can distinguish perceptual content and we have a negative account of its nature: it is not statemental. As it seems, we have no positive account of the character of perceptual content which does not involve qualia. In the absence of a positive account which does not involve qualia, I myself shall put up with having none at all. Better to have an incomplete philosophy of mind, and perhaps to admit limits to self-reflection, than to put the unbelievable wall of qualia into a lacuna.

My third conclusion, then, is that the doctrine of qualia has been owed to the conviction of Mental Realism and the need to distinguish perceptual experiences, but that we here find no sufficient ground for the doctrine. The conclusion leads to my last subject, which has hardly been out of view in our reflections so far.

4 Positing the World

Implicit and indeed explicit in the doctrine of qualia are answers to the ontological question of the nature of the world and the epistemological question of our knowledge of it. The answers have at their centre the proposition that we posit the world. I have my quale and I posit or in a funny sense perceive the table behind it. The world of ordinary physical objects is a matter of theory in the fundamental sense: it consists in theoretical entities of which we lack experience but which explain that of which we have experience, the data. What we do is imagine the world, call it into being in order to simplify our experience. We call into existence the cat in order to explain, or help explain, why a cat-quale moves towards a chair-quale from the left, disappears, and subsequently is succeeded by a qualitatively similar cat-quale moving away from the chair to the right.

This positing, further, is not a matter of asserting a fact. It is 'a means of organizing our experience in a systematic fashion', and 'we could have used posits of a quite different order, which, although no doubt inferior in explanatory value, would have been equally consonant with the bare facts of experience.'[22]

If what I have said against the existence of qualia is true, then a fundamental part of this line of thought about positing is false. If we do not have certain data, then there is no sense in talk of explaining it, no sense in speaking of theoretical entities which lie behind and simplify or organize it. *It* does not exist. We do not get to the point of having to ask about the worth of an inference to that of which, *ex hypothesi*, we can never have experience. We do not get to the point of having to consider a further question of what sense can be made of taking the simplifying cat to be a decision on our part rather than a fact (cf. Strawson, op. cit., 44–47). Is this conclusion somehow doubtful? Well, that will depend mainly on the alternative account of perception that has been suggested, an account free of qualia.

That account, which I hope is not so naive as to require more than the name of just Realism, is that to perceive is to acquire, without peculiar inference or the like, beliefs of a certain distinctive if baffling character about nothing less than ordinary physical objects. More particularly, as needs to be added, we acquire such beliefs about or in certain properties of ordinary physical objects. These are not, as we know, their properties of being public, being open to several senses, and existing unperceived. They are, very simply, their primary and secondary qualities— with both conceived, of course, in terms of perceptual contents which are not qualia. To speak differently, in line with a certain good idea of physical objects, we perceive space occupants with secondary properties (Quinton, 1973, 46–53).

Would it not be mistaken, on the basis of this view, to take a certain step prompted by the recollection of what Ayer and the other philosophers in his tradition believe about the *certainty* of quale statements? They begin with qualia and the like, as Ayer remarks, because they take propositions as to their occurrence to be indubitable (*CQ*, 58f). Would it not be a mistaken step to conclude, on the different basis that to perceive is without inference to acquire certain distinctive beliefs about physical objects, that those beliefs are *true*? No doubt they are, generally, but surely this does not follow from the given view? Is there not room left for scepticism? Surely scepticism does not have the doctrine of qualia as a necessary condition? Surely Realism does not exclude scepticism?

---

[22] *OP*, 303. For an admirable examination of the related views of Carnap and Reichenbach, see Hilary Putnam's paper in this volume.

Ted Honderich

Let us suppose this for a few moments. Are we now able to see that it is somehow doubtful to assert that the proposition that we posit the world is strictly speaking false since it is bound up with qualia? The answer to that seems to be no. The question posed by scepticism, given the new view of perception to which we have come, is simply this: Are any of our distinctive perceptual beliefs true? It is not a certain kind of request for an explanation or challenge to provide one, the kind such that a possible response is a supposition about something which lies behind and simplifies or organizes a set of data—theoretical entities. It is not a question to which positing is an answer. Of course, if we take up a very capacious and vague notion of positing, *all* questions of truth without exception may be said to be open to answers in terms of it. Here a posit is just *an answer*.

It is my fourth conclusion, then, that a defensible account of perception, a qualia-free account of perception, rules out the proposition that we posit the world. That conclusion leaves certain nearby questions untouched.

One is the question of whether it is true in any way or sense whatever that we decide on, choose, or opt for the existence of the world, where that is not to be ruled by a matter of fact, but to be guided by such a consideration as simplicity. That question, obviously, is most naturally raised by way of the view of perception we have rejected. It may be that it cannot be freed of the idea, which we have rejected, that we are aware of certain data and proceed to a theory about hidden entities which help to explain it.

To my mind *any* proposition to the effect that the world is not a matter of fact is as extraordinary as any in the history of philosophy. What stands in the way of taking it seriously is surely no mere 'psychological' resistance. Despite an inclination to assign an epistemological priority to qualia as against physical objects, an inclination to think of truth in their connection, Ayer suggests an argument in favour of this pragmatism. It is to the effect that in deciding between (i) anything like phenomenalism or the later view of his which we have been considering or (ii) a view which takes what exists to be unproblematically the world, we have no *criteria* for decision as to truth (*CQ*, 108–111; *OP*, 303, 329–336). I take it he means that there can be nothing outside of the subject-matter of these all-encompassing views against which we can check them for truth, or that we have no access to any such thing. My own response to this is that any conflict between the world as fact and any philosophical doctrine of criteria must be a short and uneven conflict. So too, incidentally, with a conflict between the world as fact and the many and yet more vulnerably theoretical considerations adduced by Quine.[23]

[23] As remarked above, they are well surveyed in Hookway (1988).

A second and related question which remains is very relevant to Ayer's treatment of scepticism, and the role he assigns to it in epistemology.[24] It is the question to which we supposed an answer for the purposes of argument a moment ago. *Does* an adequate account of perception, one which excludes qualia, also exclude scepticism? If I am tempted despite difficulties towards answering yes, and thus into a kind of agreement with Davidson and McDowell (Davidson, 1989; McDowell, 1986), I shall not say anything at all of that, but end with something else.

It is that while I have not found much to agree with in Ayer's answers to the questions with which we began, that is also my situation in connection with David Hume and his questions, as it is the situation of so many philosophers. We do not think much the less of Hume for that.

---

[24] *CQ*, 65; *PK*, 85–90. On scepticism about scepticism, cf. the last section of Putnam's paper in this volume.

Three Varieties of Knowledge

DONALD DAVIDSON

I know, for the most part, what I think, want, and intend, and what my sensations are. In addition, I know a great deal about the world around me. I also sometimes know what goes on in other people's minds. Each of these three kinds of empirical knowledge has its distinctive characteristics. What I know about the contents of my own mind I generally know without investigation or appeal to evidence. There are exceptions, but the primacy of unmediated self-knowledge is attested by the fact that we distrust the exceptions until they can be reconciled with the unmediated. My knowledge of the world outside of myself, on the other hand, depends on the functioning of my sense organs, and this causal dependence on the senses makes my beliefs about the world of nature open to a sort of uncertainty that arises only rarely in the case of beliefs about my own states of mind. Many of my simple perceptions of what is going on in the world are not based on further evidence; my perceptual beliefs are simply caused directly by the events and objects around me. But my knowledge of the propositional contents of other minds is never immediate in this sense; I would have no access to what others think and value if I could not note their behaviour.

Of course all three varieties of knowledge are concerned with aspects of the same reality; where they differ is in the mode of access to reality.

The relations among the three sorts of empirical knowledge, particularly questions of conceptual priority, have long headed the list of philosophers' epistemological concerns, and they are my subject here. These issues dominated much of Freddie Ayer's philosophical writing, and so I dedicate this essay to his memory. This is, I hope, appropriate, especially since I disagree with him on most of the essential points. For there was nothing Freddie enjoyed so much as confronting a thesis he felt to be roundly mistaken, and which he could, with his usual vigour and wit, take to pieces. It is my great loss, and yours, that he is not here to tell me off, but it is a measure of the vitality of his work that you will have no difficulty imagining his response.

Many familiar approaches to the question how the three sorts of knowledge are related take self-knowledge as primary, perhaps because of its directness and relative certainty, and then attempt to derive knowledge of the "external world" from it; as a final step, they try to base knowledge of other minds on observations of behaviour. This is not, needless to say, the only direction the derivation can take; one may instead accept knowledge of the external world, at least in some of its manifestations, as basic, and try to relate or reduce the other forms of knowledge to it. The elaboration of such reductive proposals, and the demonstration of their failure, constitutes much of the history of philosophy from Descartes to the present. If philosophers have tended to turn away from these problems in recent years, it is not because the problems are thought to have been solved, but because the problems seem intractable. There is also, of course, the wistful hope that the problems themselves are illusory.

This cannot be the case. There are compelling reasons for accepting the view that none of the three forms of knowledge is reducible to one or both of the others. Before I am finished I shall give my own reasons for believing this; but I take the hopelessness of finding effective modes of reduction to be apparent from the almost universal rejection of standard reductionist programmes. Scepticism in various of its familiar guises is our grudging tribute to the apparent impossibility of unifying the three varieties of knowledge: one form of scepticism springs from the difficulty of accounting for our knowledge of the external world on the basis of our knowledge of our own minds; another recognizes that our knowledge of other minds cannot consist only in what we can observe from the outside. The intractability of the mind-body problem is another such tribute.

It is striking the extent to which philosophers, even those who have been sceptics about the possibility of justifying beliefs about the external world, have put aside these doubts when they have come to consider the problem of other minds; striking, since the latter problem can arise only if knowledge of behaviour, and hence of the external world, is possible. Holding the problems apart has the unfortunate effect of obscuring the fact that the two problems rest on a common assumption. The assumption is that the truth concerning what a person believes about the world is logically independent of the truth of those beliefs. This certainly seems to be the case, for surely the totality of a person's beliefs and subjective experiences is logically consistent with the falsity of any of those beliefs. So no amount of knowledge of the contents of one's own mind insures the truth of a belief about the external world. The logical independence of the mental works equally in the other direction: no amount of knowledge of the external world entails the truth about the workings of a mind. If there is a logical or epistemic barrier between the mind and nature, it not only prevents us from seeing out; it also blocks a view from outside in.

It is sometimes thought that if we separate the problem of knowing what is in a mind from the problem of knowing about anything whatever outside of ourselves, then the problem of knowledge of other minds is solved when we recognize that it is part of the concept of a mental state or event that certain forms of behaviour, or other outward signs, count as evidence for the existence of that mental state or event. No doubt it is true that it is part of the concept of a mental state or event that behaviour is evidence for it. What is unclear is how this answers the sceptic. For the fact that behaviour is evidence for what is in a mind offers no explanation of the asymmetry between the indirect knowledge we have of other minds and the direct knowledge we have of our own mind. The proffered solution insists that behavioural evidence can suffice for the justified attribution of mental states to others, while it recognizes that such evidence is generally irrelevant to self-ascriptions of the same states. But if we are given no explanation of this striking asymmetry, we ought to conclude that there are really two kinds of concepts: mental concepts that apply to others, and mental concepts that apply to ourselves. If the mental states of others are known only through their behavioural and other outward manifestations, while this is not true of our own mental states, why should we think our own mental states are anything like those of others? We might also wonder why, if this answer to the problem of knowledge of other minds is satisfactory, we should not accept an analogous solution to the problem of our knowledge of the external world. Yet it is widely recognized that this answer to general scepticism is unacceptable. Do we distinguish between the problems because we suppose that while we have no access to the outside world except through experience, we nevertheless can intelligibly extrapolate to the experiences of others, since we have access to experience in our own case? But this supposition begs the question, since it assumes without argument that what we call the mental states of others are similar to what we identify as mental states in ourselves.

I have been rehearsing these well worn problems and perplexities because I want, first of all, to stress the apparent oddity of the fact that we have three irreducibly different varieties of empirical knowledge. We need an overall picture which not only accommodates all three modes of knowing, but makes sense of their relations to one another. Without such a general picture we should be deeply puzzled that the same world is known to us in three such different ways. And, second, it is essential to appreciate the extent to which problems that have usually been taken one at a time are interrelated. There are three basic problems: how a mind can know the world of nature, how it is possible for one mind to know another, and how it is possible to know the contents of our own minds without resort to observation or evidence. It is a mistake, I shall urge, to suppose that these questions can be collapsed into two, or taken in isolation.

In trying to form a picture of the relations among the three kinds of knowledge we must do much more than show *that* they are mutually

Donald Davidson

irreducible; we must see *why* they are irreducible. This in turn will involve bringing out the respective conceptual roles played by each of the forms of knowledge, and showing why each of the three sorts of knowledge is indispensable—why we could not get along without all of them. Of course, if I am right that each of the three varieties of empirical knowledge is indispensable, scepticism of the senses and scepticism about other minds must be dismissed. For the Cartesian or Humean sceptic about the external world holds that it is all too obvious that we can get along without knowledge of the world of nature—what we know of our own mind is self-sufficient, and may be all the knowledge we have. The sceptic about other minds is equally convinced that we can get along without knowledge of other minds—this must be possible if we are forever uncertain whether we have it.

It may seem at first that we could rather easily get along without a form of words to express our beliefs about the mental states of others or of ourselves. I think this is imaginable; but the issue with which I am concerned is primarily epistemic, not linguistic. It is whether we could get along without knowledge of minds, both our own and those of others. I shall argue that we could not. What we could not do is get along without a way of expressing, and thus communicating, our thoughts about the natural world. But if such communication is possible, the transition to also being able to attribute thoughts is relatively simple, and it would be astonishing if this step were not taken. With respect to our own thoughts, it is no more than the difference between saying assertively, 'Snow is white' and saying assertively, 'I believe that snow is white.' The truth conditions of these assertions are not the same, but anyone who understands the first assertion knows the truth conditions of the second, even if he does not command a sentence with those truth conditions. This is because anyone who understands speech can recognize assertions, and knows that someone who makes an assertion represents himself as believing what he says. Similarly, someone who says to Jones that snow is white knows the truth conditions of 'Jones believes that snow is white' (even if he does not know English nor have a way of expressing belief).

Belief is a condition of knowledge. But to have a belief it is not enough to discriminate among aspects of the world, to behave in different ways in different circumstances; an earthworm or a sunflower does this. Having a belief demands in addition appreciating the contrast between true belief and false, between appearance and reality, mere seeming and being. We can, of course, say that a sunflower has made a mistake if it turns toward an artificial light as if it were the sun, but we do not suppose the sunflower can think it has made a mistake, and so we do not attribute a belief to the sunflower. Someone who has a belief about the world—or anything else—must grasp the concept of objective truth, of what is the case independently of what he or she thinks. We must ask, therefore, after the source of the concept of truth.

I believe Wittgenstein put us on the track of the only possible answer to this question. The source of the concept of objective truth is interpersonal communication. Thought depends on communication. This follows at once if we suppose that language is essential to thought, and we agree with Wittgenstein that there cannot be a private language.[1] The central argument against private languages is that unless a language is shared there is no way to distinguish between using the language correctly and using it incorrectly; only communication with another can supply an objective check. If only communication can provide a check on the correct use of words, only communication can supply a standard of objectivity in other domains, as we shall see. We have no grounds for crediting a creature with the distinction between what is thought to be the case and what is the case unless the creature has the standard provided by a shared language; and without this distinction there is nothing that can clearly be called thought.

In communication, what a speaker and the speaker's interpreter must share is an understanding of what the speaker means by what he says. How is this possible? It would be good if we could say how language came into existence in the first place, or at least give an account of how an individual learns his first language, given that others in his environment are already linguistically accomplished. These matters are, however, beyond the bounds of reasonable philosophic speculation. What as philosophers we can do instead to ask how a competent interpreter (one with adequate conceptual resources and a language of his own) can come to understand the speaker of an alien tongue. An answer to this question can reveal essential features of communication, and will throw indirect light on what makes possible a first entry into language.

The practiced interpreter seeks to assign a propositional content to the utterances of a speaker. In effect he assigns a sentence of his own to each of the sentences of the speaker. To the extent that he gets things right, the interpreter's sentences provide the truth conditions of the speaker's sentences, and hence supply the basis for an interpretation of the speaker's utterances. The result can be thought of as a recursive

---

[1] I make no claims about how broadly Wittgenstein intended his thesis about private languages to be interpreted; perhaps he intended his argument to apply only to those concepts which are necessarily private. But I, like Saul Kripke, think the argument applies to language quite generally and so (I would say) to all propositional thought. See Kripke, *Wittgenstein on Rules and Private Language* (1982). I should add that while I accept the idea that communication is the source of objectivity, I do not think it depends on speakers using the same words to express the same thoughts. The use to which I put the Wittgensteinian insight will emerge presently.

characterization of truth, by the interpreter, of the sentences, and hence potential utterances, of the speaker.

An interpreter cannot directly observe another person's propositional attitudes; beliefs, desires, intentions, including the intentions which partly determine the meanings of utterances, are invisible to the naked eye. The interpreter can, however, attend to the utterances themselves, and we can assume without circularity that it is possible for him to detect one or another attitude a speaker has toward her own utterances, and from this infer attitudes to sentences. The sort of attitudes I have in mind are: holding a sentence true at a time, or wanting a sentence to be true, or preferring that one sentence rather than another be true. The assumption that such attitudes can be detected does not beg the question of how we endow the attitudes with content, since a relation, such as holding true, between a speaker and an utterance is an extensional relation which can be known to hold without knowing what the sentence means. I call such attitudes **non-individuative**, for though they are psychological in nature, they do not bestow individual propositional contents on the attitudes.

In *Word and Object* Quine (1960) appealed to the non-individuative attitude of **prompted assent.** Since someone assents to an utterance, or holds a sentence true, in part because of what he believes and in part because of what the utterance or sentence means in his language, Quine's problem was to separate out these two elements on the basis of evidence that combined their influence. If the separation succeeds, the result is a theory of both belief and meaning for the speaker, for it must yield an interpretation of the speaker's utterances, and if one knows both that the speaker assents to the utterance, and what it means in his mouth, one also knows what he believes.

The process of separating meaning and opinion invokes two key principles which must be applicable if a speaker is interpretable: the Principle of Coherence and the Principle of Correspondence. The Principle of Coherence prompts the interpreter to discover a degree of logical consistency in the thought of the speaker; the Principle of Correspondence prompts the interpreter to take the speaker to be responding to the same features of the world that he (the interpreter) would be responding to under similar circumstances. Both principles can be (and have been) called principles of charity: one principle endows the speaker with a modicum of logical truth, the other endows him with a degree of true belief about the world. Successful interpretation necessarily invests the person interpreted with basic rationality. It follows from the nature of correct interpretation that an interpersonal standard of consistency and correspondence to the facts applies to both the speaker and the speaker's interpreter, to their utterances and to their beliefs.

Two questions now obtrude. The first is: why should an interpersonal standard be an objective standard, that is, why should what people agree on be true? The second is: even if it is the case that communication assumes an objective standard of truth, why should this be the only way such a standard can be established?

Here is a way of responding to these questions. All creatures classify objects and aspects of the world in the sense that they treat some stimuli as more alike than others. The objective criterion of such classification is similarity of response. Evolution and subsequent learning no doubt explain these patterns of behaviour. But from what point of view can these be called patterns? The criterion on the basis of which a creature can be said to be treating stimuli as similar, as belonging to a class, is the similarity of the creature's responses to those stimuli; but what is the criterion of the similarity of the responses? *This* criterion cannot be derived from the creature's responses; it can come only from the responses of an observer to the responses of the creature. And it is only when an observer consciously correlates the responses of another creature with objects and events in the observer's world that there is any basis for saying the creature is responding to those objects or events (rather than any other source of the creature's stimuli). As would be interpreters of the verbal behaviour of the speaker of an alien language, we group distinct verbal acts of the speaker together: 'Mother', 'Snow', 'Table', when repeated as one word sentences, sound similar if we are appropriately attuned. If we discover kinds of objects or events in the world that we can correlate with the utterances of a speaker, we are on the way to interpreting the simplest linguistic behaviour.

If we are teaching someone a language, the situation becomes more complex, but more clearly interpersonal. What seems basic is this: an observer (or teacher) finds (or instills) a regularity in the verbal behaviour of the informant (or learner) which he can correlate with events and objects in the environment. This much can take place without developed thought on the part of the observed, of course, but it is a necessary condition for attributing thoughts and meanings to the person observed. For until the triangle is completed connecting two creatures, and each creature with common features of the world, there can be no answer to the question whether a creature, in discriminating between stimuli, is discriminating between stimuli at the sensory surfaces or somewhere further out, or further in. Without this sharing of reactions to common stimuli, thought and speech would have no particular content—that is, no content at all. It takes two points of view to give a location to the cause of a thought, and thus to define its content. We may think of it as a form of triangulation: each of two people is reacting differentially to sensory stimuli streaming in from a certain direction. If we project the incoming lines outward, their intersection is the common cause. If the two people now note each others' reactions (in the case of language, verbal reactions), each can correlate these observed reactions with his or her stimuli from the world. The common cause can now determine the contents of an utterance and a thought. The triangle which gives content to thought and speech is complete. But it takes two to triangulate. Two, or, of course, more.

Until a base line has been established by communication with someone else, there is no point in saying a person's thoughts or words have a propositional content. If this is so, then it is clear that knowledge of another mind is essential to all thought and all knowledge. Knowledge of another mind is possible, however, only if one has knowledge of the world, for the triangulation which is essential to thought requires that those in communication recognize that they occupy positions in a shared world. So knowledge of other minds and knowledge of the world are mutually dependent; neither is possible without the other. Ayer was surely right when he said, '. . . it is only with the use of language that truth and error, certainty and uncertainty, come fully upon the scene'. (*PK*, 54)

Knowledge of the propositional contents of our own minds is not possible without the other forms of knowledge since without communication propositional thought is impossible. It is also the case that we are not in a position to attribute thoughts to others unless we have our own thoughts, and know what they are, for the attribution of thought to others is a matter of matching the verbal and other behaviour of others to our own propositions or meaningful sentences. Knowledge of our own minds and of the minds of others are mutually dependent.

It should now be clear what ensures that our view of the world is, in its plainest features, largely correct. The reason is that the stimuli that cause our most basic verbal responses also determine what those verbal responses mean, and the content of the beliefs that accompany them. The nature of correct interpretation guarantees both that a large number of our simplest beliefs are true, and that the nature of these beliefs is known to others. Of course many beliefs are given content by their relations to further beliefs, or are caused by misleading sensations; any particular belief or set of beliefs about the world around us may be false. What cannot be the case is that our general picture of the world and our place in it is mistaken, for it is this picture which informs the rest of our beliefs, whether they be true or false, and makes them intelligible.

The assumption that the truth about what we believe is logically independent of the truth of what we believe is revealed as ambiguous. Any particular belief may indeed be false; but enough in the framework and fabric of our beliefs must be true to give content to the rest. The conceptual connections between our knowledge of our own minds and our knowledge of the world of nature are not definitional but holistic.

The same is true of the conceptual connections between our knowledge of behaviour and our knowledge of other minds.

There are, then, no 'barriers', logical or epistemic, between the three varieties of knowledge. On the other hand, the very way in which each depends on the others shows why none can be eliminated, or reduced to the others.

As noted above, we may think of an interpreter who aims to understand a speaker as matching up sentences of his own with the utterances and states of mind of the speaker. The totality of evidence available to the interpreter determines no unique theory of truth for a given speaker, not just because actually available evidence is finite while the theory has an infinity of testable consequences, but because all possible evidence cannot limit acceptable theories to one. Given the richness of the structure represented by the set of one's own sentences, and the nature of the connections between the members of this set and the world, we should not be surprised if there are many ways of assigning our own sentences to the sentences and thoughts of someone else that capture everything of relevant significance.

The situation is analogous to the measurement of weight or temperature by assigning numbers to objects. Even supposing there are no errors of measurement, and that all possible observations have been made, an assignment of numbers to objects that correctly registers their weights is not unique: given one such assignment, another can be produced by multiplying all the numbers by any positive constant. In the case of ordinary temperature (not absolute temperature), any correct assignment of numbers can be converted to another by a linear transformation. Because there are many different but equally acceptable ways of interpreting an agent, we may say, if we please, that interpretation or translation is indeterminate, or that there is no fact of the matter as to what someone means by his or her words. In the same vein, we could speak of the indeterminacy of weight or temperature. But we normally accentuate the positive by being clear about what is invariant from one assignment of numbers to the next, for it is what is invariant that is empirically significant. The invariant *is* the fact of the matter. We can afford to look at translation and the content of mental states in the same light.[2]

I once thought that the indeterminacy of translation supplied a reason for supposing there are no strict laws connecting mental and physical concepts, and so supported the claim that mental concepts are not even nomologically reducible to physical concepts. I was wrong:

---

[2] Here I accept Quine's thesis of the indeterminacy of translation, and extend it to the interpretation of thought generally. The analogy with measurement is my own.

indeterminancy turns up in both domains. But one source of indeterminancy in the case of the mental is that the line between empirical truth and truth due to meaning cannot in general be clearly defined on behavioural grounds; and behavioural grounds are all we have for determining what speakers mean. It is here that the irreducible difference between mental concepts and physical concepts begins to emerge: the former, at least in so far as they are intentional in nature, require the interpreter to consider how best to render the creature being interpreted intelligible, that is, as a creature endowed with reason. As a consequence, an interpreter must separate meaning from opinion in part on normative grounds, by deciding what, from his point of view, maximizes intelligibility. In this endeavour, the interpreter has, of course, no other standards of rationality to fall back on than his own. When we try to understand the world as physicists, we necessarily employ our own norms, but we do not aim to discover rationality in the phenomena.

How does the normative element in mental concepts prevent their reduction to physical concepts? Perhaps it is obvious that definitional reduction is out of the question; but why cannot there be laws—strict laws—that connect each mental event or state with events or states described in the vocabulary of an advanced physics? When writing about this twenty years ago I said, in effect, that one can hope for strict connecting laws only when the concepts connected by the laws are based on criteria of the same sort, and so a strict law could not combine normative with non-normative concepts.[3] This answer still seems to me right as far as it goes, but it has understandably been found inconclusive by many. I now want to add some further considerations.

One further consideration is this: strict laws do not employ causal concepts, while most, if not all, mental concepts are irreducibly causal. An action, for example, must be intentional under some description, but an action is intentional only if it is caused by mental factors such as beliefs and desires. Beliefs and desires are identified in part by the sorts of action they are prone to cause, given the right conditions. Most of the concepts that feature in common sense explanations are causal in this way. An accident was caused by fact that the road was slippery; something is slippery if it causes appropriate objects to slip under appropriate circumstances. We explain why the wing of an airplane does not break when it bends by noting that it is made of partially elastic materials; a material is elastic if there is something about it that causes it, under appropriate conditions, to return to its original shape after deformation. Such explanations do not lend themselves to precision for

[3] In 'Mental Events', reprinted in my *Essays on Actions and Events* (1980).

two reasons: we cannot spell out in detail when the circumstances are appropriate, and the appeal to causality finesses part of what a full scale explanation would make manifest. Descriptions of objects, states and events that are needed to instantiate strict, exceptionless laws do not contain causal concepts. (Which is not to say that laws which contain only non-causal concepts are not causal laws.)

In the case of causal properties like elasticity, slipperiness, malleability, or solubility we tend to think, right or wrongly, that what they leave unexplained can be (or already has been) explained by the advance of science. We would not be changing the subject if we were to drop the concept of elasticity in favour of a specification of the microstructure of the materials in the airplane wing that cause it to return to its original shape when exposed to certain forces. Mental concepts and explanations are not like this. They appeal to causality because they are designed, like the concept of causality itself, to single out from the totality of circumstances which conspire to cause a given event just those factors that satisfy some particular explanatory interest. When we want to explain an action, for example, we want to know the agent's reasons, so we can see for ourselves what it was about the action that appealed to the agent. But it would be foolish to suppose that there are strict laws that stipulate that whenever an agent has certain reasons he will perform a given action.

The normative and the causal properties of mental concepts are related. If we were to drop the normative aspect from psychological explanations, they would no longer serve the purposes they do. We have such a keen interest in the reasons for actions and other psychological phenomena that we are willing to settle for explanations that cannot be made to fit perfectly with the laws of physics. Physics, on the other hand has as an aim laws that are as complete and precise as we can make them; a different aim. The causal element in mental concepts helps make up for the precision they lack: it is part of the concept of an intentional action that it is caused and explained by beliefs and desires; it is part of the concept of a belief or a desire that it tends to cause and so explain actions of certain sorts.

Much of what I have said about what distinguishes mental concepts from the concepts of a developed physics could also be said to distinguished the concepts of many of the special sciences such as biology, geology, and meteorology. So even if I am right that the normative and causal character of mental concepts divide them definitionally and nomologically from the concepts of a developed physics, it may seem that there must be something more basic or foundational that accounts for this division. I think there is.

Knowledge of the contents of our own minds must, in most cases, be trivial. The reason is that, apart from special cases, the problem of interpretation cannot arise. When I am asked about the propositional contents of my mind, I must use my own sentences. The answer is usually absurdly obvious: my sentence 'Snow is white', like my thought that snow is white, is true if and only if snow is white. My knowledge of the contents of another mind is possible, I have argued, only in the context of a generally correct, and shared, view of the world. But such knowledge differs from the knowledge I have of my own mind since it is necessarily inferential, and depends, among other things, on observed correlations between the speech and other behaviour of the person and events in our communal environment.

The fundamental difference between my knowledge of another mind and my knowledge of the shared physical world has a different source. Communication, and the knowledge of other minds that it presupposes, is the basis of our concept of objectivity, our recognition of a distinction between false and true belief. There is no going outside this standard to check whether we have things right, any more than we can check whether the platinum-iridium standard kept at the International Bureau of Weights and Standards in Sèvres, France, weighs a kilogram. We can, of course, turn to a third party and a fourth to broaden and secure the interpersonal standard of the real, but this leads not to something intrinsically different, just to more of the same, though the augmentation may be welcome.

I spoke before of an analogy between how we assign numbers to keep track of the relations among objects with respect to temperature or weight and how we use our own sentences to identify the contents of the thoughts and utterances of others. But the analogy is imperfect: the nature of the scaling device differs in the two cases. We depend on our linguistic interactions with others to yield agreement on the properties of numbers and the sort of structures in nature that allow us to represent those structures in the numbers. We cannot in the same way agree on the structure of sentences or thoughts we use to chart the thoughts and meanings of others, for the attempt to reach such an agreement simply sends us back to the very process of interpretation on which all agreement depends.

It is here, I suggest, that we come to the ultimate springs of the difference between understanding minds and understanding the world as physical. A community of minds is the basis of knowledge; it provides the measure of all things. It makes no sense to question the adequacy of this measure, or to seek a more ultimate standard.

We have dwelt at length on the inescapability of the objective aspect of all thought. What remains of the subjective aspect? We have not, clearly, obliterated the difference between self-knowledge and knowledge of other minds: the first remains direct and the second inferential. And objectivity itself we have traced to the intersections of points of view; for each person, the relation between his own reactions to the world and those of others. These differences are real. Our thoughts are 'inner' and 'subjective' in that we know what they are in a way no one else can. But though *possession* of a thought is necessarily individual, what gives it content is not. The thoughts we form and entertain are located conceptually in the world we inhabit, and know we inhabit, with others. Even our thoughts about our own mental states occupy the same conceptual space and are located on the same public map.

The philosophical conception of subjectivity is burdened with a history and a set of assumptions about the nature of mind and meaning that sever the meaning of an utterance or the content of a thought from questions about external reality, thus creating a logical gap between 'my' world and the world as it appears to others. This common conception holds that the subjective is prior to the objective, that there is a subjective world prior to knowledge of external reality. It is evident that the picture of thought and meaning I have sketched here leaves no room for such priority since it predicates self-knowledge on knowledge of other minds and of the world. The objective and the inter-subjective are thus essential to anything we can call subjectivity, and constitute the context in which it takes form. Collingwood put it succinctly:

> The child's discovery of itself as a person is also its discovery of itself as a member of a world of persons . . . The discovery of myself as a person is the discovery that I can speak, and am thus a *persona* or speaker; in speaking I am both speaker and hearer; and since the discovery of myself as a person is also the discovery of other persons around me, it it the discovery of speakers and hearers other than myself. (Collingwood, 1938, 248)

It may seem that if sharing a general view of the world is a condition of thought, the differences in intellectual and imaginative character among minds and cultures will be lost to sight. If I have given this impression it is because I have wanted to concentrate on what seems to me primary, and so apt to go unnoticed: the necessary degree of communality essential to understanding another individual, and the extent to which such understanding provides the foundation of the concept of truth and reality upon which all thought depends. But I do not want to suggest that we cannot understand those with whom we differ on vast tracts of physical and moral opinion. It is also the case that understanding is a matter of degree: others may know things we do not, or even perhaps cannot. What is certain is that the clarity and effectiveness of our concepts grows with the growth of our understanding of others. There are no definite limits to how far dialogue can or will take us.

Donald Davidson

Some philosophers worry that if all our knowledge, at least our propositional knowledge, is objective, we will lose touch with an essential aspect of reality: our personal, private outlook. I think this worry is groundless. If I am right, our propositional knowledge has its basis not in the impersonal but in the interpersonal. When we look at the natural world we share with others we do not lose contact with ourselves, but rather acknowledge membership in a society of minds. If I did not know what others think I would have no thoughts of my own and so would not know what I think. If I did not know what I think, I would lack the ability to gauge the thought of others. Gauging the thoughts of others requires that I live in the same world with them, sharing many reactions to its major features, including its values. So there is no danger that in viewing the world objectively we will lose touch with ourselves. The three sorts of knowledge form a tripod: if any leg were lost, no part would stand.

The Importance of 'If'

JOHN WATLING

Every week of term, on Wednesday afternoons, during most of his years at University College, Ayer held a seminar. Strangely, he makes no mention of that seminar in his autobiography, although it was a more serious and productive affair than his Monday evening seminar, which he does mention. At the Wednesday seminar, conditionals were often the subject for discussion. They are intriguing things in themselves but the attention they received must have been due, in large part, to their central role in Ayer's philosophy. Ayer was a phenomenalist, but he did not go so far as that prince of phenomenalists, George Berkeley, and assert that the things around us in space, chairs and tables, trees and rocks and lakes, the sun, moon and stars, were sensations, sensations of various kinds. Ayer's view was more that of John Stuart Mill, that these things were permanent possibilities of sensation. To assert the existence of a lake was to assert that *if* certain characteristic sensations occurred, then certain other characteristic sensations would follow. In that way, conditionals played a central role in Ayer's phenomenalism. That phenomenalism, however, needed to agree with an even more central element of his thought, the positivism he derived, perhaps from the philosophy of the Vienna Circle, perhaps from David Hume. According to that positivism, experience sets limits to understanding. If we can experience nothing but the presence or absence of sensations, then propositions concerning the presence or absence of sensations are all we can understand. Now a conditional concerning sensations does not imply the presence of sensations and, although it does imply the absence of sensations, it implies more besides. What Ayer's phenomenalism required, his positivism could not allow.

Ayer always believed that the problem could be resolved. Some members of the Wednesday seminar would have agreed with him, others would not. In one of his later books, *Probability and Evidence*, published in 1972, he outlines a resolution, although by that time both his phenomenalism and his positivism had undergone some modification. I shall not be concerned directly with Ayer's problem in what follows. I take up a problem posed to me not so long since by someone who, as it happens, was a member of Ayer's seminar of long ago, at least in its first years, but the considerations I bring forward establish, I think, that the problem cannot be resolved in the way Ayer proposes, indeed, that it cannot be resolved at all. That conclusion is not the importance of 'if' I intend by the title of this lecture. What that is will become clear.

The lecture relates to Ayer in several ways: to a central problem of his philosophy, to a view he took in resolution of that problem and to the work and thought of some of the people who took part in that Wednesday seminar with such interest and profit. If anyone should think it inappropriate in a memorial lecture to offer a refutation of one of its subject's cherished views, then he might be right about memorial lectures for others but not about a lecture for Freddie Ayer. He delighted in being contradicted. It was not, of course, that he always accepted the argument against him. Often one could not prevent the expression 'water off a duck's back' coming to mind. One of his cherished views was the incorrigibility, as he called it, of beliefs concerning the immediate data of sense. I remember his coming into the department one morning and announcing that he had concluded that sense-datum propositions were corrigible after all. 'Good heavens,' I said, 'for the reasons that Martin and I have been urging all these years?' 'No,' he said, 'No, for no reason at all really.' I must not give a wrong impression here. Ayer was a marvellous teacher and was so largely because he made evident the value he placed on the work and thought of his students. Without that trait, you might as well give up teaching philosophy. Ayer had it to a pre-eminent degree.

So I come to my topic, set by the question 'What do we need to know about the future to guide our actions?' A few years ago now, Martin Shearn said to me that he was puzzled why it was that if you were trying to do something, all information about what was going to happen was relevant, except the information that you would not succeed. I found that puzzling too, but I came to think that it was wrong and so I wrote this paper.

Knowledge as a guide to action: the future

It is often held that when scientific knowledge enables us to achieve our ends it does so by enabling us to foretell what will and what will not happen. David Hume, for example, takes that for granted in his *Enquiry Concerning Human Understanding*, for he offers an explanation of how experience leads us to form correct expectations concerning the future and considers he has explained how it is that we are able to adjust means to ends and how it is that our species subsists. 'Custom, then,' he says, 'is the great guide of human life,' and, since custom is his explanation of how we come to form correct expectations, he there takes it for granted that if we can foretell we can guide our actions. What he most often asserts is that foreknowledge is essential for the ability to guide our actions, and that, at least, seems correct. If we do not know what will happen, how can we plan our actions to take advantage of it or to minimize its ill effects? Let us consider a simple example of such a calculation.

Suppose I wish to reach a certain town and decide to catch a bus. I see one approaching a stop a little distance away. If I run, I can reach the stop by the time the bus does, but will it stop? It seems important to know, for, if it is going to stop, I can run and reach the stop in time. If it is not, I shall only waste my breath by running. That reasoning is fallacious. Suppose the truth is that the bus is not going to stop. Does that show that it would be useless to run? Not at all. Perhaps, if I were to run, the driver would see me running and stop. The fact that the bus is not going to stop is quite consistent with that. Again, suppose the truth is that the bus is going to stop. That does not show that it would be sensible to run, so as to be at the stop in time. Perhaps, if I were to run, the driver would see me running and drive past. The fact that something will happen does not mean that I can plan my actions to take advantage of it; the fact that it will not, does not mean that I have to do without it. What I need to know is not whether the bus will stop, but whether it would stop, if I were to run.

The bus driver is a human agent but that is not what makes the reasoning fallacious. The fact that the surface of a bog will remain flat for the next hour is not something I can take advantage of to walk across it. It will remain flat but, if I were to walk into it, it would not. Perhaps the reasoning is fallacious because drivers and soft wet ground are sensitive things. Surely, knowledge of the future states of insensitive things is something upon which we can base our plans? The ebb and flow of the tide is a good example. If, having hired a boat upon a tidal river, I know the time at which the tide will turn, then I may be able to row quite a long way down the river, counting upon turning with the tide and having its help in both directions. Without that knowledge I could not venture so far, for fear of a hard row back against the current. Here is a fact that I seem to be able to take advantage of. However, just as before, what I need to know is when the tide would turn if I were to row down the river on it and, just as before, that fact does not follow from a fact concerning when it will turn. If I were to justify my plan by the fact concerning the time at which the tide will turn, my reasoning would be as fallacious as before. There is, indeed, something I know about the river, that its current is not much affected by small boats rowing on its surface, which, together with my knowledge of when the tide will turn, does enable me to justify my plan. This fact, which I can take advantage of, is not merely about the future of the river, for it is about its insensitivity: it is the fact that, whether or not my plan were put into effect, the tide would turn at the time at which it will turn. Therefore, although when I am dealing with insensitive things knowledge of their future is of great value, it is of no use by itself. Moreover, although of great value, it may not be indispensible; it may be possible to discover what their future would be without employing any knowledge of what it will be. Of course, knowledge of what will or will not happen in the future, combined with knowledge that a plan is one I shall adopt, is relevant to the assessment of the plan. That is why I can look back later and, knowing that I did adopt the plan and that I did not achieve what I set out to achieve, judge the plan a bad one. However, when I assess a plan in order to decide whether to adopt it, the information that I shall adopt it is lacking.

The fallacy that I have been trying to expose is that of arguing from what will happen to what would happen if. There is a particular form of that argument, equally fallacious, which sometimes leads people to think that a knowledge of what will happen enables us to guide our actions. They sometimes think that if they know that one or other of two things will happen, that both will not fail, then they can conclude that by preventing one of them they can ensure the other. That, too, is a delusion. The fact that one or other of them will happen is quite consistent with the fact that neither would if one were prevented. Suppose it is a fact that either I shall not run or the bus will stop. It cannot be that this implies that by running I can stop the bus, for it is itself implied by the fact that the bus will stop and that fact does not imply that my running would stop it. The fact that the bus will stop is quite compatible with the fact that my running would ensure that it did not. People fail to notice examples like that and think only of ones like this, that a certain piece of iron will not be heated without expanding. That, of course, is implied by the fact that either it will not be heated or will expand and seems to them to justify the conclusion that by heating the piece of iron they can make it expand. That conclusion is true, but that fact is no reason for it. Perhaps they know that the conclusion is true, but the knowledge concerning the future of the piece of iron does not enable them to prove it. Of course, those who accept this implication must feel uncomfortable about the other conclusion that ought, on this form of argument, equally to follow, that I can ensure that the piece of iron will remain cool by preventing it from expanding. They can hardly feel confident that that is true.

Sometimes the words we use to speak of what will happen are so close to those we use to speak about what would happen if, that it is difficult to avoid confusing the one with the other. Suppose that I am going to miss the bus. Then it is difficult not to agree that whatever I do I shall miss the bus. However, the words 'Whatever I do, I shall miss the bus' seem to express the very same conclusion that might have been expressed by the words 'Whatever I were to do, I should miss the bus', words which express something which implies that there is nothing I can do to catch the bus. Yet the fact that I shall miss the bus does not imply that there is nothing I can do to catch it. What has gone wrong? The trouble lies in the ambiguity of the words 'Whatever I do, I shall miss the bus'. They might be taken to mean that every one of the things I shall do will be followed by my missing the bus. Taken in that sense, they express something which follows from the fact that I shall miss the bus but does not imply that I cannot catch it. They might, however, be taken to mean that every one of the things I can do, not just the things I shall do, would be followed, if I were to do it, by my missing the bus. That is a very different thing. It does not follow from the fact that I shall miss the bus but does imply that I cannot catch it. To know that, among all the things I shall do, none will be followed by my catching the bus is to know only that I shall miss it. To know that, among all the things I can do, none would be followed by my catching it is to know more. If we confuse these two ways of taking the words, then we may be deceived into thinking that the fact that I shall miss the bus implies that I cannot catch it.

There is another confusion arising over the word 'if' which can make these fallacious forms of inference seem valid. James Thomson, a member of Ayer's seminar in its earlier years, was perhaps the first philosopher to exploit it. Someone who argues from the premise that either he will not run or the bus will stop together with the further premise that he will run can rightly conclude that the bus will stop. He might put this by saying 'Either I shan't run or the bus will stop. So, since I shall run, the bus will stop.' If he was not sure whether or nor he was going to run, he might express the validity of the same argument, without embracing the conclusion, by saying 'Either I shall not run or the bus will stop. So, if I run, the bus will stop.' Since the argument is valid, it must be right for him to say that but, in saying that, is he not arguing from the premise that either he will not run or the bus will stop to the conclusion that if he runs the bus will stop? Therefore, from the validity of argument of the form 'One or other of these things is true, the first isn't, so the second is' we seem to have established the validity of argument of the form I have been declaring fallacious, and which is indeed fallacious, 'One or other of these things is true, so, if the first weren't true the second would be'. Where is the mistake here?

It is natural to assume that, when we express an argument, the words with which we follow the word 'so' are words we employ in the expression of our conclusion. In fact we often employ those words in other ways. We do so in the expression of the first of the two arguments just considered, for that was expressed 'Either I won't run or the bus will stop, so, since I will run, the bus will stop.' The words 'since I will run' follow the word 'so' but, far from entering into the expression of the conclusion of the argument, they introduce one of its premises. To believe otherwise, you would have to accept that words such as 'since I will run, the bus will stop' could serve to express a conclusion that someone might draw. They could not, for the word 'since' introduces an argument, not an opinion which might be arrived at on the basis of argument. Now the word 'if', in the second of the two arguments, has the same function as the word 'since' in the first: it introduces a premise, not a conclusion. The conclusion is that the bus will stop and the argument to that conclusion is valid. Once we recognize that the word 'if' can be used, not to express a conclusion, but to add a further premise, there is no temptation to identify the valid argument 'Either this or that, so, if not this, that' with the invalid argument 'Either this or that, so, if this were not true, that would be.' These are two quite different things that the word 'if' can be used to do. One is to introduce a further premise, or, perhaps it would be better to say, to indicate a further premise that someone might be in a position to introduce because he knew it to be true. The other is to express a conclusion that may enable us to assess a plan of action, a conclusion of the form 'If that were true, this would be.' It was by discussion with Peter Long, another member of the seminar, that I came to that view of the matter. His own view is more complex. It is set out in a forthcoming monograph.

Unfortunately, it is not always possible to tell from the words someone employs which of the two arguments he intends. If he says 'Either you won't run or you will catch the bus, so, if you run, you will catch the bus' there is nothing about his words to enable us to judge whether he is trying to convince us that running for the bus would be a good plan on the inadequate grounds that either we shall not run or the bus will stop, grounds which might hold only because we are not going to run, or whether he is quite reasonably pointing out that if we know that we shall run he has information to contribute that would allow the two of us, putting our knowledge together, to complete a proof that the bus will stop. There is, however, a grammatical question we can put to him to decide the matter. Could what he intends be expressed equally well with the verb following the word 'if' in the subjunctive mood? If it could, then he intends the invalid argument. The sentence 'Either you won't run or the bus will stop so, if you were to run, the bus would stop' could not express the valid argument from the premise that either you will not run or the bus will stop together with the premise, supposed true, that you will run to the conclusion that the bus will stop. If what he intends could not be expressed in that way, then he intends the valid argument. The subjunctive mood for its verb is a sign that the word 'if' is being used in a certain way, to express the sort of thing we need to know in order to assess our plans, but the absence of the subjunctive mood, that is, the presence of the indicative mood, is not a sign that the word is not being used in that way. That is why the grammatical question may be required.

It seems that we must recognize, corresponding to these two ways of using the word 'if', two different things which are both commonly called 'supposing'. In one, we argue from a supposition in order, perhaps, to determine its truth or in order to determine what conclusions we could reach if we discovered it to be true. In the other, we argue to the effects and other consequences of the supposition. In supposition of the first kind, every truth is relevant. For example, once we have found something to be true that contradicts the supposition, then the purpose of supposing it has been achieved and the supposition can be rejected. In supposition of the second kind, many truths are irrelevant. I have been arguing that many truths about what will happen in the future are. The effects and other consequences of a supposition, which is what we investigate in supposition of the second kind, are what we need to know in order to assess the wisdom of bringing something about, of not preventing it, or of preventing it. It is what we need to know in order to decide, not whether something is true, but whether it would be a good thing if it were. Therefore the knowledge we seek when we make suppositions of the second kind is the most important knowledge we can have. If there is no such knowledge, then we never assess plans or act for reasons and, if science does not provide such knowledge, it is of no help in any practical matter. There cannot be knowledge of this kind if there are not facts concerning what would be true if, facts of conditional form. Science cannot provide such knowledge if it is no part of the business of science to investigate such facts.

It is surprising, therefore, to find that many people who have thought about these matters have concluded that there are no such facts and no such knowledge. Ayer was one of them, as a reading of the chapter 'The Problem of Conditionals' will show. There he denies that conditionals, which he speaks of as 'non-truth-functional conditionals', state facts or have truth values. Evidently nothing that lacked a truth value could be known to be true, let alone be part of the most important knowledge we have. I find it evident that we do act for reasons and do assess plans. I find it evident that science does provide information which enables us to devise means of achieving ends we could not otherwise achieve. So I argue that there must be such knowledge and such facts. It is important, however, not to ignore the case against them. Perhaps it is not strong enough to stand against the evidence to which I have just pointed but it must be cogent to have impressed people so much. In this lecture, I want to insist only upon the importance of questions of the form 'What would happen if . . .?' They are so important that, if they cannot be answered, no other questions have any importance at all.

Knowledge as a guide to action: the past

To assess a plan we need to know, not what will happen, but what would happen if the plan were carried out. Is it equally true that we need to know, not what has happened, but what would have happened were the plan were now carried out? The words 'What would have happened if the plan were now carried out?' have an awkward ring and some people reject the idea that they express any question at all. It is not easy to say why the awkwardness arises but there are good reasons against treating it as a ground for rejecting such questions. Perhaps the awkwardness arises from the natural expectation that when someone begins 'If that were done' he is about to make a remark about what would follow. That would show the question to be unusual but not to be unacceptable. Perhaps, again, the words 'What would have happened if the plan were adopted?' have an awkward ring because the question they express seems to have the same answer as the question 'What has happened?' That might lead people to identify the two questions, to forget about the more complicated one and to employ the simpler one in its place. If that neglect is how the awkwardness of the words arises, it is an awkwardness we should face, for there is good reason to doubt whether the neglect is justified. Is what would have happened if a plan were now adopted always what has happened? Is it, if what has happened prevents the adoption of the plan? When a bus has not stopped and its not stopping prevents my getting on it would seem to follow that, if I were to get on, the bus would, earlier, have stopped. What would have happened if I were to get on and what did happen would not be the same. That argument can be given a slightly different form. Although a bus has not stopped someone who did not know whether it did or not might say, with truth, that if the bus had not stopped I would not now get on. Argument by contraposition, of the form 'Since, if this were not true that would not be, if that were true this would be', is commonly held valid. If such argument is valid, then it may be concluded that if I were to get on the bus would have stopped. Once again, what would have happened if I were to get on and what did happen would not be the same.

Perhaps, yet again, the awkwardness arises because, when we wonder whether to adopt a plan, we are concerned largely with the effects of adopting it. To ask about the effects of a prospective action upon events that have already taken place does seem absurd, for it suggests that an action might affect what has already happened. However, it is not true that when we consider adopting a plan we are concerned only with its effects. There are circumstances which we know our plan will not affect, as the time at which the tide will turn is not affected by my rowing down the river, but concerning which we nevertheless need to know how they would stand if we were to adopt the plan. Circumstances before the moment for which action is planned will, of course, not be affected by our plans, but there will be much the same reasons for wishing to know how they would stand if the plan were adopted. The circumstances following the adoption of the plan may, indeed, arise from circumstances preceding it, as the turn of the tide arises from the entry of a tidal wave into the river mouth, so that knowledge concerning the preceding circumstances seems important. It seems possible that the feeling of awkwardness does arise from such a suggestion of causation but, if it does, the feeling is a misleading one. I am inclined to conclude that these questions cannot be rejected and may be important. If that is so, then the problem posed at first, 'Which do we need to know in order to assess a plan, what has happened or what would have happened if the plan were carried out?' is a real one. How should it be answered?

Suppose that I am on a beach from which it is dangerous to swim during the third hour after high tide, that the tide was high two hours ago and that there is a life guard on duty who would prevent me swimming if I attempted to do so. Would swimming now be a good idea? If I were to swim now, would I be in danger? If it is correct to argue from what has happened, then the answer is that swimming would be a bad idea and that if I were to swim now I would be in danger. The tide was high two hours ago and swimming in the third hour after high tide is dangerous. If, on the other hand, it is correct to argue from what would have happened earlier if the plan were adopted, then swimming would be a good idea and if I were to swim I would be safe, for if I were to swim the tide would not have been high two hours ago. Thanks to the life guard, I cannot swim during the third hour after high tide. The truth is, I think, that swimming now is a bad idea, for swimming now would put me in danger, but that, if I were to swim now, the tide would not have been high two hours ago so that I should be safe. In other words, swimming now would put me in danger but if I were to swim now I should not be in danger. Certainly, my answer seems a very paradoxical one. Can the appearance of paradox be removed?

The paradox is present because the question whether swimming now would put me in danger seems to rest upon the question whether if I were to swim now I should be in danger, yet I have suggested that the former is true and the latter false. In the last chapter I assumed that

what we need to know in order to assess a plan was what would happen
if the plan were now adopted. That assumption seems an eminently
sensible one. What could be wrong with it? This might be: that there is
a distinction among *what would happen if* questions, some being what
we need to know in order to assess a plan, others not. I shall attempt to
show that to be the case.

When I considered the example about my trying to catch a bus I
argued that the fact that the bus was going to stop did not show that if I
were to run to catch it I should get on it. The fact that the bus was going
to stop was consistent with the possibility that if I were to run to catch it
it would not. I want now to emphasize that, in the example, it is true
that if the bus were going to stop and I were going to run for it, then I
would succeed in getting on. It must be, therefore, that that fact,
together with the fact that the bus is going to stop, does not imply that if
I were to run for the bus I would succeed in getting on. Although if I
were to run and it were to stop I would succeed in getting on and
although it is going to stop, it may not be true that if I were to run I
would succeed in getting on. Argument of that form, 'if this and that
were true, the other would be; that is true, so if this were true the other
would be,' is called argument by exportation. Here it is the premise 'It
is going to stop' that suffers exportation. Such argument must in
general be invalid, since this example of it certainly is. This is important, so consider a more graphic example. You and I are on a see-saw, at
opposite ends. The one who is up can see over the fence. If you were up
and I were up, we could both see over the fence. Is it valid to argue: 'If
you were up and I were up, we could both see over the fence. I am up.
So, if you were up, we could both see over the fence'? That is argument
by exportation, where the premise 'I am up' is exported. Obviously it is
not valid. If you were up, I should be down.

Now consider the swimming example once more. If it were two
hours after high tide and I were to swim, I should be in danger. Is it
correct to argue by exportation that, since it is two hours after high tide,
if I were to swim I should be in danger? I suggest that this example of
exportation is as invalid as the other and that, although it is true that the
tide was high two hours ago and true that if the tide had been high two
hours ago and I were to go swimming now I should be in danger, it is
not true that if I were to go swimming now I should be in danger. On
the other hand, I admit that the conclusion that swimming now would
put me in danger can be validly drawn. How can argument to the latter,
causal, conclusion be valid if argument to the former is not?

That would be possible if, when we ask whether swimming now
would put me in danger, which is a question about causation, about
what effects swimming now would have, we were asking whether, if
things had been as they were and I were to swim, I should be in danger,

for that is not at all the same thing as asking whether if I were to swim I should be in danger. The answer to the former question is yes. The tide was high two hours ago, so that if things had been as they were and I were to go swimming I should be in danger. The answer to the second is no, since, if I were to swim, the tide would not have been high two hours ago. Since exportation is invalid for conditionals, these two answers are compatible with each other and together compatible with the fact that the tide was high two hours ago. If that is right, then although exportation does not hold for conditionals it does hold for causation. Obviously, that is what we always assume. When we want to know what effects an action would have, we look at the situation as it has been and as it is. We argue that, since the currents are strong, going swimming would be a dangerous thing to do. Confronted with a taut rope, we conclude that, since it is taut, a jerk at one end would produce a jerk at the other. We do not conclude that, since if it were loose and jerked at one end the other end would not move, a jerk at one end would not produce a jerk at the other. We argue that, since the atmosphere is present, a suction pump will draw water from a well that is not too deep. We do not argue that, since if the atmosphere were not present and a suction pump were operated no water would rise, a suction pump will not draw water from a well.

Peter Downing, yet another seminar member, who was the first to call attention to this difficulty concerning the relationship between conditionals and causation, drew a different lesson from it. His conclusion in the example of the high tide would be, I think, that the presence of the lifeguard does not show that if I were now to swim the tide would not have been high and, not showing that, does not show that if I were now to swim I should not be in danger. His view is that antecedents concerning times earlier than the moment for which action is planned can be validly exported from a conditional, those concerning times later than that moment cannot. That suggestion that the validity of an argument involving conditionals should depend upon the temporal order of the events with which the antecedents are concerned struck many people as a great implausibility. Not everything implausible is false, but the suggestion does attribute to conditionals in general peculiarities which might be thought to belong only to those concerning causation. For that reason a resolution deriving from the nature of causal conditionals seems better. By a causal conditional I mean one concerning what would be produced or prevented, if an event or action occurred.

If causal conditionals have the character I have suggested, then it cannot be that any later event produces or influences an earlier one, however firmly the two may be linked together. There is a link, it might be thought, that allows us to argue from the fact that a lighted match has been thrown into a tank containing a half and half mixture of air and petrol vapour to the conclusion that an explosion will follow. That same link allows us to argue from the absence of an explosion to the conclusion that no lighted match was thrown into a tank containing a half and half mixture of air and petrol vapour. The fact that the link enables us to make inferences as surely in one direction as in the other leaves many people puzzled about why we accept that throwing a match into such a tank would cause an explosion but would not for a moment accept that the absence of an explosion would prevent a match having earlier been thrown into such a tank. However, if, as I have suggested, the causal question is not 'What would happen if a match were thrown into such a tank?' but 'What would happen if, things having been as they were until now, a match were now thrown into such a tank?' and, correspondingly, not 'What would happen if no explosion were to occur?' but 'What would happen if, things having been as they were until now, no explosion were now to occur?', then when we ask what the effect of throwing the match would have been we do not assume that no explosion would occur, whereas, when we ask what the effect of there being no explosion would have been we do assume that a match would have been thrown.

To see this clearly, consider the situation in which a match was thrown into such a tank and an explosion followed. If my suggestion is correct, then it is not true that the absence of an explosion at the time at which the explosion occurred would have prevented a match being thrown earlier, since it is not true that if things had been as they were until the time of the explosion and no explosion had occurred, then no match would have been thrown. A match was thrown, so, if things had been as they were until the time of the explosion, a match would have been thrown. That explains why we accept that throwing a match into such a tank would cause an explosion but would not for a moment accept that the absence of an explosion would prevent a match having been thrown.

The suggestion fits well with the way we argue about causation and the way we assess plans. Probably anyone who saw that to ask what would happen if a plan were now adopted is one thing and that to ask what would happen if things had been as they have been and the plan were now adopted is another would choose the latter as the right question for investigating the consequences of adopting the plan and for assessing it. Unfortunately, it is difficult to explain why that should be the right question or to prove that it is. Perhaps it is correct, when considering what effects an event or action would now have, to consider what would happen if it were now to follow the things that have happened, but why would it not be more sensible to consider what would happen if it were now to follow the things that would have happened if it were now to happen? If the former is correct, it is easy to see that a later event cannot prevent an earlier one, but without an explanation of why it is correct, there is no explanation of why it cannot. Indeed it seems as plausible to explain why we ask about what would happen if, things having been as they have been, the event were to happen by pointing to the fact that the event could not affect how things have been, as it does to explain why the event could not affect how things have been by pointing to the fact that in order to investigate the effects of an event we ask, not what would have happened, but what would have happened had things been as they have.

That observation suggests that there might be another way of resolving the problem set in the example of the high tide, that of maintaining that to assess a plan the knowledge we need is always knowledge of its effects, of what its adoption would produce and what prevent. To answer that question, it might be held, what has and what has not happened and what will and will not happen are relevant, if the adoption of the plan would not affect them; if it would, they are not relevant. The fact that the tide was high two hours ago is relevant to the question whether swimming now would be a good idea because swimming now could not affect the time of the last high tide. The fact that the bus will stop may be irrelevant to the question whether running to catch it would be a good idea because running to catch it may affect the career of the bus. The fact that the tide will turn at five o'clock is relevant to the plan of rowing down the river because rowing down the river could not affect that occurrence. That resolution of the problem would introduce the temporal relationships between the things that have happened or will happen, on the one hand, and the moment at which the plan is to be adopted or the event to occur, on the other, only indirectly. The fact that later events cannot affect earlier ones would be invoked to explain why facts concerning what has already happened are relevant to the assessment of a plan, while those concerning what will happen may not be. Some facts concerning what will happen later, those concerning happenings that could not be affected by the plan, will be as relevant as those concerning what has already happened. However, this approach to the problem, sensible as it seems, faces a dilemma. If causal questions are questions concerning what would happen if, then the problem posed by the example of swimming from the dangerous beach arises, for that is an example of an event, the tide's having been high two hours ago, that could not be affected by the plan of going swimming but which is, nevertheless, irrelevant to what would happen if the plan were adopted, irrelevant because, if I were to swim, the tide would not have been high. Yet the idea that causal questions are not questions about what would happen if is difficult to accept. Even those philosophers, such as David Hume and John Stuart Mill, whose accounts of causation exclude all consideration of what would happen if, assume, when off guard, that that is what they are about. It is to that dilemma that the suggestion that causal questions are a special sort of *what would happen if* question, of the *what would happen in present circumstances if* form, offers a solution.

I conclude that there is an asymmetry concerning the knowledge we need in order to assess a plan of action. About the past, or, better, about times before the moment for which action is planned, we need to know what has happened. About the future, about times after the moment for which action is planned, we need to know what would happen if, things having been as they have been until that moment, the plan were put into effect. How things will be is irrelevant.

In the chapter 'Problems of Conditionals', to which I have referred before, Ayer discusses the argument of Peter Downing's on which I founded my example posing the question 'If I were to swim now, would I or would I not be in danger?' Ayer concludes that both answers are right. If you think that only one can be, he says, you are taking 'a naively realistic view of non-truth-functional conditionals.' But could it really be that questions we need to settle in order to decide how to act have two correct answers, 'Yes' and 'No'? If you think that, are you not taking a disastrously unrealistic view of human action?

If I am right, Ayer failed to see the importance of 'if', as so many philosophers have.

Ayer's Ethical Theory: Emotivism or Subjectivism?*

DAVID WIGGINS

1. In 1936, in a chapter of *Language, Truth and Logic* clearly influenced by Hume (though inconsistent with Hume) and influenced also (Ayer later conjectured) by Ogden's and Richards's *The Meaning of Meaning* (1923), Ayer claimed that judgments of value, in so far as they are not scientific statements, are not in the literal sense significant but are simply expressions of emotion which can be neither true nor false. To say 'You acted wrongly in stealing that money' is not to state any more than one would have stated by merely saying 'you stole that money'. To add that the action was wrong is not to make a further statement about it, but simply to evince one's moral disapproval. 'It is as if I had said "you stole that money" in a peculiar tone of horror, or written it with the addition of some special exclamation mark. The tone or the exclamation mark adds nothing to the literal meaning of the sentence. It merely serves to show that the expression of it is attended by certain feelings of the speaker' (*LTL*, 107).

Ayer adds that ethical terms like 'wrong' not only express feeling. 'They are also calculated to arouse feeling and to stimulate action' (*LTL*, 108). Some, for instance, like the term 'duty' as it occurs in 'It is your duty to tell the truth', may be regarded both as the expression of a certain sort of feeling about truthfulness and as the expression of a command, 'Tell the truth'. What distinguishes the phrases 'You ought to' and 'it is good to' from 'It is your duty to' is simply a diminution of emphasis that can reduce a command such as 'Tell the truth' to a less categorical command and then to a mere suggestion. 'In fact, we may define the meaning of the various ethical words in terms of the different feelings they are ordinarily taken to express and the different responses they are calculated to provoke' (*LTL*, 108).

2. What this implies about moral disagreement, Ayer says, is that, since there are really no specifically moral *statements*, strictly speaking (whatever their makers may think) there is no moral disagreement.

---

*This essay is excerpted, with kind permission of the editor and publisher, from a fuller treatment of the same matter, 'Ayer on Morality and Feeling: from Subjectivism to Emotivism and back?', to appear in Lewis E. Hahn (ed.). *The Philosophy of A. J. Ayer* (Library of Living Philosophers).

David Wiggins

'Another man may disagree with me about the wrongness of stealing, in the sense that he may not have the same feelings about stealing as I have, and he may quarrel with me on account of my moral sentiments. But he cannot, strictly speaking, *contradict me*. For in saying that a certain type of actions is right or wrong, I am not making any factual statement, not even a statement about my own state of mind. I am merely expressing certain moral sentiments' (*LTL*, 107, my italics). The quarrel feels like real disagreement, perhaps. But given the real nature of the conflict, which is revealed by philosophy, Ayer claims that there is no point in asking which of the parties is *in the right*.

3. This is the moment to say that Ayer's emotivism was shaped by his positivism. At the time of writing *Language, Truth and Logic*, Ayer held that every significant sentence was either analytic and, as such, the (however complex or indirect) upshot of symbolic conventions, or else synthetic and, as such, possessed of a content controlled (and strictly speaking exhausted) by the method associated with the sentence of accepting or rejecting the sentence on the basis of sense perception. Such a position leaves no room to construe moral judgments as declarative. So one cannot help but ask what we are now to think about positivism. The view I take of the matter is that logical positivism fails badly on both sides of the division it makes between analytic and non-analytic statements.

In the case of the analytic, its first difficulty is that, if we say that an analytic statement is one that is true in virtue of meaning, then, since our grasp of the meanings of most verbs, substantives and adjectives is actually *a posteriori*, it seems there is a real danger that most of the sentences that Ayer wanted to say expressed analytic truths will be *a posteriori*. If Ayer responds to this unwelcome conclusion by reverting to Frege's much clearer and less fugitive definition of 'analytic' (see Frege, 1953, 4) to say that an analytic sentence is one whose truth follows from logic and explicit definitions, then our second difficulty is that terribly few verbs, substantives or adjectives have the explicit definitions that Fregean analytically will require. This is surely a reflection of our grasp of these senses being empirically conditioned. And our third difficulty is that it is perfectly obscure, in any case, how the stipulative theory of the *a priori*, or any other account that seeks in positivist fashion to demystify non-empirical truths and cut them down to size in this way, can furnish an account of 'follows from' that will confer upon analytic sentences the property of *truth* (contrast the property of being an accepted stipulation) that analytic sentences aspire to. How in particular can they share in the very same property of truth that is enjoyed by non-analytic sentences, or stand side by side with the non-analytic in arguments that are advertised as preserving that property? How can stipulation confer on a sentence the same property that another sentence gets by empirical confirmation?

But that is not the worst of it. Further difficulties make their appearance when we pass from the positivist's attempt to explain all in one go how necessary truths have their meaning and status to his attempt to show how contingent judgments in general, or (coextensively for the positivist) synthetic judgments in general, are meaningful. If it is obscure (and surely it is obscure) how a species of brute sensation can sustain the meaning of a synthetic sentence, and if it seems arbitrary to try to delimit in advance just how far a meaningful sentence can sit from direct observation without lapsing into cognitive meaninglessness, then it is hard to find any non-arbitrary ruling about what else can sustain the full cognitive import or understanding of a sentence.

I conclude that the situation is this. It seems—I readily concede this to Ayer—that to every declarative sentence that actually declares anything there must correspond something that is at issue or something on which the truth of falsity of the sentence turns or depends. So maybe it is right that to every *a posteriori* sentence (indeed to every sentence) there corresponds some kind of test that can help, however weakly, in some suitable context to confirm it. Certainly there is something special about the test of observation. Observation is one of the things that can force us independently of our will, albeit not independently of cognitive background, into a belief or out of a belief. That is what we want truth to be like. That is why stipulation was so mysterious a way of making truths. But waiving any need there may be to qualify the claim I have allowed about every sentence possessing a test, the relation thus claimed to hold between cognitive meaning and tests of truth provides no remit for us to reverse the order of quantifiers and make a stronger assertion: namely that there is a kind of test such that, for every non *a priori* sentence, a test of that kind can confirm the sentence. For there is simply no prospect of rolling up once and for all, in terms of tests or observation as the positivist understands these (or in terms of any other single thing), the nature and extent of non-analytic truths. How *could* one delimit in advance the whole province of non-analytic cognitive meaning? We can say, if we like, that for every sentence there has to be *some* way that arises from its sense of making the claim stick that is made by the sentence. But at most this is a schema for the piecemeal criticism of different kinds of cognitive pretension.

4. If what was convincing in positivism can create no *general* presumption against the cognitive aspirations even of moral discourse, the next question is what sound reasons Ayer had to think that his emotivism was 'valid on its own account'. This is the claim he made in the 1946 preface for the second edition of *Language, Truth and Logic*.

David Wiggins

First, I suppose, there is the plausible point that it represents human morality as independent of revelation and as a matter to be determined by human assessment.

Second, emotivism is in harmony with explanatory (or Humean) naturalism, the sensible and defensible position (not to be confused with the reductive moral naturalism that provoked the passion and fury of Moore) that tries to see man as part of nature and tries to explain morality as arising out of man's nature and situation.

The third point is more special to morals as such. The emotivist theory delivers, vindicates and explains the independently manifest truth, (or so Ayer and I would count it) that, in tens of thousands of uses (even if not in all, e.g. as used in questions or conditionals or some past-tense statement etc.), evaluative sentences both express feelings and arouse feelings, some of these being feelings that are strong enough to issue directly or indirectly in action. Thus acceptance of a judgment *commits* us to respond in a certain way. Even if emotivism is not alone in having this merit, it vividly portrays at least some of the connections that exist between judgment and action.

5. These are substantial virtues in a theory of morals. Not only that. They are independent of positivism. The chief question is whether the non-descriptive analysis of moral language that distinguishes emotivism from its predecessors is essential to their attainment. The question is important because the non-descriptive analysis offered by emotivism appears both as the source of all the difficulties of the position and as inessential to the emotivist's claim that valuational language is expressive.

6. The non-descriptive analysis appears inessential to the expressiveness of moral language because in the right context I can surely express a feeling such as hate by saying in the right way, either to or about the person hated, any of all sorts of things. I can say imperatively 'There go my heart's abhorrence' or 'Water your damned flower pots do.' Or interrogatively, I can say 'If hate killed men, would not mine kill you?' Or simply indicatively, I can come out with the words 'You are odious'. In the right context (a Spanish cloister, an allotment, a back garden) any or all of these will represent expressions of hatred.

The non-descriptive analysis appears as a source of difficulty for emotivism for two reasons. First because one finds it hard to understand, along the lines that the emotivist suggests, the negative or conditional uses of valuational language or its use in judgments about things remote from all present concern. (Whereas a descriptive analysis would make it easy to understand these things and easy to predict which of the more straightforward uses are likely to turn out to be apt vehicles for the expression of feeling. All this will be especially easy if an account can be offered of how feelings enter into the determination of the sense of valuational language.) The second difficulty with the non-descriptive analysis offered by emotivism is that, if one looks outwards to real life, it is simply not believable that, when I say 'x is odious', all that I am doing is making as if to growl 'G-r-r-r!' at x. One can find this no more credible than that, when one makes the fully fledged and sufficiently reflected utterance 'That hurts', one is simply doing as if to say 'Ouch.'

On this last claim, I offer one more point. When I say 'x is odious', I give voice to a reaction in which I expect others to concur with me, and to concur not mindlessly but on the normal basis that this man really does 'possess qualities whose tendency is pernicious' (as Hume puts it, *Inquiry Concerning the principles of Morals*, Section IX, part 1). But surely I do then say something about x. Just as I say something when, instead of crying 'Ouch', I say I am in pain or that that hurts. When I say that I am in pain, I can expect to be asked how it hurts and how that resulted from whatever else happened to me. In each of these cases, the valuational and the mental, what one says in the fully fledged case can have its *origin* in something expressive like 'G-r-r-r' or 'Ouch'. But in the sophisticated language that we actually speak, things have moved a long way from that simple origin. If the declarative has indeed come into existence out of the expressive, it now has an altogether new relation to the expressive.

7. All these points about emotivism and its doubtful claim to unique possession of the three advantages it does possess I should labour much more if it did not seem that Ayer had come very close even in 1936 to conceding that one can express one thing by making the declaration of another (see *LTL*, 111), if the 'Grrr'/'Ouch' comparison were not suggested by what Ayer himself wrote, and if Ayer himself had not more recently, that is in 1984, volunteered another important concession. This is that there is even

something to be said for devising an assertoric form which could be adapted to the use of emotive expressions in conditional contexts and apparently deductive reasoning. Suppose that we render 'This is good' as 'This is to be approved of', where 'is to be' is construed in a purely prescriptive fashion. Then we can rewrite our examples ['if he did that, he acted rightly' and 'He would have been a better man if he had had a stricter upbringing'], admittedly in a somewhat clumsy English, as 'if he did that, he is to be approved of', 'He would be more to be approved of if he had been more strictly brought up', and [in the case of 'If A is better than B and B is better than C then A is better than C'], more straightforwardly, as 'If A is more to be approved of than B and B is more to be approved of than C, then A is more to be approved of than C'. This device has the advantage of locating the emotive reaction in the present, whatever the dating of its 'object', and whether the object is actual or hypothetical, and it also has the advantage of bringing out the prescriptive element in our use of ethical terms. (*FM*, 30).

It may be unclear that this quotation, conveying what I claim is the third of Ayer's three concessions, really amounts to what I say it does, however. So I shall offer a commentary on it before going any further.

Ayer says that that 'there is something to be aside for devising [the] assertoric form' ['this is to be approved of']. At least one thing Ayer means to discourage by his careful choice of language in the passage I have just quoted is the idea that the use of the assertoric form carries with it some automatic commitment to find full-blooded truth in normative or value judgments so paraphrased. In this I concur. That is indeed a further question. (See sections 12 and 20 below.) But what are we to make of Ayer's claim that in 'this is to be approved of' the 'is to be' is to be 'construed' in a 'purely prescriptive' fashion? Scarcely that the form 'is to be approved of' is a variant of 'Hurrah' that just happens— this being the *only* difference—to behave as a predicate. That would be tantamount to the denial that there was ever any difficulty in the first place. If such a variant were possible then we ought to have been able to do what we found we could not and understand 'Hurrah' itself *both* in the ordinary way *and simultaneously* as a predicate. But if indeed we cannot do that, then it seems that Ayer must be deemed to have allowed that it is possible for a value predicate to have transcended the condition of 'Hurrah' and to have graduated, with some corresponding semantic shift, to the status of a genuine predicate—the transition from 'Ouch' to 'That hurts' again points the way—and all this *without* loss of prescriptivity, i.e. without any weakening in the link between assenting and being motivated. But if so much is true, then surely 'is to be approved of' must really mean '*merits* or *deserves* approval' or 'is such as to make approval *appropriate*'.

The immediate importance of this is that it appears that, by 1984, Ayer no longer saw the rejection of the indicative construal of moral language as essential to the general view he wanted to take of evaluative judgments. In effect he had *given up* any idea that his position required any analytical reduction of moral language, still less any reduction of the normative to the non-normative.[1] One with Ayer's world-view need not dismiss ethics. (Of course, he never did dismiss it: he tirelessly debated ethical questions, from a broadly utilitarian point of view.) But he need not give definitions of its content. What he has to do is to try to

---

[1] Thus Ayer comes by his own route to anticipate a conclusion reached in different ways and with different motivations from his by John McDowell, (1985, 117–120) and by myself at p. 187 of 'A Sensible Subjectivism?', in (Wiggins, 1987, 187).

understand it better, first in its own terms and then perhaps in more ambitious terms (see below section 11 foll.).

8. So much for the commentary upon the third of three points I take Ayer to have in some way conceded about the special difficulties of emotivism, and so much for the possibility of gaining all the advantages of emotivism without actually embracing the claims that chiefly distinguished the position from all its predecessors. But in the course of the argument I think it has become plain that there is a further interest in the conclusion that Ayer arrived at so many years after writing *Language, Truth and Logic*. What we catch sight of in the passage from the 1984 essay is the possibility of a reconciliation between emotivism and an older position that went under the name of subjectivism. (I do not mean by this the position that Ayer calls subjectivism. Ayer means by 'subjectivism' the position G. E. Moore attacked but never even attempted to impute to Hume.) Such a reconciliation may be all the easier to effect if the older position can be brought to life by allowing Hume's authority to outweigh Moore's over what exactly that position is.

9. Ayer's 1984 proposal is that x is good if and only if x is to be approved of. (A suggestion we may see as furnishing a schema that one could elaborate further: x is [a] good [f] if and only if x is good [as among the fs] if and only if x is to be approved of [as within the reference group of fs] . . . and similarly *mutatis mutandis* for other value predicates.) Whereas Hume, for his part, declares that he defines virtue to be any mental quality that occasions an agreeable sentiment of approbation in the observer, and that 'when you pronounce any action or character to be vicious, you mean nothing but that from the constitution of your nature you have a feeling or sentiment of blame from the contemplation of it' (T.469).

There are similarities and there are differences here, and there is room for mutual accommodation. In so far as what we have here are rival models for the *philosophical analysis* of moral terms, Ayer's version obviously comes closer to satisfying the subtle and exacting standards of necessity and sufficiency to which Ayer himself worked and encouraged others to work.[2]

---

[2] I would also note that, if Hume's claims were amended on the model of Ayer's (using his 'is to be approved of'), the possibility would loom that Hume was not irrevocably committed by his subjective starting point or by his doctrine of the sovereignty of moral subjects to the claim (*Treatise*, 547) that 'There is just so much vice or virtue in any character as every one places in it and 'tis impossible in this particular *we can ever be mistaken*.' The subjectivist can say something more subtle than this. Hume makes a start upon this himself in 'Of the Standard of Taste'.

On the other hand, there could be an accommodation in the opposite direction. As Ayer himself perceived on occasions when he wrote directly about Hume, it seems that, even when Hume said he would 'define' virtue or vice, Hume's real concern was not definition or analysis as twentieth-century philosophers have conceived this, but explanation and commentary. Had Hume been confronted with the delicate questions of analysis that exercised G. E. Moore in *Principia Ethica* (1903) and *Ethics* (1912) and Ayer in *Language, Truth and Logic* then, so far from responding to them either with Ayer's device or with the 'x is good if and only if I approve of x' type of equivalence implausibly attributed to the subjectivist by Moore, he would surely have done best to respond by saying that, wherever taste or morals 'gilds' or stains natural objects with colours borrowed from natural sentiment' (*Inquiry into Principles of Morals*, Appendix One), what they raise up is always 'in a manner a new creation'—not, that is, something it is the business of the moral scientist (or of any sane philosophy) to try to define or analyse, but something *sui generis* that can be recognized as *sui generis* by explanatory naturalist and positivist alike. The philosopher's or moral scientist's business, he might have said, is not to reduce the content of what is said to something else, but to explain as well and as fully as he can the enabling conditions of its emergence (see below, section 11 foll.) and to determine in detail the contribution of feeling to the fixing of the sense of the language that conveys this content. Roughly speaking, value terms will have their sense by being annexed to that which in *the object* calls for certain shareable responses of feeling and action, namely the responses it *makes appropriate*.[3]

In proposing this possibility of alliance between Ayer and the tradition of Hume, I am asserting in effect that the important thing is to disentangle the central aims and insights of proper subjectivism—the real position of Protagoras, Hobbes, Hume and (I like to think) Ayer—from niceties of linguistic analysis that were as inessential to Ayer's world-view as they were to Hume's. It is true that it was an important theme of *Language, Truth and Logic* that the proper business of philosophy was analysis. (Yet another thing Ayer inherited from G. E. Moore.) But in time Ayer came to insist less and less upon this. (There are other signs, for instance in the 1984 essay from which I have quoted, that Ayer was in retreat from that general stand about the nature of philosophy.)[4] And in any case, as I said, we are invited in the preface to

---

[3] See notes 1 and 2.

[4] In *Language, Truth and Logic* Ayer had a fourfold division of ethical propositions. These were roughly (1) definitions (2) descriptions of the phenomena of moral experience (3) exhortations (4) actual ethical judgments.

the 2nd edition of *Language, Truth and Logic* to consider Ayer's moral philosophy both independently of positivism and strictly on its own merits. Once we acquiesce in that invitation and reassess the attractions of subjectivism in that light, I think it is apparent that subjectivism was not only a position that Ayer needed to borrow from (as he did) but a position he should have embraced on equal terms as an ally to his main philosophical concerns.

A further claim I would now make—but this is potentially more controversial—is that it would then have been open to Ayer, if he had proceeded in this way, to decide that it was not essential to subjectivism as such that the theory be introduced either by philosophical denials of the type with which Hume introduces the theory in the *Treatise* (some of these being wisely relegated in the *Inquiry* to an appendix) or by the *enfant terrible* pronouncements about moral judgments with which Ogden and Richards, Winston F. Barnes, Ayer and others affrighted polite society and the worlds of learning and letters. What really matters is not to issue shocking and imprecise denials but to elaborate and refine some positive account of the genesis in feeling and emotion of morality and moral language and then to study and improve an account like Hume's of how a social process that ignores partial sentiments, but reinforces sentiments and judgments which depart from our private and particular situation and appeal to the point of view that shall be common to one person with another, can cause there to emerge public standards, standards at once contestable and impersonal, for the assessment of personal merit and the discrimination of right and wrong acts. It may pose a problem for positivism that the moral language that is talked at the end of this process is fully as declarative in its aspirations as the language that is talked at the end of the process by which psychological states come to be singled out and described by their possessors. But it need not pose any problem for that world-view itself to which Ayer gave expression in his positivism. Or so I claim.

10. The position I am commending to Ayer is a naturalist position in the familiar sense in which Hume's speculations were naturalist. But it is not naturalist in Moore's sense, or in any sense that ought to have worried Ayer.

Reading G. E. Moore's *Principia Ethica* in the way I suggest we should read it (a way further encouraged and fortified by Casimir Lewy's résumé and interpretation of the preface Moore drafted for a reprint of *Principia Ethica* but never in the event published (Lewy, 1964)), a naturalistic property is *either* one with which it is the business

---

The analysis of (4) was the only thing Ayer invested with strictly philosophical interest. For Ayer's relaxation of this restrictive ruling, see 'Are there objective values?', op. cit. paragraph 3 following; also the sixth paragraph from the end.

of the natural sciences of experimental psychology to deal (cf. *Principia*, 40) or a property which can be completely defined in terms of such properties.[5] Naturalism is then the philosophical position that seeks to *define* good by predicates that stand for such naturalistic properties. But now one notes that there is simply no reason why the Humean position that Ayer's 1984 declaration revives should engage at all in such forbidden definitions.

11. Concentrating on what subjectivist doctrine positively asserts about the origin and basis of morality, rather than on what Hume and Ayer deny about the prospects of morality's constituting a subject matter in which there can be knowledge or truth, what I think we shall find is that the negative claim Hume and Ayer put into the exposition of subjectivism turns up rather in the guise of a real, undecided *question*, a question that has to be resolved by *working out* the consequences of the positive subjective view. Pending that working out, we shall have non-natural predicates with a distinctive sentiment-involving kind of sense, which may or may not turn out to stand for genuine or real properties. In the only serious and appropriate sense of 'real', they will stand for real properties according as whether the indicative form 'x is good' (etc) does or does not prove capable of sustaining a more than merely formal attribution of truth. Having sought in conversation with him to interest Ayer in my own view (expressed elsewhere[6]) of what it turns on whether or not value-statements can sustain such an attribution, I shall not however, pursue that particular matter much further now. For if we are to focus on Ayer's own views, it seems much more urgent to fill out the subjectivism we have recovered from his emotivism by drawing for this purpose upon Ayer's account of moral dispute and disagreement.

12. Ayer's account of moral dispute and moral disagreement may be reproduced as follows:

(α) We hold that one really never does dispute about questions of value. This may seem at first sight, to be a very paradoxical assertion. For we certainly do engage in disputes which are ordinarily regarded as disputes about questions of value. But, in all such cases, we find, if we consider the matter closely, that the dispute is not really about a question of value, but about a question of fact. When someone disagrees with us about the moral value of a certain action or type of action, we do admittedly resort to argument in order to win him over

[5] Then in *Principia* the idea of the natural is extended to the metaphysical. A metaphysical property is a property that stands to some supersensible object in the same relation in which natural properties stand to natural objects. See Lewy, 1964–5.

[6] See my 'A Sensible Subjectivism' and chapter 4 of (Wiggins, 1987 also, ibid. Postscript sections 3, 4).

to our way of thinking. But we do not attempt to show by our arguments that he has the 'wrong' ethical feeling towards a situation whose nature he has correctly apprehended. What we attempt to show is that he is mistaken about the facts of the case. We argue that he has misconceived the agent's motive: or that he has misjudged the effects of the action, or its probable effects in view of the agent's knowledge; or that he has failed to take into account the special circumstances in which the agent was placed. Or else we employ more general arguments about the effects which actions of a certain type tend to produce, or the qualities which are usually manifested in their performance. We do this in the hope that we have only to get our opponent to agree with us about the nature of the empirical facts for him to adopt the same moral attitude towards them as we do. (*LTL*, 119–20)

(β) '. . . if our opponent happens to have undergone a different process of moral 'conditioning' from ourselves, so that, even when he acknowledges all the facts, he still disagrees with us about the moral value of the actions under discussion, then we abandon the attempt to convince him by argument. We say that it is impossible to argue with him because he has a distorted or undeveloped moral sense; which signifies merely that he employs a different set of values from our own. We feel that our own system of values is superior, and therefore speak in such derogatory terms of his.' (*LTL*, 120; Cf. *LTL*, 2nd edn, intro., 22)

(γ) 'But we cannot bring forward any arguments to show that our system is superior. For our judgement that it is so is itself a judgement of value, and accordingly outside the scope of argument. It is because argument fails us when we come to deal with pure questions of value, as distinct from questions of fact, that we finally resort to mere abuse.' (*LTL*, 120)

(δ) 'In short, we find that argument is possible on moral questions only if some system of values is presupposed. If our opponent concurs with us in expressing moral disapproval of all actions of a given type t, then we may get him to condemn a particular action A, by bringing forward arguments to show that A is of type t. For the question whether A does or does not belong to that type is a plain question of fact. Given that a man has certain moral principles, we argue that he must, in order to be consistent, react morally to certain things in a certain way. What we do not and cannot argue about is the validity of theses moral principles. We merely praise or condemn them in the light of our own feelings.' (*LTL*, 120)

13. Here, as so often in Humean and latter-day subjectivist writings, one finds much to admire in what is affirmed positively about the

David Wiggins

nature and substance of morals and moral disputation [especially e.g. under (α)], but one finds precipitate and less persuasive the negative claims, which may or may not turn out to be correct when the subjectivist viewpoint is properly recovered and more fully developed. It may turn out that vindicating explanations of moral beliefs, explanations that explain the existence of beliefs by virtue of their correctness, can be mustered for the more important contentions of morality as subjectively conceived. Or it may not turn out that way. But until the possibility is disproved, it is premature to declare that the only response to deep-seated disagreement is abuse [see (γ)].

Another assumption that Ayer makes, and that seems unwarranted by the emotivist or subjectivist starting point, concerns the inner structure and cohesion of a moral outlook. Ayer's picture of a person's moral outlook in potential collision with the moral outlook of some other person is that of a tree-like structure, in which less general beliefs and context-dependent reactions to practical questions or to actions or situations, are directly or indirectly supported by one or more general attitudes which either *are* or *repose upon* fully general attitudes, attitudes that are pictured as basic, as mutually independent and (if not as immutable) as not mutable by ordinary moral persuasion. (Which, by having always to presuppose more basic principles, cf. (δ), is seen by Ayer as cut off from the scrutiny of the most basic, load-bearing principles.) But I should say that Ayer has no adequate reason to embrace this particular picture or conception. Conceiving morality as the subjectivist conceives it, Ayer should be wide open to the possibility that what sustains it is a vast multiplicity of sentiments of varying origin and strength, and he should be ready for the possibility that logically distinguishable feelings or sentiments (sentiments intentionally directed, sentiments that are thoughts) can be either loosely or tightly intertwined in the economy of feeling. Why should these not sustain one another *without* standing in formal relations of entailment? Why is Ayer not open to the possibility that in some cases, contrary to what he assumes, more general beliefs are sustained by much *less* general particular responses and tendencies? It is a matter of fact, an empirical question, not something to be settled by philosophical preconception (especially not by misconceived analogy with the case of a theory that is susceptible to being hypothetico-deductively presented), how to picture the structure of a moral outlook and how best to understand what happens when disputants with different moral outlooks find themselves in serious conflict over what to say about an object of shared attention or about an act that both agree that some agent has done. As long as this empirical question goes unexplored, there is *no clear thing to mean* by a distinction between fundamental and non-fundamental moral disagreements, and there is no reason to believe that, if we imagine two people agreeing over all non-moral facts but disagreeing in their moral reaction to some shared object of attention, then we are imagining a case where no scope remains for anything beside abuse. For any x and any y, for x and y to dispute with one another there must be something x and y agree about. No doubt. But perhaps there is nothing such that x and y must agree about this in order that they dispute—not even some basic thing. We do not, I repeat, know yet what 'basic' means here. For all that subjectivism says, perhaps x and y can begin almost anywhere. No doubt it is culture and context that combine with human nature to determine a moral outlook. But it is an open question what forms of moral argument this determination must in a given case foreclose or render for ever ineffective. In advance, there is nothing a subjectivist or emotivist is committed to think about *any* of this.

14. So much for what seems unconvincing. It is what Ayer says under (*α*) that seems fresh, admirable, and capable of taking on an altogether new life if Ayer's theory forms an alliance with subjectivism, especially if this is a version of subjectivism that accepts that moral thinking is as it is (namely persistent in what it sees as the pursuit of consistency, agreement and truth) and that leaves open the possibility that the moral is a subspecies of the factual, while at the same time refraining from seeking to ground the moral within the non-moral or searching for formal implications from the non-moral to the moral.

Ayer begins by boldly denying that we dispute at all about questions of value. But his real view is that we do dispute. All he wants to deny here is that for us to dispute is for us to seek to show anyone who disagrees with us the wrongness of their ethical feeling towards some act or situation whose nature they have correctly apprehended. Rather, what we do is try to show our opponent that he has misconceived what has happened or been done, or misconceived either the agent's motive or the circumstances in which his act was undertaken. We do *not* try to dispute with our opponent about right and wrong ways, as it were, of hooking attitudes of appraisal to agreed descriptions—as if moral disagreement standardly consisted in the participants to a disagreement being adherents of different ways of moving from statements of how things are to statements of how things ought to be or ought to have been.[7] For what is at issue is not normally a question of moving from an '-is-' judgment to an '-ought-' verdict at all. Rather it is a question of moving from some object or situation, concretely given, to 'good' or to 'ought' or 'must'. What is centrally typical of moral difference, including the moral difference that issues in actual disagreement, is that, in the face of one and the same action or context (some actual object of

---

[7] Even if isolated cases of this could be produced, the point is that they are not at all typical of normal disagreement.

awareness), different moral agents begin by bringing different sensibilities or different moral emphases to bear. They respond to significantly different properties or features of the object. Each can try to persuade the other to be party to his or her own way of seeing things, as Ayer says, and each can seek to understand the other's way. To this end, all sorts of things can be said or conveyed or pointed to. But, at least for a subjectivist, there is simply no reason to insist that what is said, either in the process of persuasion or in the course of justification of the stand taken up, should stand in a relation of *implying* the judgment for which the disputant is trying to gain favour. What the disputant mainly needs to do is to draw full attention to the saliency that engages with the sentiment which he expects the object to draw down upon itself, and which, if it does not already do that, he seeks to enable the other disputant to learn to catch onto when confronted with such an object. For in so far as the two disputants are within dialectical reach of one another, the language in which they dispute is language whose understanding *presupposes* the great fund of sentiments in which those who learn that language can learn to concur. What they have to find ways to do is to cause one another to exploit the *full* range, reach and resonance of these sentiments.

Here I think Ayer's positive claim (if I have not transduced it altogether by transposing it to the context of subjectivism) solves at one stroke the problem that so many of Hume's commentators have bogged down upon in their attempts to understand how, and with what putative special precautions, Hume himself proposed to get from 'the usual copulations, *is* and *is not*' to 'the new relation or affirmation' of an '*ought* or an *ought not*' (cf. *Treatise* 3.1.1). Ayer's proposal simply removes that problem by forcing upon us the thought that what disputants must focus upon is the object of attention itself.

15. Of course, Ayer's claim (α) postpones the question of what else goes on when moral disputants seek to get the measure of one another, and it postpones other business too. What the doctrine would have to do next is to say how property-mediated linkages between kinds of thing and kinds of subjective response are altered and refined in the processes of instruction and persuasion.[8] But that is not what I ought to attempt here. It is more urgent, if the alliance I have suggested is to have any claim to coherence or point, that I distinguish the objective/non-objective distinction, which needs (I claim) to be characterized in terms of the prospects of a class of judgments attaining substantial truth, from the non-subjective/subjective distinction. I suggest that the latter distinction may best be characterized in terms of the senses of certain kinds of sentences involving or not involving (or not always involving) for

[8] Hume's essay 'Of the Standard of Taste' points the way here.

their proper elucidation some allusion to the states or responses of conscious subjects. These distinctions are different, and they have *prima facie* different points. If we call Hume's position subjectivism, then this should be to evoke (in the first instance, at least) the non-subjective/subjective distinction, not the objective/non-objective distinction. For, if we concentrate on what the theory says positively about morality, then it leaves open such possibilities as this:

> The interest, on which justice is founded, is the greatest imaginable, and extends to all times and places. It cannot possibly be serv'd by any other invention. It is obvious, and discovers itself on the very first formation of society. All these causes render the rules of justice [i.e. such things as property rules] stedfast and immutable; at least, as immutable as human nature. And if they were founded on original instincts, cou'd they have any greater stability? (*Treatise*, 620)

This is a species of objectivity, and not one Ayer has any need to reject.

16. Confronted with this proposal of alliance and the claim that one might move forward from such Humean avowals (and his claim that between vice and virtue there is a *real distinction*) to something better than a merely nominal objectivity, I think Ayer would ask this question: If you think that ways of thinking can emerge and find their own subject matter; if you distinguish, as you have advocated that we should, between morality as the contribution of conscious subjects, on the one hand, and how that contribution represents things as being, on the other; and if you persuade us not to constrain the search for the thing represented by the criterion of observationality but rather by what you will claim to be the rational criteria that are immanent within the practices that make up that contribution; then is there any limit to what we shall end up countenancing? Could we not end up satisfied by saying almost anything about the absolute or Mumbo-Jumbo or whatever else at all? Could Mumbo Jumbo discourse not bring itself into being and then claim to have caught up with Mumbo Jumbo himself? What could one in the theoretical position you advocate say in criticism of the supposition that this had actually been done, and that Mumbo Jumbo himself had been 'identified'?

The reply to this question must hark back to my section 3 and what I claimed there about positivism. To every sentence there corresponds *something* that its correctness must turn upon, even perhaps some test that can help in some suitable context to confirm it. But this is consistent (I claimed) with there being no prospect of circumscribing in advance or once and for all what can *count* as a test or as a thing at issue. We have to take each purported case on its merits, and accredit or discredit it on these individual merits. What Ayer wants is some non-vacuous *general* criterion of success or failure. Is there such a thing? It would indeed be wonderful to have a substantial but completely general account of what can force us (malgré nous, as Leibniz would say) to believe or disbelieve something. But are we utterly lost if we cannot find this? Why can Ayer not see it as more than enough of a problem for those who want to talk of God that, habitually (or so one like Ayer or me might declare), *either* these people say nothing that even a disbeliever need reject *or* they put forward an account of things that is internally incoherent *or* they put forward an account of the origin and nature of the world that generates at least as many questions as it answers? Why is it not enough of a challenge to theology for Ayer to ask it to find a way to do better than that? If Ayer thinks it is not enough and this is Ayer's ground for rejecting the option I offer him (an option which leaves it an open question, remember, whether or not a subjective morality will admit truth, knowledge and objectivity, and which does not '*postulate*' its own adequacy to do that!), if Ayer insists that he must have belt *and* braces, then he will force me to suppose that he has not really given up the difficult old business of trying to establish the bounds of sense from within the bounds of sense. He will force me to doubt what I previously did not doubt, namely the separateness you remember he claimed in 1946 of his original subscription to emotivism and his original and (it will seem) residually persisting subscription to positivism.

Subjectivism and Toleration

BERNARD WILLIAMS

Bertrand Russell said more than once that he was uncomfortable about a conflict, as he saw it, between two things: the strength of the conviction with which he held his ethical beliefs, and the philosophical opinions that he had about the status of those ethical beliefs—opinions which were non-cognitivist, and in some sense subjectivist. Russell felt that, in some way, if he did not think that his ethical beliefs were objective, he had no right to hold them so passionately. This discomfort was not something that Ayer noted or discussed in his account of Russell's moral philosophy and ethical opinions, at least in the book that he wrote for the *Modern Masters* series (*RS*). Perhaps this was because it was not a kind of discomfort that Ayer felt himself. His own philosophical views about the status of ethics were at all periods at any rate non-cognitivist, and I think that he did not mind them being called 'subjectivist'. He did indeed argue that the supposed difference between objectivism and subjectivism in ethics did no work, and that philosophers who took themselves to be objectivists could not achieve anything more than those who admitted they were subjectivists. Ayer based this mainly on the idea that the claims made by objectivists for the factuality, objective truth, and so forth of moral judgments added nothing to those judgments—so far as moral conclusions were concerned, the objectivist was saying the same as the subjectivist but in a louder voice.

While, in this way, he thought that the extra claims of objectivism did no real work, Ayer did not conclude from this that the distinction between subjectivism and objectivism had no content at all. He did not reject the distinction altogether, because he thought that there was a meta-ethical view which he held and any objectivist would reject, namely that moral utterances were not fact-stating, were not (really) true or false. Indeed, in saying that no real work was done by claims to the effect that moral utterances could state facts, Ayer took himself to be disagreeing with an objectivist—so there had to be some difference between his own position and the objectivist's. The assertion of vacuity was not itself vacuous.

Ayer admitted that many moral utterances—the claim that someone was a coward, for instance—did have what on anyone's view would be a factual component: this, by a well-known style of analysis, was supposed to be separated out from the distinctively moral dimension of the utterance. He further admitted that in ordinary speech moral utterances were often called 'true' or 'false': this he traced to comprehensible prejudice. However, there is a problem about what more he supposed was necessary for them to be *really* true or false: that is to say, what it precisely was that, according to him, the objectivist believed and he did not. A diluted version of the verification principle was typically invoked here: if moral claims were really true or false, there would have to be some agreed procedures, inherent in the meaning of those claims, for checking up on them. This is what he had in mind when he attacked objectivism in the form of the intuitionism that was associated with the Oxford of his earlier days, in particular with Prichard and Ross. Because the intuitionists' theory provided no way of verifying the supposed truths of morality, Ayer held that a claim that we could have knowledge of them or reasoned belief in them was false, and from this he perhaps concluded that it was equally false to hold that they were truths at all. Since Ayer agreed that one could indeed hold moral views, it was implicit in his position, as in any other that denies truth-value to moral claims but does not reject them altogether, that one can hold a moral position (assent to it, etc.) without holding that it is true. If the attitude to moral propositions that one holds can be called 'belief', then there are propositions that one can believe without believing them to be true.

Ayer resisted this conclusion by denying that the favourable attitude to moral propositions is, properly speaking, belief. He preferred to express his position on this in terms of speech-acts; the claim was that the moral utterer (as such) was not stating facts, but rather doing something else. In *Language, Truth and Logic* the candidate for the other speech-act was 'expressing one's feelings'; by 1949 it was such things as prescribing, giving leave, showing oneself favourably disposed, expressing a resolution, and so on. Indeed from at least 1949 onwards Ayer seems to have adopted a simple version of prescriptivism, the kind of theory that R. M. Hare was to express in a more complex form in *The Language of Morals*.

This appeal to an alternative speech-act may provide a formula for avoiding the difficulties about belief and truth, but it does not provide (as Ayer and others perhaps believed) any independent way of understanding the claim that moral utterances do not state facts or have a truth value. People when they make moral remarks do not typically think of themselves as just prescribing, expressing a resolution, and so on—this may be illustrated by their ordinary use of 'true' and 'false', which was mentioned before—and they usually think it about others only when they think the others' claims are baseless. The philosophical theory that what people are (really) (only) doing is prescribing, expressing resolutions, and so forth, gets any force it has from the view, independently supported, that they cannot be stating facts. Indeed the phenomenology of moral thought is in some ways notably resistant to a prescriptivist interpretation, a point I shall come back to.

Ayer did introduce in 1949 the idea of having reasons for a moral prescription; this was supposed to make a wider range of moral comments comprehensible than emotivism did. As he put it:[1]

> In saying that Brutus or Raskolnikov acted rightly, I am giving myself and others leave to imitate them should similar circumstances arise . . . Similarly, in saying that they acted wrongly, I express a resolution not to imitate them, and endeavour also to discourage others. It may be thought that the mere use of the dyslogistic word 'wrongly' is not much of a discouragement, although it does have some emotive force. But that is where reasons come in. I discourage others, or at any rate hope to discourage them, by telling them why I think the action wrong . . .

There are several implausible things in this passage, for instance the idea that it is up to me to give someone leave to imitate these characters. More generally, there is something very puzzling in the idea that the considerations it offers could be enough to give a sense to 'why I think the action wrong'. What Ayer goes on to say does not give that content, but simply explains when I may be able to modify someone else's attitude. The connections between having a reason, giving a reason, and trying to persuade someone else, are a great deal more complex than this implies. In part, this is a problem left over from emotivism, and in part, a problem shared by prescriptivism.

It was characteristic of Ayer's outlook that the shift to prescriptivism did not do much more than suggest new modes of persuasion. It could have done more, by alerting Ayer to a different idea of objectivity, associated with the possibility that moral statements might express objectively universal prescriptions (as in Hare's later work and, in a different form, in Kant.) Such a view of course separates the question of objectivity from the question whether moral discourse is as such fact-stating: on the Kantian view, the correct moral principles and their foundation, the Categorical Imperative, are *objective*, because supposedly grounded in the requirements of practical reason, but they are not fact-stating, because they are imperatives. The objectivity is that of a construction, not of a discovery. Ayer never considered such a possibility. For him, in line with positivist concerns, issues of objectivity and of (roughly) cognitivism were always the same.

[1] 'On the Analysis of Moral Judgements', originally published in *Horizon* xx (1949), reprinted in *PE*; this quotation is from pp. 237–238 in that reprint.

Bernard Williams

Ayer insisted that his meta-ethical analysis had no implications for first-order moral thought. His argument for this was a standard prescriptivist version of the fact-value distinction, together with the claim that meta-ethical analysis, because analysis, is descriptive. Ayer was concerned to emphasize the point that the subjectivist analysis does not lead to a nihilist conclusion that moral considerations are trivial or unimportant. This was as near as he came to meeting, though he did not share, Russell's worry, and he was perhaps encouraged to make the point by criticisms from Christians, Cyril Joad and others who tended to accuse positivism of moral frivolity or worse. Equally, Ayer did not suppose that the meta-ethical analysis had any implications in the opposite direction; he did not think that subjectivist considerations might be used to support some more positive conclusions, such as toleration. This is another difference from Russell, who—in entirely comprehensible conflict with his worry about his subjectivism and the strength of his convictions—was disposed to agree with J. S. Mill that bigots were fortified in their bigotry by cognitivism, at least of some varieties.

Of course, even granted Ayer's assumptions, we are not told what philosophy should do: the assumptions themselves show us why they cannot tell us that. If we are to conclude, as Ayer and many other partisans of the fact/value distinction concluded, that philosophy is not in the business of morality, we need a further premise, which Ayer accepted, to the effect that philosophy is confined to analysis. Moreover, the idea that philosophy could not support any distinctive moral conclusions was helped by the belief that 'supports' had to mean one of two things: either 'entails' or, alternatively, 'by a statistical law encourages people to think . . .' Ayer accepted this too, another positivist legacy. That left it open whether the profession of certain philosophical views might turn out, as a matter of statistical fact, to encourage certain moral or political attitudes, and in this empirical sense 'support' them. But Ayer also seemed to think that if this did turn out to be so, it would not follow that the philosopher who professed the views had any responsibility in that direction—the misunderstanding was, so to speak, the hearers' fault. There is something innocent, or (on a harsher view) conventionally academic, in this outlook. The content of moral utterances is boldly reduced to their force, and their force virtually reduced to their effects. But the remarks of philosophy, the results of analysis, remain secure in their conceptual content, and mean no more or less than they say. Any effects they may have are seen as firmly separated from them.

Granted these views, it was something of an aberration when, in the Eleanor Rathbone Lecture that he gave in 1965,[2] Ayer explained in

[2] 'Philosophy and Politics', published 1967 by the Liverpool University Press, reprinted in *MCS*; the quotation is from pp. 259–260 of the reprint.

historical and political terms the fact that French philosophers had offered more (moral) views about politics than British philosophers had. He did not say simply, as he must have thought he was entitled to say, that British philosophers stuck to philosophy. Nevertheless, he remained faithful to the separation that he accepted between philosophy and first-order political views, and indeed enacted it with surrealistic exaggeration in this lecture. In the first part of it he ran through a well-known tutorial rehearsing thirteen reasons that have been given for why one should obey the law. He then moved to give, unphilosophically, an account of his own, somewhat muted, liberal views:

> In this matter I am like the rest; I have nothing new to offer. Only the old familiar liberal principles; old, but not so firmly established that we can afford to take them for granted. Representative government, universal suffrage, freedom of speech, freedom of the press, the right of collective bargaining, equality before the law, and all that goes with the so-called welfare state. It is not a heady brew. Such principles nowadays are a ground for excitement, a source of enthusiasm, only when they appear to be violated. For most of us participation in politics takes the form of protest; protest against war, against the aggressive actions of the major powers, against the maltreatment of political prisoners, against censorship, against capital or corporal punishment, against the persecution of homosexuals, against racial discrimination; there is still quite a lot to be against. It would be more romantic to be marching forward shoulder to shoulder under some bright new banner towards a brave new world. But I do not know: perhaps it is the effect of age. I do not really feel the need for anything to replace this mainly utilitarian, mainly tolerant, undramatic type of radicalism.

In this passage he is in more than one way unfair to himself. He is unfair to the vigour with which he indeed campaigned for these causes; he is unfair in the implication that aged 55, as he then was, he was anywhere near the end of his energies or his commitment to those campaigns. But perhaps the most touching implication of the lecture as a whole is its suggestion, contrary to the tenor of what he believed in philosophy, that if politics were more ideological, political philosophy would be livelier than it was—livelier, indeed, than the demonstration that he himself gave of it.

Another consequence that Ayer insisted did not follow from his meta-ethical view was relativism. In particular, the meta-ethical view cannot entail a particular kind of relativistic attitude, one that is marked by toleration of divergent moral practices. If in making moral utte-

201

rances, I prescribe, then I indeed prescribe, and for everyone. There must be some truth in this; toleration is a substantive attitude, and it is certainly not going to spring out of an analysis of moral language. Yet, at the same time, many people have thought, as (I mentioned earlier) Russell thought, that subjectivism could have something to do with toleration: that there was something more general to be learned from the fact that some bigots are particularly vigorous objectivists. Perhaps if we relax the notion of a 'consequence' somewhat, and allow a rather broader kind of reflection than Ayer allowed, it may be a real question whether consciousness of subjectivism should not have some consequences for toleration and, in those terms, for liberalism. This is the question I shall consider for the rest of this paper.

Some cognitivist views certainly provide added motives to bigotry, for instance by holding out hopes of divine reward, suggesting divine encouragement of zeal, offering assurances that the benighted are being assisted and so on. A more sceptical philosophy might hope to clear away some of these inducements, a point that has been familiar at least since Montaigne, and which is standard in Enlightenment thought. Ayer did not make much of this line of argument, perhaps because he thought that if the cognitivist content were identifiably religious, then the views would be 'factual' and not moral. The only moral element, on his analysis, will be the prescription to obey God or whatever it may be. So this might be said, if rather narrowly, not to be a point about moral cognitivism as such. Moreover, it is of course true that there could be other cognitivist considerations, whether of a religious character or not, that had a more tolerant tendency. But the broadly positivist outlook of which Ayer's subjectivism was part was devoted, as a progressive view, to rejecting myths, and among the myths it rejected were some that institutionally or psychologically opposed toleration. This constitutes an *historical* association, at least, between subjectivism and toleration.

I said earlier that prescriptivist and similar theories do not fit altogether easily with the phenomenology of moral thought. In part, this is because one's moral beliefs do not seem to be things that one acquires by decision. More broadly, the subject of seeking to arrive at a moral conclusion is left out. Ayer himself always presents the moral subject as already holding views, opposed to some others' views; the subject is not represented as in doubt about what views to hold. This does not allow enough for the part that is played in moral experience by such thoughts as that other views are possible, that they might be more satisfactory, that someone else could be right, that there can be explanations of why they might be right. To some degree, these thoughts encourage cognitivist or other objectivist pictures: the thought that I might be wrong and someone else might be right invites the further thought that there must be something that we can be right or wrong about.

However, thoughts of this kind may equally encourage one to reflect in a different direction, about possible moralities other than the one that happens to be one's own, and those reflections do not uniquely favour objectivism: they may lead us to some broader associations between subjectivism and toleration. 'A possible morality' means here not just an empirically possible human phenomenon, but something that could be acknowledged on the basis of one's understanding of human life as an intelligible solution to the requirements of a human society in certain circumstances. The thought that there are various possible moralities is perhaps compatible with some forms of cognitivism, but those forms are likely to represent the moral 'facts' as very general or indeterminate. If, however, objectivism—and not merely cognitivism—is false, the class of possible moralities is open. This is opposed to an assumption of standard morality, identified by Nietzsche, that morality is unique, the only morality—an assumption which is oddly carried over into the structure of Ayer's prescriptivism, where it is used in the way I have already mentioned, in order to shout down relativism.

To accept that there are various possible moralities does not, certainly, lead directly to a relativism or to toleration. One reason for this is obvious, that the content of a morality must to some extent determine one's attitude to other, and conflicting, moralities. If I am opposed to what, on my view of things, is called the subjection of women, then this does not leave me indifferent to the merits of moralities that practise, as it seems to me, the subjection of women. Not being indifferent, it is likely, equally, that I shall not be tolerant. This does not mean that I will support the suppression of these practices by force, but I may campaign against them, urge legal restraints, and so forth. Since this is obviously so, it may well seem that the relations between subjectivism and toleration do not extend further than an historical association. It may well be true that the same movements of ideas have supported both, and this is very comprehensible, but it may still be difficult to find any deeper connection between them. It is simply that those who hold subjectivist views also hold distinctive moral opinions, some of which, on certain matters, are more tolerant.

Is this all there is to it? The connections, it seems to me, can be pressed rather further. First, there is the consideration that on a subjectivist account of the matter, the function of holding a moral outlook is basically to regulate and define one's relations to other people. To the extent that this is clearly understood, moral outlooks will have a tendency to lose impetus if their expressions are not directed to people with whom one's relations need to be regulated and defined:

in particular, if they are directed to people remote in time. Subjectivism tends to support what I have elsewhere (1985) called 'the relativism of distance'. Cognitivism is less likely to be sympathetic to such an outlook: if the aim of moral speech is to set out how things stand with the moral, then distance in itself has no effect.

There are some results of this asymmetry, but they are not very spectacular. On the one hand, even robust forms of cognitivism can presumably embrace the thought that some moral truths are more worth announcing (by a given speaker at a given time) than others: addressing oneself at length to the merits of Brutus or the demerits of Caligula may seem just as pointless if you think that you are pointing out timeless truths of morality as it does if you think you are doing the things that Ayer thought you were doing. In fact, comments on the distant may come into question more with matters of general practice, concerning whole moral outlooks; but then it is very unlikely that *mere* distance will be the issue. There will be substantive social differences between the two situations, and then cognitivism can deploy familiar resources to explain why the same view need not be taken of two different situations.

It is true that there is a difference between thinking, as a subjectivist perhaps may, that moral opinions simply do not apply to the distant, and thinking, as a cognitivist can perhaps at most think, that judgments at a distance apply but may not be worth announcing. One difficulty in putting much weight on this is that the subjectivist may actually be reluctant to use his distinctive resources. As Ayer's own peculiar account of our relations to Brutus illustrates, once the question of the distant is raised, moral judgments seem to find it quite easy to work up the energy to reach the target. A sophisticated subjectivism will have no difficulty in explaining, in turn, that fact, but of course it cannot at the same time use the supposed asymmetry in support of its position: there will not be an asymmetry, but rather two different explanations of why there is not one.

In any case, a mere relativism of distance will not distinctively support toleration. The most that it could support would be a form of indifference, towards the distant. It can be said that indifference is actually inconsistent with toleration—if you are indifferent, you do not need to be tolerant. But that is true, if at all, only about tolerance as a personal virtue, not about toleration as a social and political practice. Indifference is no doubt one route to toleration as a practice; it can scarcely be denied that toleration of religious variation has increased with a decline of enthusiasm for religion and religious issues. But indifference *merely to the distant* is no route to toleration. Toleration essentially involves attitudes to those who are not at a distance, and the issues it raises are in the first instance issues for people living in the same social space.

Perhaps there is a different asymmetry between cognitivism (at least) and subjectivism, one that bears on the situation in which toleration may be called for. It may be expressed in terms of paternalism. On a cognitivist view, if X believes some moral P, and Y does not, X can have this thought: if Y were to come to believe P, not only would there be the advantages that follow merely from that change (among them, less conflict with me), but Y's views would be nearer to the truth. How much content there is to this thought depends on the type of cognitivism. But if there seems to be some content, this can (though it need not) provide X with reasons for making it more probable that Y acquire this belief, in ways perhaps offensive to liberalism. In particular, since Y can be credited with an interest in coming to know the truth, X can invoke paternalist reasons for helping to enlighten Y. If cognitivism is false, there can be no such reasons. Cognitivism adds a possible paternalist argument for altering others' beliefs.

This represents a real asymmetry, which is important as far as it goes. The additional paternalist consideration is no more than a possible addition, since cognitivism might have its own arguments for liberal toleration, such as an appeal to the virtues of people finding things out for themselves. This illustrates a general point which has come out already: subjectivism is unlikely to achieve any unique results in this area. For any consequence of subjectivism in favour of toleration, there will be some version of cognitivism or other forms of objectivism that can yield the same result. (This is one of the many phenomena that make it obscure, as these types of theories are progressively elaborated, how much distance is going to be left between them.) The only issue is whether there are features of subjectivism that make it natural, by more than an historical association, to expect it to support toleration.

It might be thought that this paternalism argument can be strongly generalized. Suppose a society in which there is a variety of conflicting beliefs about moral issues. Then, it might be argued, the subjectivist, on reflection, will see that an attempt to make the other parties agree with one's own view would be a mere act of will, whereas for the objectivist it would not. This is another application of the point made in the paternalism argument, that the objectivist has another description of what is going on when the other parties' beliefs change. But a mere act of will by one party against another must be inconsistent with the conditions of co-existing in a society at all: to curb such acts of will is a basic point of society's existence. Hence subjectivism yields, it may be claimed, from this obvious premise, an argument for toleration which is lacking to objectivism.

Bernard Williams

This argument cannot be sound as it stands. The sense in which any society is committed to curbing 'mere acts of will' is one in which such acts are contrasted with procedures that are supported by certain kinds of reason: 'I want it because it serves my interests' will not count as a justifying reason, while 'it must be stopped because it damages the interests of many' may serve as such a reason, and action done for that reason will not, correspondingly, count as a 'mere act of will'. But when the argument deploys from its account of subjectivism the notion of a 'mere act of will', this is a notion that applies to any act at all that is based on a moral reason; or, perhaps, to any act based on a moral reason which another party does not accept; or, at the very least, to any act which involves an imposition on another party and which is done for a moral reason that the other party does not accept. The idea of a mere act of will which is derived from a subjectivist account of what a moral judgment is, is not the same as the idea of a mere act of will as what is excluded by the basis of social arrangements. That is unsurprising, since the first is, as it were, a 'transcendental' idea, derived from the mere idea of a moral judgment, whereas the latter is based in a distinction between some kinds of reasons and others.

Can the argument be improved? It can be improved only if subjectivism, in some way or another, can make a contribution to the question of what reasons might, and what reasons might not, justify the suppression or other social discouragement of deviant moral belief and behaviour. If we ask what contribution might be made at that level of generality, it looks as though the only answer to be found would lie in the requirement that no justification could be offered that turned solely on the values of truth, or consist simply in the consideration that it was better for a group to believe the moral truth rather than moral falsehood.

But this restriction, beyond the bounds of the paternalism argument itself, can exercise vey little distinctive influence. In factual matters, after all, the claim that some theories rather than others should be taught in school, while it will be supported by the claim that those theories are true, will not be supported by that claim and no more; it will be supported by whatever reasons make one think that those theories are true. Similarly, the claim that some moral beliefs should prevail over others—at the limit, not permit the toleration of practices based on them—would be supported by the objectivist not with the simple claim that those beliefs are true, but by bringing forward whatever reasons supposedly support those beliefs; in the more drastic case, the further claim that the beliefs need to be enforced would have to be supported by reasons going beyond the mere claim that the beliefs were true. (If not, we are back in the territory of the paternalism argument.) An argument on the matter will be an argument about, and in terms of, the reasons: in the first instance, it will be an argument with the parties to be coerced, and if that argument breaks down, then reasons will have to be deployed among the other, dominant, parties to explain to themselves and to anyone else who may be interested why, in this case, they think coercion is justified.

None of those activities, in themselves, derives special strength or encouragement from either a subjectivist or an objectivist meta-ethic. These activities, of course, presuppose that the society is, broadly, in the business of giving reasons for its various moral beliefs and for its tolerant or intolerant practices. All societies must be to some degree in that business, though clearly they may differ a good deal in the extent to which that is so, in the range of groups between which reasons have to be given, and in the degree of specificity that is demanded for particular policies, as opposed to generalized appeals to legitimacy. If a meta-ethical theory is adequate to give an account of what it is for anyone to have a reason for any moral attitude, it seems plausible to suppose that it will have some materials in terms of which these issues can be discussed. If a version of subjectivism or objectivism can meet the more basic requirement of giving an account of reasons in moral discussion, then it should be able to give some account of the role of reason-giving in, in particular, a liberal society, and hence of the requirements and possibilities of toleration.

If this outline discussion is right, it looks as though, with the limited exception of the paternalism argument, there may be less intrinsic, as opposed to historical, connection between subjectivism and toleration than some have supposed. However, it must not be forgotten how important the historical connections themselves are. The mere fact that the question can now look like this, and adequately sophisticated versions of subjectivism and objectivism can now seem difficult to distinguish, is a tribute to the fact that more fanatical claims have been laid aside. It might well be claimed at this point, and Ayer might have claimed it, that the symmetries that seem now to extend over most of these matters are not themselves symmetrical in their implications, because it is various forms of objectivism, in particular religious forms, that have lost their fanatical impulse. It can be pointed out that it was traditionally objectivism that supposed so much to turn on the issue of the debate between objectivism and subjectivism, and if less now seems to turn on that debate, the significance of that fact is itself not symmetrical: it implies that objectivism, in particular, has lost some of its force.

No doubt paradoxes can be conjured from that statement of the situation. But Ayer himself, certainly, would have supposed that such paradoxes were a great deal less important than the fact that if fanatical religious intolerance (and with it, some particularly unrepentant forms of objectivism) is not prominent in philosophy, that is a point about philosophy, not yet one about the world. Ayer himself would have thought that this put these discussions into a correct perspective: he devoted a good deal more energy to the defence of toleration than to the discussion of meta-ethics.

An Interview with A. J. Ayer[1]

TED HONDERICH

Ted Honderich: Professor Ayer, you wrote *Language, Truth and Logic* when you were only twenty-four, in 1935, and achieved fame by way of it. Tell us a bit about the writing.

A. J. Ayer: After I'd taken my Schools at Oxford—I read Greats—my tutor Gilbert Ryle suggested that I go away for a couple of terms. I had already been appointed Lecturer at Christ Church, and I wanted to go to Cambridge to study under Wittgenstein, but Gilbert said no, don't do that. We've got a lot of people going to Cambridge and we've a vague idea of what Wittgenstein is up to, but I believe something very interesting is happening in Vienna, under Moritz Schlick. Why don't you go to Vienna?

I'd just got married for the first time, and I thought Vienna would be a nice place to go to for a honeymoon. At this point I didn't speak much German, but I thought I'd pick up some, which I did, and so I went and worked with the Vienna Circle. I couldn't really take much part in their debates, but I understood what was going on and came back very enthusiastic about what they were doing. They were extremely empiricist, very anti-metaphysical, anti-religious, and this suited my cast of mind very much. I immediately started lecturing at Oxford on—I think it was Russell, Wittgenstein and Quine. Russell was at that time almost a forbidden subject at Oxford, and Wittgenstein and Quine were people who'd not been heard of.

I was very passionate, and Isaiah Berlin said to me—Well look, Freddie, why don't you write a book before you lose your enthusiasm? I said—I shan't lose my enthusiasm, but it's quite a good idea to write a book. So I sat down and I thought to myself—Well, it's no good writing a book which isn't going to be published, I'd better get a contract first. I knew someone who worked in Gollancz's office, and I went and got an introduction to Gollancz, and interviewed him, and said, very brashly—I'm going to write a book you'll want to publish. He was slightly surprised, but to get rid of me, I think, gave me a contract. I

[1] This interview was recorded on 27 April 1989 and was subsequently broadcast on BBC Radio 3. The transcript of the interview has been edited by Ted Honderich. (Further footnotes are added by the volume editor.)

wrote the book, and eighteen months later, when I was twenty-four, I gave it to him.

He was horrified. At that time he was only interested in politics and not in philosophy. He thought nobody would want to read this book, so he published an edition of 250 copies, or maybe it was 500. And they were sold out in a month. He thought—By Gum, people are mad! He published another 250 copies and they were sold out. And in the end, up to the war, the book went to as many as four impressions, but only 2,000 copies of it in all.

TH: Were you pleased with the controversy it created? Was it attacked immediately?

AA: Not really seriously. It was attacked by a man called Tomlin,[2] who was a sort of amateur metaphysician, in *Scrutiny*, Leavis's periodical. He attacked it savagely, but otherwise, it got rather good reviews. It particularly got a very good review from Susan Stebbing in *Mind*. There were attacks, but not much in public. There was one really interesting episode—slightly flattering to me, but I will repeat it—in Blackwell's, the bookshop in Oxford.

There were two terrible old monsters called Pritchard and Joseph, both pupils of Cook Wilson, who were dominating philosophy at Oxford at that time, and very, very reactionary. Pritchard wasn't a bad moral philosopher. Joseph was a great tremendous counterpuncher, and William James said of him 'I often feel that Mr Joseph pounces on my words before they get out of my mouth.' He was exactly like that. They disliked everything that was new, or had anything to do with Cambridge.

They were in Blackwell's and my book had just been published, and they were saying—Oh, how disgraceful, the publishers will publish anything these days. This book should never have been published. Collingwood, Professor of Metaphysics at that time, an Idealist himself, was standing by and he said—Gentlemen, this book will be read when your names are forgotten. That's true, but the episode didn't endear me to them.

TH: What would you say have been the effects on your life of having early intellectual fame?

AA: Well, I didn't have so much fame, you see, at that time. The book was a success in a fairly narrow circle of some professional philosophers, but great success only came a good deal later, after the War.

[2] Tomlin, 1936.

Gollancz let it go out of print during the war, and I wrote to him saying was he going to reprint it, and he said he would if I wrote a new introduction. I did. And then it took off, in about 1947. I began to become famous.

TH: One might think it's a bit of a disadvantage to have a burst of intellectual fame so early on. One must feel the rest of one's life is perhaps a running-down?

AA: But I didn't really have a great burst of intellectual fame. I became fairly celebrated in the profession, but I didn't become a public figure until very much later, in the '50's, by which time I had become Grote Professor at University College, where in fact you first met me. I was already then over forty years old, and became famous through appearing on a television programme called The Brains Trust. Otherwise, I was well-known only in the philosophical world. I've never had an exaggerated opinion of myself as a philosopher. I think I'm good. In Scottish football for example, they have a Premier Division, a First Division and a Second Division. In the Premier Division, in this century, I put Russell and Wittgenstein. I put myself, Ryle, Quine, etc. in the First Division.

TH: That is a decent standing. To go back to before *Language, Truth and Logic*, do you remember a first encounter with philosophy, a first encounter with a philosophical argument or problem, perhaps at Eton?

AA: Yes indeed. I was a classical scholar at Eton and read Plato. We were taught Plato pretty well but only for the Greek—I mean, philologically. I was interested also in the ideas, and that introduced me to philosophy. Also, we had a master who had come from Oxford, no from Cambridge, I think. He gave us some lessons on the pre-Socratics, not for examination purposes, just for fun. I enjoyed those. But I think even before that, I discovered philosophy on my own.

The first book I ever read was Bertrand Russell's *Sceptical Essays*,[3] with that marvellous beginning— I can't quote it verbatim—to the effect that he was going to propose something extremely revolutionary, that one shouldn't believe a proposition if there was no reason for thinking it true. (This he said would destroy all the income of bishops and so on.) I've always believed that. I also at that time was interested in aesthetics—an interest I've not kept up—and I read Clive Bell's little book on art. He defends the view that beauty, like good, is an unanalysable non-natural quality. He says that for the arguments in

[3] Russell, 1928.

211

favour of this view, he recommends Moore's *Principia Ethica*.[4] I dutifully went out and bought it, and for several years, I believed Moore. Only in my second year at Oxford did I realize that this view was untrue.

TH: Do you think that you've always been attracted to the audacious in philosophy, perhaps out of your personality? As some might say, attracted to the audacious at the expense occasionally of truth?

AA: I hope never at the expense of truth. Not anyhow voluntarily at the expense of truth. I think I've always been fairly brave intellectually, yes. Rather inclined to—well, to be sceptical about traditional views. As a boy, I was a very militant aetheist from the age of about sixteen onwards.

TH: You have a place in the tradition of British Empiricism, the philosophy founded by Locke, Berkeley and Hume, and carried forward by John Stuart Mill and Bertrand Russell. How would you characterize that tradition?

AA: I think it's a commonsensical tradition. Even Berkeley, who was as you know a Subjective Idealist, thought he was the very epitome of commonsense. It has respect for science, though not too much respect—Berkeley being the exception. Sticking close to the facts, and close to observation, and not being carried away by German Romanticism, high falutin' talk, obscurity, metaphysics. It's a tradition, on the whole, of good prose. That is very important. If you write good prose, you can't succumb to the sort of nonsense we get from Germany and now also from France.

TH: It is remarkable that commonsense, as you call it, should issue in such extravagant conclusions as Berkeley's and perhaps one or two of your own?

AA: Well, the conclusion is not all that extravagant. Berkeley's conclusions arise out of Phenomenalism, the theory that in the end, everything we say can be analysed in terms of what's immediately observed. This is in a way very practical. Berkeley's argument against Locke was that Locke took away our ordinary chairs that we look at and sit on, in favour of a notion of matter that wasn't commonsensical at all. Berkeley, in restoring the phenomenal world, the things having colour

---

[4] Moore, 1903.

and sound and so on, was much closer to the man in the street than Locke had been.

TH: Still, all in the mind.

AA: Yes, well we have to bracket that.

TH: Might this British empiricism be regarded as a bit insular in more than a literal sense?

AA: I don't think it's literally insular. It isn't exclusively British. You find it in America. It's very interesting how close the Logical Positivism which I am supposed to be the chief exponent of, anyhow in this country, is to pragmatism. If you read a book like Lewis's *Mind and the World Order,*[5] it's a pragmatist book. Or even C. S. Peirce's early pragmatist essays. They're very close to what the Vienna Circle was saying and very close to what I said in *Language, Truth and Logic.* In fact my book could have been a pragmatist book. You get much the same view in Scandinavia. They have a tradition the same as ours. Hard-headed, empiricist, knowing their facts, dubious of metaphysics. British Empiricism is insular in the sense that it has its counterpart in political attitudes in England and so on. We are on the whole a people rather sceptical of high-falutin' talk.

TH: If you will let me speak of four periods or episodes in your philosophical career, they might be said to be Logical Positivism, Phenomenalism, an Epistemological period, and finally something I would like to call Constructionism. The first of those, Logical Positivism, has as its centre the Verification Principle. You struggled a long time with the formulation of the Verification Principle. What do you take to be its best brief formulation now?

AA: It was a theory of meaning or the centrepiece of a theory of meaning, according to which what could be significantly said was divided into two classes. First of all, sentences that expressed propositions that were formally true, like those of logic and mathematics. Following Wittgenstein, we adherents of the principle took these propositions to be saying nothing about reality. If I tell you either it's raining or not raining, I'm not telling what the weather is. Apart from that, we required of a proposition that it should be testable by observation.

The difficulty in formulating the principle perhaps hasn't yet been solved, although Crispin Wright has come up now with a bit of formula

[5] Lewis, 1929.

that looks to me to be possibly watertight. The difficulty has been that any attempt to formalize confirmation has so far been such that it allowed anything in. My original attempt was very crude. A more sophisticated attempt was shown by Alonzo Church also not to be immune from this very fatal objection. But of course, this doesn't really destroy the principle. The notion of confirmation is quite a good one, even though it can't be defined in terms of logical deduction, which was what I tried to do.

TH: At the very centre, the idea is that an utterance has a truth value only if it is, as you say, analytic—necessarily true, a matter of the meanings of words—or alternatively, it is in the second category, verifiable by sense experience.

AA: Yes, that's what I held.

TH: Why did you put it in a rather different and much more dramatic way—something is *meaningful* only if either analytic or verifiable by sense experience?

AA: I think I was vey much influenced—perhaps not altogether consciously, because I made no acknowledgment to them—by Ogden and Richards' *Meaning of Meaning*,[6] which had come out in the early '20's. They divided meaningful utterances into two classes, those that were literally meaningful, and those that were only meaningful, as they put it, emotively. I said when I put the Verification Principle forward that it was a criterion of literal meaning, not meaning in general. I also had emotive meaning for moral propositions.

TH: All of that excluded as either true or false religious utterances, moral utterances and various other utterances. What is your attitude now to the question of the nature of moral judgments?

AA: I've never put religion and morals together. I always said that religion was absolute verbiage. It might possibly have some poetical meaning, but that is all.

TH: Do you still think that 'God exists' . . .

AA: Oh no.

TH: . . . is neither true nor false?

[6] Ogden and Richards, 1923.

214

AA: No. Well, I think on many interpretations it's neither true nor false, just nonsense. But I think you can treat, if you're very careful, the affirmation of God's existence as a vacuous hypothesis, in which case it would be, I suppose, false. And you could explain everything that happened in the world in terms of purely psychical occurrences—a series of experiences that you then thought of as preceding everything else, and somehow causally responsible for everything else. This would not be satisfactory to religious people who wanted to believe in a transcendant deity, and also would be hopeless because it wouldn't explain anything.

TH: Right.

AA: I would now say—Well, if it offends people to call religion nonsensical, let's call it false. I've become much milder in my old age. As for morals, I hold my old view. I published a book about ten years ago—perhaps a little less—in which I said I thought that my old theory of ethics was still better than anything else.

TH: Which is to the effect that moral judgments are expressions of emotion?

AA: Well I've widened that a bit. Expressions, say, of attitude, and also prescriptive.

TH: Speaking of a related matter, politics, are you now returning to the fold of the Labour Party?

AA: Well, I'm in no man's land at the moment. Having been a Labour supporter since the middle '30's, and twice I think offered myself for election to local government in Westminster—once managing 24 votes—I joined the SDP, if it was called that then. They seemed perfectly right at the moment. The Labour Party had made an absolute fool of itself, and the Conservatives were unspeakably awful—they still are. I thought the SDP showed some hope. But now, it's gone into a nothing. I don't like the Labour Party, I don't think they've got themselves together yet, but I think I probably will rejoin it sooner or later.

TH: Let us leave that scene of disaster and come back to a matter of greater importance, what I spoke of as a second episode in your thought, Phenomenalism. It might even be called solipsism. What I had principally in mind was your book *The Foundations of Empirical*

Knowledge, published at the beginning of the war. The idea is that what each person is aware of in experience is private to that person. As you and I peer out of the window, what each of us is immediately aware of is a separate and distinct thing. Might you expound something of that outlook, Phenomenalism or solipsism?

AA: Well, it's perhaps a somewhat unfair way of putting it, because most phenomenalists don't at all want to be solipsists. On the contrary, try their utmost to avoid solipsism.

TH: Still, according to the view I'm in my private world of experience, and you're in your private world of experience.

AA: Well this probably is true in any case. But let's take it a little slower. Phenomenalism was a theory held by Berkeley, I suppose, if you deprive him of God. In a way, it was held by Hume, though not explicitly. It was certainly held by Mill, held at one time by Russell, very nearly held by my predecessor at Oxford—Henry Price—and certainly at the outset by me. And by Schlick of the Vienna Circle as well. It is the theory that everything that's said about ordinary commonplace objects, chairs and tables, etc., can be translated into a series of statements about what Russell and Moore called sense-data.

The difficulty is that if you regard these data as private, you are in danger of reaching the conclusion that everything you say refers to your own actual and possible experience. I mean it's very hard to see how you can have any reason to believe in the existence of other people. On this view, you will be constructed out of my sense data, and I'm not quite clear how I can indeed intelligibly ascribe to you a similar experience of your own. This is a problem all Phenomenalists have wrestled with. I came to the conclusion, just after the War, that Phenomenalism wouldn't work. You couldn't carry out the translation.

TH: Let us save that. We'll come on to your development of the later view.

AA: All right. Anyway, I was left with the problem, which has been with me all my career, of justifying my belief in other minds. In *Language, Truth and Logic*, I took a view which is actually inconsistent. I said my own experiences had to be interpreted mentally, and yours would have to be interpreted behaviouristically. But I then generalized this and said this is true of everybody. This was incoherent. If I can only understand the statements about your experiences behaviouristically I can't suppose that you understand them mentally, because your understanding of them mentally would have no meaning for me. I got into this hopeless position, pointed out by one of my pupils, a psychologist called Martin Shearn. I tried various expedients and never quite got round it. And then I thought—well, my way round this problem comes in my Constructivism, and I don't know whether you want to get on to that?

TH: We will indeed get to it, but first could we spend a moment more on your phenomenalist period, and an attack made on *The Foundations of Empirical Knowledge* by J. L. Austin, who was the doyen of Ordinary Language Philosophy. In retrospect, what do you think of his attack on your Phenomenalism in his book *Sense and Sensibilia*?[7]

AA: I think it's full of good jokes. I think it's philosophically very weak indeed. And in fact, I replied to it at great length in an essay called 'Has Austin Refuted the Sense-Datum Theory?' which I published in a Swedish journal and reprinted in one of my books. I think it's in *Metaphysics and Commonsense*. Anyhow, I picked out fourteen arguments that Austin could be supposed to have put forward—I was a bit generous to him there—and refuted them all. I think it was, as a serious piece of philosophy, not worthy of him. I had a high respect for Austin. I thought he was very clever. I think one of his books, *How To Do Things With Words*,[8] is interesting, and some of his articles are interesting, but *Sense and Sensibilia* I thought was a poor book. Not because he attacked me. I didn't mind that at all. The arguments are very bad. To do him justice, he never would have published it in that form. It was published posthumously by his faithful followers—I think Warnock in this case. I think Austin would never, never really let it appear in that form. He was far too clever.

He also really disliked philosophy. He was a philologist, and he thought that people should not be bothering themselves with these philosophical questions but should be studying language. I was one of the rivals to his view. I was taking philosophy seriously. Any stick was good enough to beat me with. He got his laughs from his audience at Oxford, from his lectures, and they went away thinking—Oh, sense-data, that's all rubbish—putting aside not just me but a whole tradition of philosophy ever since Descartes.

Why would Descartes, Locke, Berkeley, Hume, Mill, Russell, Moore—not all of them fools—believe in sense-data philosophy if it was really such an absurdity as Austin made out? He only attacked two pages of my book, the first two pages. That was enough for the whole

[7] Austin, 1962.
[8] Austin, 1971.

series of lectures which he repeated year after year until I came to Oxford. That was a shoddy performance.

TH: The *Foundations of Empirical Knowledge* was published at the beginning of the war. To speak of the war, briefly, were you a good spy?

AA: Not really, no. I started out much more grandly as a Guards Officer. I started out as a Guardsman Recruit. I corrected the proofs of that book in the barrack room. I said to Sergeant Jackson, my Squad Sergeant—Sergeant Jackson, can I put your name in the Preface of my book, mention Sergeant Jackson's squad? He said—You're not going to make a bloody fool of me. I said—Sergeant Jackson, I offer you a chance of immortality. He wasn't having it.

TH: Still, you went on to do a bit of spying after that didn't you?

AA: Well, after about two years' masquerading as a Guards Officer, it was discovered I spoke languages. I was sent to America—I spoke Spanish at that time—to go down to South America and put poison in the coffee-cups of Nazis and so on. I was trained in unarmed combat. At that stage I could in theory have killed someone with my bare hands. (It seemed to me to depend, though, on their doing nothing in self-defence.) I never put it to the test. But then the Americans came into the war, and said they weren't having any Limeys killing people in South America. The only killings that were going to be done they were going to do themselves. So I stayed in New York for about a year, just collecting intelligence from South America. Then I felt guilty and came back to England. They sent me to West Africa on a totally fruitless mission.

Finally, I did get into the French Section, as I am almost bilingual, and I did end up in France, but not really dangerously. I went in with the Americans, in the Southern landing, in August '44, and was a Liaison Officer with the French Resistance. By that time the Germans were all in retreat. I can't say I was ever in any serious danger. I had a good, amusing time, particularly when I raised a little private army and was proposing to invade Spain, but then my office arrested me and . . .

TH: Why?

AA: . . . they sent me back to England.

TH: I think that after the war, having survived the war, you then suffered excommunication by Ludwig Wittgenstein?

AA: Well, yes. That was a sad business really. I'd been taken by my tutor, Gilbert Ryle, to see Wittgenstein, as early as 1932. I was very impressed by him. I had been enormously impressed by the *Tractatus* and I was very impressed by Wittgenstein personally. He had a very, very strong personality, and piercing blue eyes. He lived in a little monk-like cell, on a staircase in Trinity Cambridge. Gilbert Ryle took me up to him and they gossiped for a bit. Then Wittgenstein suddenly turned to me and said—What was the last book you read? It could easily have been Agatha Christie, but fortunately it wasn't. I truthfully said it was Calderon's *La vida es sueño*⁹—*Life is a Dream*. Wittgenstein was very impressed by this, particularly when I said I didn't understand it very well, meaning my Spanish wasn't very good. He thought I was saying it was too profound for me. He thought I was a marvellous person. Throughout the '30's, whenever I went to Cambridge, he attended my meetings. He would say I think what Ayer means is this, and then say something much cleverer than anything I'd meant, and I would rather wickedly nod—Yes, that's what I meant.

But then, alas, I published a lecture in which I referred, perhaps slightly flippantly, to the conclusion of the *Tractatus*, which was that philosophers could only wait till someone has said something and then say it was not nonsensical. I went on to say I didn't know what Wittgenstein was then writing, but I understood it was rather assimilating philosophy to psycho-analysis. I then went on to talk about his pupil—well, not his pupil, but his colleague, John Wisdom—and this was what offended him. He denied that his method was like that of psycho-analysis—I think perhaps not quite truly. He couldn't bear being compared to anybody else, let alone someone junior to himself at Cambridge, Wisdom. So he excommunicated me.

When I went to Cambridge a week later, to read a paper, he attended the meeting but wouldn't speak to me, spoke only to Wisdom, and then stalked out of the room, with a great clatter, followed by Miss Anscombe. He pretended afterwards never to have heard of me. It was very, very sad. But he was an extraordinary man. He was perhaps not a very nice man, though I think a genius.

TH: To come on to your third period, as we're calling it, what I have in mind is the book *The Problem of Knowledge*, published in 1956, which I think you sometimes have spoken of as your best book. It is essentially an epistemological book, about the nature of knowledge and the question of how far our claims to knowledge can be justified. Have your views changed a lot about, say, memory and scepticism?

⁹ Calderon, 1876.

AA: About memory, I think not at all. Did I have a special view of memory there? I think I have the same view of memory I always had. I always think that memory can't be justified in anything but a circular fashion. I mean, you can correct one memory by another, but you can't justify memory in general. I think I've always held that, and still do hold it. I still think that talking of direct access to the past is a fraud. It just means that you have memories that you trust.

As to Scepticism, I do take it still very, very seriously. I think the chief merit of my book, and its chief originality, was that it did show the whole Theory of Knowledge as a set of different answers towards a standard sceptical argument. The sceptical argument being that in every case, our conclusions make an impossible jump from the premises. We get to the external world by making, according to the sceptic, an unjustified leap from sense-data. At another level, we get to other minds making, according to the sceptic, an unjustified leap from physical behaviour. We get to the past through making an unjustified leap from present memory-images. We get to the future by relying on an unjustified method of induction. I think that the way I did that was very good. I do think it is the best thing I've done. Well, that and Constructivism perhaps—we're coming to that. But I think I cheated and took away from the Sceptic the victory he'd won, like a bribed referee at a boxing match.

TH: What the sceptic essentially says is that the premises don't entail the conclusion. My present recollection of having left Hampstead this morning, doesn't mean that it is actually true that I did leave Hampstead this morning. But one might say—Who cares? You're putting much too strong a test on our knowledge or . . .

AA: Oh no, you're underrating the sceptic's argument. He says not only is there no entailment there, but there's no inductive argument either. Induction only gets you from sense-data to sense-data. Induction gets you from behaviour to more behaviour. Induction will never make a vertical jump. For a vertical jump, entailment doesn't work, and there's nothing else.

TH: And yet you believe it's true beyond question of doubt that you had a bath this morning?

AA: Not beyond question of doubt, no, because I think I might easily . . .

TH: Oh, go on!

AA: No, no. There's often a failure of hot water in this house, and so I don't get a bath every morning, I can never quite remember whether I had a bath this morning or yesterday morning. It's not so important to me. So it might well be that I think I had a bath this morning and in the end it might have been yesterday's bath. I agree, I believe I did have a bath this morning, but it's not beyond reasonable doubt.

TH: At about his time, when you were engaged in these epistemological enquiries and writing *The Problems of Knowledge*, you were Grote Professor at University College London. You seemed to me—a graduate student come lately from the colonies, as I was—to be living a social life that was pretty near to perfervid. Has it ever got in the way of your work?

AA: No, I wouldn't describe it as perfervid, but I've always been a fairly gregarious person. But as I get older, I can take social life or leave it. I spent most of the past year in France—I've a house in Provence—seeing almost nobody, and working away quite happily. I've always been very lucky in that I can concentrate very hard when I'm writing, and then switch off. When I'm working on a book, I make it the habit to work perhaps three hours in a morning and perhaps an hour in the evening—at about five or six—and perhaps in four hours I can get three or four hundred words written. If you do that every day, you can very quickly compile a whole book. I do try to do that—I don't always succeed, but I do succeed on the whole. Once I've finished working, I put it aside and I'm perfectly free to do anything else. I do lots of other things.

I like playing chess, I like watching sport, or anyway I did when I was younger. I used regularly to watch the Spurs play soccer, and Middlesex play cricket. Now I watch them on television or listen to them on the wireless. I like conversation. I used to like drinking—I can't drink so much now. I have made many friends. So I live a very full sort of social life. I fortunately have a very good head, and so I don't suffer much from hangovers, and settle down to work the next morning. Connolly said there were two different persons—or Philip Toynbee I think said it—there was A. J. Ayer and there was Freddie Ayer, and they were quite different and never quite got together. Cyril Connolly made that joke—called me the 'London Freddie Ayer'. I think it's true I have this rather mixed personality.

TH: When you returned to Oxford from University College London, I think in 1959, did the opposition of J. L. Austin—he of *Sense and*

Ted Honderich

Sensibilia—much bother you? I think you once said to me you should have remained in London.

AA: Well in many ways, I wish I had remained in London. I went on living in London, and never actually settled down in Oxford. I used to spend the week in New College, where I had very nice rooms, and then come home for the weekend. I went to Oxford to combat Austin, not because he had attacked me in *Sense and Sensibilia*—I didn't even know about *Sense and Sensibilia* at that time—but because I disliked very much the extreme concentration on ordinary English usage that he was responsible for. I thought that this was a perversion of the views that I had put forward in *Language, Truth and Logic*—that philosophy had to be to some extent a critique of language. But not in that rather pedestrian way. I thought that he was leading philosophy up a blind alley. So I did go back to Oxford mainly to try to counteract his influence. Austin had organized a group of younger philosophy lecturers and fellows which used to meet on Saturday mornings and was very much dominated by him. I organized a counter-group which wasn't so hierarchical and was much more informal. That still exists after thirty years. I'm very proud of that.

TH: Excellent.

AA: But Austin died at the end of my first term at Oxford, so I'd really gone back to fight something that wasn't there any more. His method of philosophy entirely depended on his strong personality, and indeed his great cleverness. Once he was dead, the whole thing just faded away. Warnock and Urmson remained faithful, but they weren't strong enough to carry it on on their own. Americans used to arrive in Oxford looking for linguistic philosophy and failing to find it.

TH: So the battle was never really joined. To come on to your fourth period, it is what we're calling Constructionism. It's laid out pretty accessibly in your *Central Questions of Philosophy*.

AA: That's right.

TH: You take yourself to have escaped Phenomenalism, the idea which perhaps in plain terms is the idea that we are imprisoned in our private experience . . .

AA: Well I wish you wouldn't call that Phenomenalism, because that is much more solipsism, isn't it?

TH: Uhuh. But none the less, our statements about the external public world are really to be understood as statements about private experience. Would you accept that as an account of Phenomenalism?

AA: Well yes. I think so.

TH: You escaped this. You break out and speak of constructing the physical world or positing it. I've always been just a little bit puzzled as to what this construction or this positing comes to.

AA: Well, I took the term 'positing' from the American philosopher W. V. Quine. In his very famous article 'Two Dogmas of Empiricism'[10] he talked of positing the physical world. The construction isn't a construction in the old sense, not a logical construction. Also I said it's hopeless if you start with private entities, so I started with neutral sense qualities, with what I called qualia—borrowing the term again from the Pragmatists, from Lewis and Nelson Goodman. A quale is something like greenness or loudness.

TH: These are neither private ideas nor public objects.

AA: They're neutral. No question of privacy arises, because privacy arises only when you've got persons and you haven't at this stage got persons. All you've got are these qualities and also patterns like bird-sound, chair-scrape and so on. These are concretized by being put in sense-fields, and so having places and times. The construction takes the form of showing how on the basis of the recurrences in our sense experience—Hume's concept of coherence, really—Kant also develops this, Price does it very thoroughly in his book on perception—we can develop a theory. It is only possible because on the whole things stay put. For example, to use commonsense language, that chair is in the same physical relationship to that ice-bucket and to that table and that box of kleenex and so on, as it was yesterday.

You get to what I call a visuo-tactical continuant, and then you have to put in causal properties and so on. I can't go into all that here. I keep the question of what there is as a question of the adoption of a theory, and I say we're going to plump for these constructs, these posited objects as what there is. And now—this is the clever move—I interpret my neutral starting-point back into the theory. I construct persons out of physical objects—physical objects out of which signs emanate—and

---

[10] Quine, 1953.

then interpret my original sense-data as states of these persons. That's how I do it. It's a trick, but I think its's a legitimate trick.

TH: We've looked at your Logical Positivism, your Phenomenalism, your Epistemological period and now finally Constructionism. These four periods leave out a lot of your other philosophy. You've attended to particular problems—the problem of induction, the problem of causation, and the problem of free will and determinism. Where do you think you've done your best? Where do you get a clear Alpha?

AA: Well I think that my dealings with scepticism on the whole merit at least an Alpha Minus. And I think that I'm rather proud of the way I deal with a whole group of problems—causality, induction and so on—without having to believe in objective physical necessity. I regard necessity as purely a logical notion. I won't have metaphysical necessity, which people now are going in for, and which seems to be horrible. Or indeed causal necessity, which I'm afraid to say you are rather tempted by. I think I give myself an Alpha for trying to stamp out that absurd heresy.

TH: We all struggle a bit against vanity, Freddie. Do you carry on a great struggle?

AA: I'm vain but not conceited. I can be described in that way. A vain man is one who's proud to display his medals. I am vain. A conceited man is one who thinks he deserves more medals than he's got. I'm not conceited.

TH: Excellent. You have the deserved acclaim of being the clearest of contemporary philosophers, absolutely pellucid. What do you make of talk which is always directed against clear philosophers, of whom you are the exemplar, to the effect that there's such a thing as superficial clarity? I think a condescending book was published some while back, not exactly about you, under the title *Clarity is Not Enough.*[11]

AA: I think you're referring to a book published by a man called Lewis, a philosopher of religion, who took the title from a much better philosopher, Price, my predecessor at Oxford. Price, who was himself rather a clear writer, wanted people to take a greater interest than they did in psychical research. He was against people just dismissing it contemptuously, and used that rather misleading title, I think it's perfectly true that people who write very clearly *may* be superficial.

[11] Lewis, 1963.

One way of writing clearly is to avoid difficult questions. But I think it isn't at all true that someone who writes clearly *has* to be superficial.

On the contrary, I think that a good philosophical writer is someone who can put difficult theories—as for instance my Constructionalism, which is extremely difficult—in a clear fashion. One of the great dangers in philosophy is woolliness, and woolliness, particularly among Germans, is always masked by very unclear writing. English philosophers, like Professor Lewis, who imitate the Germans, are, to my mind, perhaps not among the very best.

TH: Your recent lecture on *The Meaning of Life* suggested that it hasn't got any meaning, and that life is really pretty nasty.

AA: Well no . . .

TH: Is that a fair summary?

AA: Well, these are two separate propositions, because I hold that life has no meaning independently of the meaning one is able to give it. But it doesn't follow from this that it's either nice or nasty. This is a historical question. I do in fact hold that for most people throughout history, life has been rather unpleasant.

TH: Sound and fury signifying nothing?

AA: Well, yes, yes. That is true, that it signifies nothing in itself, but it can be made to signify something. I think my life, for me, has been full of meaning—lots of things that I cared to do, and some I've done fairly well. On the whole I've had a happy life.

TH: What have you pursued above all?

AA: Oh, you mean like Hume—literary fame?

TH: I wondered.

AA: I suppose Truth. I suppose Truth. I suppose that I care more about having got some things right in philosophy, if I have got anything right, than having written elegantly. Although I like that too.

TH: Some months ago, in hospital, you 'died'—or at any rate had a 'near-death' experience, and after that, you seemed to write a little more tolerantly of the idea that we might survive our deaths.

AA: Well I did write more tolerantly in an article that was published in *The Sunday Telegraph*. Then I took it back in a subsequent article published in *The Spectator* and said—No, I still retain my belief we don't survive our deaths. The effect of the experience, though, was to make me more interested in the possibility of survival. Without thinking it *was* a possibility. I was more interested in the question of what circumstances might make it true that one had survived.

I've always hoped to be able to establish a Humean theory of personal identity, namely one in terms of relationships between experiences, divorced from their physical attachment. But I have never been able to do this and decided that probably it can't be done. So I'm not even sure that survival in that sense is logically possible. I think reincarnation might be possible, if one just legislated. That's to say, supposing it were the case that people did remember, as if it were their own experience, the experience of someone dead. One might choose to say they were the same person. That's the sort of thing that Derek Parfit explored in his book.[12] I became as a result of my experience more interested in that kind of speculation. That's all.

TH: But you were and are in no danger of a death-bed recantation, I think?

AA: Oh, no, no. No, none whatsoever. I don't know, I might go ga-ga—but as long as I maintain my present intelligence, no.

TH: Thank you very much.

AA: Thank you.

---

[12] Parfit, 1984..

Notes on Contributors

Frederick Copleston is Emeritus Professor of the University of London and Vice-Presdient of the Royal Institute. His monumental *History of Philosophy* was published in nine volumes between 1946 and 1975. He is a priest of the Society of Jesus.

Donald Davidson is Professor of Philosophy at the University of California, Berkeley. Amongst other works is his *Essays on Actions and Events* which was published in 1980. (*See also page 3 of this volume.*)

Ted Honderich is the Grote Professor of Mind and Logic at University College, London, and a member of the Council of the Royal Institute. He is the author of *A Theory of Determinism* (1988).

Stephan Körner, for many years a member of the Council of the Royal Institute, is Professor Emeritus, University of Bristol and Yale University. Among his books is *Metaphysics: Its Structure and Function*, published in 1984.

Donald MacKinnon was a colleague of Ayer's at Oxford as a Fellow of Keble College in the late 'thirties, and afterwards became Professor of Divinity at the University of Cambridge. His *Problems of Metaphysics* was published in 1974.

D. H. Mellor is Professor of Philosophy at the University of Cambridge, and a member of the Council of the Royal Institute. His latest book is *Matters of Metaphysics*, published in 1991.

Hilary Putnam is Professor of Philosophy at Harvard University. His sixth book, based on his Gifford Lectures, *Renewing Philosophy*, will be published by the Harvard University Press in 1992. (*See also page 3 of this volume.*)

Anthony Quinton (Baron Quinton of Holywell;, was formerly President of Trinity College Oxford. He is the President of the Royal Institute. Among his book are *The Nature of Things*, 1973, and *thoughts and Thinkers*, 1982.

Stewart Sutherland, formerly Professor of the History and Philosophy of Religion, and subsequently Principal, at King's College, University of London, is now that University's Vice-Chancellor. He is the Chairman of the Royal Institute of Philosophy. His *Jesus, God and Belief* was published in 1984.

John Watling was a colleague of Ayer's for many years at University College, London. His *Bertrand Russel* was published in 1970.

David Wiggins is Professor of Philosophy at Birbeck College, University of London. His third book, *Needs, Values, Truth* was published in 1988.

Bernard Williams is White's Professor of Moral Philosophy at the University of Oxford. His *Ethics and the Limits of Philosophy* was published in 1985. He is a member of the Council of the Royal Institute.

Richard Wollheim was a colleague of Ayer's at University College, London, and is now Professor at the University of California, Berkeley and Davies. Among his books are *F. H. Bradley* and *On Art and Mind*.

References

References to works by A. J. Ayer are given as follows:

CQ   1973. *The Central Questions of Philosophy* (London: Wiedenfeld and Nicholson).

CP   1963. *The Concept of a Person and other essays* (London: Macmillan).

FEK   1940. *The Foundations of Empirical Knowledge* (London: Macmillan).

FM   1984. *Freedom and Morality and other essays* (Oxford: Clarendon Press).

HM   1980. *Hume* (London: Oxford University Press).

IM   1934 'Demonstration of the Impossibility of Metaphysics', *Mind*.

LP   (ed.) 1963. *Logical Positivism* (New York: Free Press).

LTL   1963. *Language, Truth and Logic* (London: Gollancz, 2nd edn, 1946).

MCS   1969. *Metaphysics and Common Sense* (London: Macmillan).

ML   1990. *The Meaning of Life and other essays,* ed. Ted Honderich (ed.) (London: Wiedenfeld and Nicholson).

OP   1968. *The Origins of Pragmatism, Studies in the Philosophies of Charles Sanders Peirce and William James* (London: Wiedenfeld and Nicholson).

PBEV   1972. *Probability and Evidence* (London: Macmillan).

PE   1954. *Philosophical Essays* (London: Macmillan).

PK   1956. *The Problem of Knowledge* (London: Macmillan).

PL   1977. *Part of my Life* (London: Collins).

PTC   1982. *Philosophy in the Twentieth Century* (London: Wiedenfeld and Nicholson).

RS   1972. *Russell* (London: Fontana).

TM   1947. *Thinking and Meaning* An Inaugural Lecture. (London: Lewis).

TP   1988. *Thomas Paine* (London: Secker and Warburg).

VL   1986. *Voltaire* (London: Wiedenfeld and Nicholson).

WT   1985. *Wittgenstein* (London: Wiedenfeld and Nicholson).

Other references:

Alexander, Samuel 1927. *Space, Time and Deity* (London: Macmillan, 1966).

Armstrong, D. M. 1961. *Perception and the Physical World* (London: Routledge and Kegan Paul).

Armstrong, D. M. 1968. *A Materialist Theory of Mind* (London: Routledge and Kegan Paul).

Armstrong, D. M. 1973. *Belief, Truth and Knowledge* (Cambridge: Cambridge University Press, 1973).

Austin, J. L. 1971. *How to Do Things with Words* (London: Oxford University Press).

References

Austin, J. L. 1962. *Sense and Sensibilia, reconstructed from the manuscript notes by G. J. Warnock* (Oxford: Clarendon Press).

Barnes, W. H. F. 1933. 'A Suggestion about Value.' *Analysis*.

Bell, Clive. 1930. *Art* (London: Chatto and Windus, 1914).

Berkeley, George *Commonplace Book*, G. Johnson (ed.) (London: Faber).

Bradley, F. H. 1914. *Essays on Truth and Reality* (Oxford: Clarendon Press).

Braithwaite, R. B. 1955. *The Eddington Memorial Lecture of 1955* (Cambridge University Press).

Brentano, F. 1973. *Psychology from an Empirical Point of View*, O. Kraus and L. MacAlister (eds) (London: Routledge and Kegan Paul).

Broad, C. D. 1925. *The Mind and its Place in Nature* (London: Routledge and Kegan Paul).

Broad, C. D. 1923. *Scientific Thought* (London: Kegan Paul).

Calderon de la Barca 1876. *La vida es Sueño: comedia en tres jornadas,* (Leipzig: Brockhaus).

Carnap, R. 1928a. *Logische Aufbau der Welt* Berlin. trans. George, D. as *The Logical Structure of the World* (London: Routledge and Kegan Paul, 1967).

Carnap, R. 1928b. *Scheinprobleme in der Philosophie: Das Fremdpsychische und der Realismusstreit* Berlin.

Carnap, R. 1932. 'Uberwindung der Metaphysik durch die Logische Analyse der Sprache.' *Erkenntnis*.

Carnap, R. 1934. *Logische Syntax der Sprache* Vienna.

Carnap, R. 1936, 1937. 'Testability and Meaning.' *Philosophy of Science* **3** 420–468.

Carnagh, R. 1937. 'Testability and Meaning'. *Philosophy of Science* **4** 1–40.

Carnap, R. 1942. *Introduction to Semantics* (Cambridge, Mass.: Harvard University Press).

Carnap, R. 1962. *Logical Foundations of Probability* 2nd edn. (Chicago: University of Chicago Press).

Cassirer, E. 1906. *Erkenntnisproblem in der Philosophie und Wissenschaft der neueren Zeit* Berlin.

Chisholm, Roderick 1957. *Perceiving: a philosophical study* (London: Oxford University Press).

Cohen, Hermann 1915. *Der Begriff der Religion im System der Philosophie* Berlin.

Collingwood, R. G. 1924. *Speculum Mentis; or, the Map of Knowledge* (Oxford: Clarendon Press).

Collingwood, R. G. 1938. *Principles of Art* (Oxford: Clarendon Press).

Collingwood, R. G. 1940. *An Essay on Metaphysics* (Oxford: Clarendon Press).

Copleston, F. 1982. *Religion and the One: Philosophies East and West* (Tunbridge Wells: Search Press).

Crane, Tim 1988. 'Concepts in Perception.' *Analysis*.

Crick, Bernard 1981. *Orwell: A Life* Rev. edn. (London: Secker and Warburg).

Crick, F. H. C. 1966. *Of Molecules and Men* University of Washington Press.

Davidson, Donald 1980. *Essays on Action and Events* (Oxford: Clarendon Press).

Davidson, Donald 1986. 'Knowing One's Own Mind.' *Proceedings of the American Philosophical Association.*

Davidson, Donald 1989. 'The Myth of the Subjective,' in M. Krausz, (ed.), *Relativism: Interpretation and Confrontation* Notre Dame.

Davidson, Donald 1990. In *Grazer Philosophische Studien*, special issue entitled *The Mind of Donald Davidson* Graz.

Day, J. P. 1986. 'Hope', *American Philosophical Quarterly, Vol. 6.*

de Finetti, B. 1931. 'Probabilism.' *Erkenntnis, 1989.*

Dewey, John 1929a. *Experience and Nature* (London: Open Court).

Dewey, John 1929b. *The Quest for Certainty* (New York: Putnam, 1929).

Dretske, F. 1981. *Knowledge and the Flow of Information* (Oxford: Blackwell).

Dummett, Michael 1979. 'Common Sense and Physics.' In Macdonald, 1979.

Eddington, A. 1928. *The Nature of the Physical World* (Cambridge: Cambridge University Press).

Eddington, A. 1939. *The Philosophy of Physical Science* (Cambridge: Cambridge University Press).

Edwards, Paul (ed.) 1967. *Encyclopaedia of Philosophy* (London: Collier Macmillan).

Feigl, H. and Brodbeck, M. (eds), 1953. *Readings in the Philosophy of Science* (New York: Appleton Century Crofts).

Field, H. 1972. 'Tarski's Theory of Truth.' *Journal of Philosophy.*

Flew, A. and MacIntyre, A. (eds.), *New Essays in Philosophical Theology* (London: SCM Press).

Foster, John 1985. *A. J. Ayer* (London: Routledge and Kegan Paul).

Frege, Gottlieb 1953. *The Foundations of Arithmetic, a logico-methodological enquiry into the concept of number*, trans. Austin, J. L. (Oxford: Blackwell).

Gasking, Douglas 1954. 'The Philosophy of John Wisdom', I and II. *Australasian Journal of Philosophy*, 1954.

Goodman, Nelson 1961. *The Structure of Appearance* (Indianapolis: Bobbs-Merril).

Hacking, I. 1983. *Representing and Intervening* (Cambridge: Cambridge University Press).

Hahn, E. and Schilpp, P. A. (eds) 1986. *The Philosophy of Quine* La Salle, (Illinois: Open Court).

Hahn, Hans 1933. *Logik, Mathematik and Naturerkennen* Vienna.

Hirst, R. J. 1957. *The Problems of Perception* (London: Allen and Unwin).

Hirst, R. J. 1967. 'Realism.' In Edwards, 1967.

Holt, E. B. & others 1912. *The New Realism: Coöperative Studies in Philosophy* (New York).

Honderich, Ted 1988. *A Theory of Determinism: The Mind, Neuroscience, and Life-Hopes* (Oxford: Clarendon Press).

Honderich, Ted 1990. *A Theory of Determinism*, Vol. I, *Mind and Brain* (Oxford: Clarendon Press).

Honderich, Ted and Burnyeat, Myles (eds) 1979. *Philosophy as it Is* (London: Allen Lane).

References

Hookway, Christopher 1988. *Quine, Language, Experience and Reality* (Cambridge: Polity).

Howson, C. and Urbach, P. 1989. *Scientific Reasoning: The Bayesian Approach* La Salle, (Illinois: Open Court).

James, William 1907. *Pragmatism, A new name for some old ways of thought* (New York: Longmans, Green).

Jeans, J. 1937. *The Mysterious Universe* London: Penguin).

Jeffrey, R. C. 1983. *The Logic of Decision* 2nd edn. (Chicago: Chicago University Press).

Joachim, H. H. 1906. *The Nature of Truth* (Oxford: Clarendon Press).

Joseph, H. W. B. 1916. *Introduction to Logic* 2nd edn. (Oxford: Clarendon Press).

Kant, Immanuel 1968. *Kritik der Praktischen Vernunft* Akademie Textausgabe Edn, Vol. V. (Berlin: de Gruyter).

Körner, S. (ed.) 1957. *Observation and Interpretation* (London: Butterworth).

Körner, S. 1966. *Experience and Theory* (London: Hutchinson).

Körner, S. 1981. 'Über Sprachspiele ünd rechtliche Institutionem,' in Morscher and Stranzinger (eds), *Proceedings of the 5th Wittgenstein Symposium* Vienna.

Körner, S. 1984. *Metaphysics, Its Structure and Function* (Cambridge: Cambridge University Press).

Kripke, Saul 1982. *Wittgenstein on Rules and Private Language, an elementary exposition* (Oxford: Blackwell).

Kyburg, H. 1978. 'Subjective probability: criticisms, reflections and problems.' *Journal of Philosophical Logic*.

Lemmon, E. J. 1966. 'Sentences, statements and propositions,' in *British Analytical Philosophy* B. Williams and A. Montefiore (eds) (London: Routledge and Kegan Paul).

Lewis, C. I. 1929. *Mind and the World Order* (New York).

Lewis, H. D. (ed.) 1963. *Clarity is Not Enough, Essays in Criticism of Linguistic Philosophy* (London: Allen and Unwin).

Lewy, Casmir. 1964. 'G. E. Moore and the Naturalistic Fallacy.' *Proceedings of the British Academy*.

Locke, John 1690. *Essay Concerning Human Understanding* London.

Macdonald, G. F. (ed.) 1979. *Perception and Identity: Essays presented to A. J. Ayer with his replies to them* (London: Macmillan).

Mackie, John 1976. *Problems from Locke* (Oxford: Clarendon Press).

Marcel, Gabriel 1951. *Homo Viator*, trans. Crauford, E. (London: Gollancz).

Marr, David 1982. *Vision, a Computational Investigation into the Human Representation and Processing of Visual Information* (San Francisco: Freeman).

McDowell, John 1985. 'Values and Secondary Qualities,' in *Morality and Objectivity; a tribute to J. L. Mackie* T. Honderich, (ed.) (London: Routledge and Kegan Paul).

McDowell, John 1986. 'Singular Thought and the Extent of Inner Space', in P. Petit and J. McDowell, (eds) *Subject, Thought and Context* (Oxford: Clarendon Press).

McTaggart, J. E. 1901. *Studies in Hegelian Cosmology* (Cambridge: Cambridge University Press).

McTaggart, J. E. 1906. *Some Dogmas of Religion* (London: Arnold).

Mellor, D. H. 1971. *The Matter of Chance* (Cambridge: Cambridge University Press).

Mellor, D. H. 1982. 'Chance and Degrees of Belief.' In *Matters of Metaphysics*, 1991. (Cambridge: Cambridge University Press).

Mellor, D. H. 1988a. 'On Raising the Chances of Effects.' In *Matters of Metaphysics*, 1991. (Cambridge: Cambridge University Press).

Mellor, D. H. 1988b. 'The Warrant of Induction.' In *Matters of Metaphysics*, 1991. (Cambridge: Cambridge University Press).

Mill, J. S. 1859. *Essay on Liberty* London.

Mill, J. S. 1861. 'Utilitarianism.' *Fraser's Magazine*.

Mill, J. S. 1865. *Examination of Sir William Hamilton's Philosophy, and of the principal questions discussed in his writings* (London: Longmans, Green).

Mill, J. S. 1873. *Autobiography* (London: Longmans, Green).

Mitchell, Basil (ed.) 1957. *Faith and Logic, Oxford essays in philosophical theology* (London: Allen and Unwin).

Moore, G. E. 1903. *Principia Ethica* (Cambridge: Cambridge University Press).

Moore, G. E. 1912. *Ethics* (London: Williams and Norgate).

Moore, G. E. 1922. 'The Refutation of Idealism.' In *Philosophical Studies* (London: Kegan Paul).

Moore, G. E. 1953. *Some Main Problems of Philosophy* (London: Allen and Unwin).

Moore, Walter. 1989. *Schrödinger: Life and Thought* (Cambridge: Cambridge University Press).

Nagel, E. 1956. *Logic without Metaphysics* Glencoe, (Illinois: Open Court).

Ogden, C. K. and Richards, I. A. 1923. *The Meaning of Meaning, a study of the influence of language upon thought and of the science of symbolism* (London: Kegan Paul).

Parfit, Derek 1984. *Reasons and Persons* (Oxford: Clarendon Press).

Peacocke, Christopher 1983. *Sense and Content, experience, thought and their relations* (Oxford: Clarendon Press).

Peirce, C. S. 1923. *Chance, Love and Logic: philosophical essays*, M. R. Cohen (ed.) (London: Kegan Paul).

Peirce, C. S. 1960. *Collected Papers*, C. Hartshorne and P. Weiss (eds) (Cambridge, Mass.: Harvard University Press), 1931–1960.

Popper, Karl 1935. *Logik der Forschung zur Erkenntnistheorie der modernen Naturwissenschaft* Vienna.

Popper, Karl 1957. 'The propensity Interpretation of the Calculus of Probabilities, and the Quantum Theory.' In Körner, 1957.

Popper, Karl 1959. *The Logic of Scientific Discovery* (London: Hutchinson).

Price, H. H. 1940. *Hume's Theory of the External World* (Oxford: Clarendon Press).

Price, H. H. 1950. *Perception* 2nd edn. (London: Methuen).

Price, H. H. 1969. *Belief* (London: Allen and Unwin).

References

Prichard, H. A. 1909. *Kant's Theory of Knowledge* (Oxford: Clarendon Press).

Putnam, Hilary 1981. *Reason, Truth and History* (Cambridge: Cambridge University Press).

Putnam, Hilary 1983. *Realism and Reason: Philosophical Papers*, Vol. 3. (Cambridge: Cambridge University Press).

Putnam, Hilary 1989. *Representation and Reality* (Boston: MIT Press).

Putnam, Hilary 1990. *Realism with Human Face* (Cambridge, Mass.: Harvard University Press).

Quine, W. V. O. 1936. 'Truth by Convention'. In H. Feigl and W. Sellars, (eds) *Philosophical Essays for Alfred North Whitehead* (New York: 1936).

Quine, W. V. O. 1939. 'Designation and Existence.' *Journal of Philosophy*.

Quine, W. V. O. 1953a. *From a Logical Point of View: 9 logico-philosophical essays* (Cambridge, Mass.: Harvard University Press).

Quine, W. V. O. 1953b. 'Two Dogmas of Empiricism.' In Quine, 1953a.

Quine, W. V. O. 1960. *Word and Object* (Cambridge, Mass.: M.I.T.).

Quinton, Anthony 1973. *The Nature of Things* (London: Routledge and Kegan Paul).

Ramsey, F. P. 1926. 'Truth and Probability.' In *Philosophical Papers*, 1990 (Cambridge: Cambridge University Press).

Ramsey, F. P. 1931. *Foundations of Mathematics and other logical essays*, R. Braithwaite (ed.), (London: Routledge).

Ramsey, F. P. 1978. *Foundations: Essays in Philosophy, Logic and Mathematics*, D. H. Mellor, (ed.) (London: Routledge and Kegan Paul).

Reichenbach, H. 1936. 'Logistic Empiricism in Germany and the Present State of its Problems.' *Journal of Philosophy*.

Reichenbach, H. 1938. *Experience and Prediction, an analysis of the structure of knowledge* (London: University of Chicago Press).

Reichenbach, H. 1939. 'Dewey's Theory of Science.' In P. A. Schilpp, (ed.), *The Philosophy of John Dewey* (New York: Open Court).

Reichenbach, H. 1951. *The Rise of Scientific Philosophy* (Berkeley and Los Angeles: University of California Press).

Reichenbach, M. and Cohen, R. (eds.) 1978. *Hans Reichenbach: Selected Writings, 1909–1953* (Holland: Reidel).

Royce, Josiah 1900. *The World and the Individual* (New York: Macmillan).

Russell, Bertrand 1912. *Problems of Philosophy* (London: Oxford University Press).

Russell, Bertrand 1914. *Our Knowledge of the External World, as a field for scientific method in philosophy* (London: Open Court).

Russell, Bertrand 1917. *Mysticism and Logic, and other essays* London: Allen and Unwin).

Russell, Bertrand 1918. 'The philosophy of Logical Atomism' in *The Monist* (Reprinted in *Logic and Logic and Knowledge*, R. C. Marsh, (ed.) London: Allen and Unwin, 1956.)

Russell, Bertrand 1921. *The Analysis of Mind* (London: Allen and Unwin).

Russell, Bertrand 1926. *Analysis of Matter* (London: Kegan Paul).

Russell, Bertrand 1928. *Sceptical Essays* (London: Allen and Unwin).

References

Russell, Bertrand 1948. *Human Knowledge, its Scope and Limits* (London: Allen and Unwin).

Ryle, Gilbert 1929. Review of Heidegger, *Sein und Zeit. Mind.*

Ryle, Gilbert 1930. 'Are there Propositions?' Aristotelian Society, *Proceedings*, Vol. 30.

Ryle, Gilbert 1932. 'Systematically Misleading Expressions.' Aristotelian Society, *Proceedings*, Vol. 32.

Ryle, Gilbert 1936. 'Unverifiability by Me.' *Analysis.*

Ryle, Gilbert 1949. *The Concept of Mind* (London: Hutchinson).

Santayana, George 1905 *The Life of Reason* 5. vols. (London: Constable).

Santayana, George 1928 *Realms of Being* Vol. 1. (London: Constable).

Sartre, J-.P. 1947 *L'Etre et le neant, essai d'ontologie phenomenologique* (Paris: Fallimard).

Scheffler, I. G. 1963. *The Anatomy of Enquiry* New York.

Schilpp, P. A. (ed.) 1963. *The Philosophy of Russell* (New York: Harper Row).

Schlick, Moritz 1918. *Allgemeine Erkenntnslehre, Naturwissenschaftliche Monographien und Lehrbucher,* Berlin.

Schlick, Moritz 1933. 'Positivismus und Realismus.' *Erkenntnis.* Reprinted as 'Positivism and Realism', trans. Rynin, D. In *LP.*

Schlick, Moritz 1934. 'Uber das Fundament der Erkenntnis.' *Erkenntnis.* Reprinted as 'The Foundation of Knowledge', trans. Rynin, D. In *LP.*

Smith, N. Kemp 1924. *Prolegomena to an Idealist of Knowledge* (London: Macmillan).

Strawson, P. F. 1959. *Individuals. An essay in descriptive Metaphysics* (London: Methuen).

Strawson, P. F. 1979. 'Perception and its Objects.' In Macdonald, 1979.

Strawson, P. F. 1985. *Scepticism and Naturalism: Some Varieties* (London: Methuen).

Sutherland, S. K. 1977. *Atheism and the Rejection of God* (London: Blackwell and Mott).

Sutherland, S. K. 1984. *Jesus, God and Belief, the legacy of theism* (Oxford: Blackwell).

Tomlin, W. F. 1936. Review of *LTL* in *Scrutiny.*

Vaihinger, H. 1911. *Die Philosophie des Als-Ob. System der theoretischen, praktischen and religiosen* Berlin.

Walsh, W. H. 1963. *Metaphysics* (London: Hutchinson).

Warnock, Geoffrey 1958. *English Philosophy since 1900* (London: Oxford University Press).

Whitehead, A. N. 1929. *Process and Reality, an essay in cosmology* (London: Oxford University Press).

Whyte, J. T. 1990. 'Success Semantics.' *Analysis.*

Wiggins, David 1987. *Needs, Values, Truth, Essays in the Philosophy of Value* (Oxford: Blackwell).

Wilson, J. Cook 1962. *Statement and Inference, with other philosophical papers,* ed. Farquaharson. (Oxford: Clarendon Press, 1926).

References

Wilson, J. Cook 1962. Reported in N. Smart, (ed.), *Historical Selections in the Philosophy of Religion* (London: SCM Press).

Wittgenstein, Ludwig 1922. *Tractus Logico-Philosophicus*, trans. C. K. Ogden, (London: Routledge).

Wittgenstein, Ludwig 1958. *Blue and Brown Books* (Oxford: Blackwell).

Wittgenstein, Ludwig 1953. *Philosophical Investigations*, trans. G. Anscombe, (Oxford: Blackwell).

Index of Names

Alexander, S., 32
Ambrose, A., 63
Ambrose, Alice, 27
Anderson, J., 32
Aristotle, 63, 97
Armstrong, D., 27
Ashton, F., 18
Augustine, St., 45
Austin, J. L., 24, 30, 41, 44, 45, 46, 47, 48, 53, 217, 221, 222

Barnes, W. H. F., 38
Barth, K., 82
Bell, Clive, 31, 211
Bentham, J., 42, 49, 57
Bergson, H., 33
Berkeley, G., 9, 12, 13, 14, 40, 53, 129, 130, 167, 212, 216
Berlin, I., 18, 24, 53, 57, 209
Black, M., 27
Boyle, R., 45
Bradley, F. H., 1, 2, 3, 33, 40, 64, 65
Braithwaite, R. B., 58
Brentano, F., 106, 142
Britten, B., 19
Broad, C. D., 9, 13, 32, 34, 40, 45, 130
Bumberg, A., 35
Burgess, G., 19

Camus, A., 60
Carnap, R., 7, 9, 11–12, 33, 35, 36, 37, 38, 40, 42, 61, 105, 105n., 106ff., 132, 149n
Carritt, E., 54
Carter, M. B., 19
Cassirer, E., 33
Cecil, D., 18
Chandler, R., 34
Chisholm, R., 142
Churchill, R., 19
Clifford, W. K., 48
Cohen, H., 33

Cohen, M. R., 46
Coleridge, S., 53
Collingwood, R. G., 31, 60, 77, 165, 210
Comte, A., 99
Connolly, C., 19, 221
Copleston, F. C., 77
Crane, T., 129n., 145
Crick, B., 79
Crick, F., 100
Croce, B., 33

Davidson, D., 3, 129n., 130, 144, 151
Descartes, R., 9, 45, 141, 217
Dewey, J., 33, 111
Dick, M., 18
Downing, P., 21, 177, 180
Dretske, F., 147
Dummett, M., 7–10

Eddington, A., 13, 50
Einstein, A., 54, 96
Eliot, T. S., 50
Evans, G., 22

Feigl, H., 35
Foster, J., 141n
Frege, G., 37, 53, 94, 96, 97, 182
Freud, S., 86

Gaitskell, H., 19
Gasking, D., 44
Gassendi, 45
Giaquinto, M., 129n
Goodman, N., 3, 7, 8, 11, 130, 223
Grice, H. P., 20
Griffiths, A., 129n

Hahn, H., 37
Hampshire, S., 21, 24
Hart, W., 129n
Hartmann, N., 33
Hegel, G., 3

237

Index

Index